Sea, Sky and Stars

Sea, Sky and Stars

An Illustrated History of Grumman Aircraft

Michael J. Hardy

ARMS AND ARMOUR PRESS

First published in Great Britain
in 1987 by Arms and Armour Press Ltd.,
Link House, West Street, Poole, Dorset BH15 1LL

Distributed in the USA by Sterling Publishing Co. Inc.,
2 Park Avenue, New York, NY 10016.

Distributed in Australia by
Capricorn Link (Australia) Pty. Ltd., P.O. Box 665,
Lane Cove, New South Wales 2066.

British Library Cataloguing in Publication data:
Hardy, M. J.
Sea, sky and stars: an illustrated history of Grumman
aircraft. 1. Grumman airplanes – History   I. Title
623.74'6   TL686.G78

ISBN 0-85368-832-X

Edited and designed at Little Oak Studios.
Typeset by Typesetters (Birmingham) Ltd.
Printed and bound in Great Britain.

Jacket illustrations: A Grumman-designed Lunar
Module and a Boeing Lunar Rover Vehicle on the surface
of the moon (left); a Grumman F-14 Tomcat in VF-84
markings (centre); and a McKinnon G-21D Turbo
Goose. (Grumman)

Half-title page: Two A-6A Intruders from VA-52 (*Kitty
Hawk*) fly over southern California. (US Navy)
Title spread: A UF-2G Albatross, the Coast Guard's
version of the UF-2/HU-16D. (Grumman)
Contents spread: F9F-8 Cougar BuNo 141140, with
flight refuelling probe installed in the nose. (Grumman)

Contents

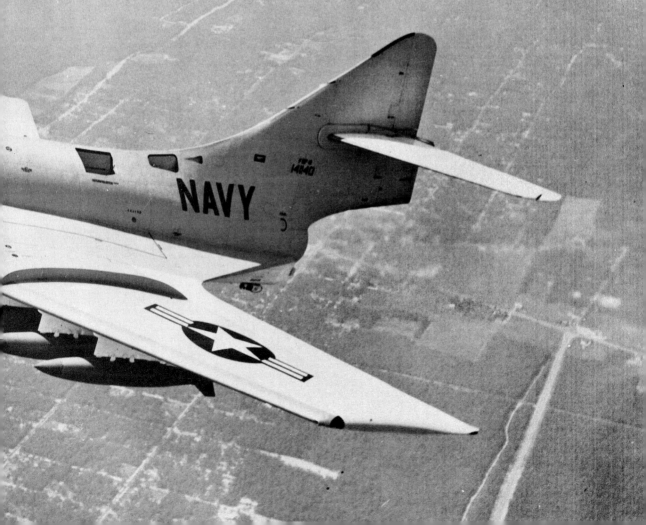

Introduction

Few manufacturers have maintained such a record of loyalty to one major military customer over so many years as has Grumman to the US Navy. For half a century now it has been predominantly a builder of Navy aircraft – especially fighters – and it was not until 1957 that it began to diversify in a big way into civil aviation with the Ag-Cat agricultural biplane, followed by the Gulfstream I and II executive transports. Now that the former Grumman American Aviation Corporation subsidiary has become a separate entity under new ownership and the new name of Gulfstream Aerospace Corporation, production of the AA-1 and AA-5 range of light aircraft which it built has ceased, and Grumman has once more become primarily a manufacturer of Navy aircraft.

During the 1920s Leroy R. Grumman worked for the Loening company, which was engaged in the production of a line of single-engined observation and utility amphibians for the US Army Air Service and the US Navy. He formed his own business, the Grumman Aircraft Engineering Corporation, on 6 December 1929, with its head office at Bethpage, Long Island, and started work on some Navy contracts for seaplane floats. Within two years Grumman were building their own FF-1 two-seat fighter, the first such Navy aircraft to have a retractable undercarriage: the two main wheels were raised manually to be stowed in an upright position in wheel wells in the fuselage sides. This form of retraction, together with the big radial engine, led to the characteristically tubby fuselage of the FF-1, F2F-1 and F3F biplane fighters, and also of the F4F Wildcat. The Loening tradition was carried on with the JF and J2F Duck single-engined utility amphibians, and these were followed in 1937 by the G-21, later named Goose, the first of a series of successful twin-engined amphibians that saw military and civil service in many countries. The number of modification and re-engining schemes devised postwar for the Goose and Widgeon by firms such as McKinnon underlines the basic soundness of their design.

The F4F Wildcat was the first of a long line of 'feline fighters' named after members of the cat family, and it is worth noting that a large proportion of the jet-engined 'cats' have been powered by British turbojets such as the Rolls-Royce Nene and Tay, licence-built by Pratt & Whitney as the J42 and J48 respectively. The F11F-1 Tiger, notable as the first ever fighter designed from the start to incorporate an area-ruled fuselage, was powered by the Wright J65, the US-built version of the Armstrong Siddeley Sapphire. With Rolls-Royce Dart turboprops in the Gulfstream I and Spey turbofans in the Gulfstream II, Grumman has used British-designed engines over a longer period in its aircraft than any other major US manufacturer. The mighty F-14A Tomcat was preceded by a remarkable pioneering effort in the XF10F-1 Jaguar, which was only the second aeroplane to fly with its wing sweep variable in flight (the Bell X-5 had been the first). Although only partly successful, the XF10F laid the foundations not only for the Tomcat but also for Grumman's co-operation with General Dynamics on the swing-wing F-111, and their development of the EF-111A variant for providing ECM jamming coverage for air strike forces.

The S-2 Tracker combined very successfully in one airframe the submarine hunter and killer capabilities of the TBM-3W/TBM-3S Avengers and AF2-W/AF-2S Guardians, and its AEW development, the WF-2 Tracer, led to the much larger and more advanced E-2 Hawkeye to fulfil the role of an airborne operations control centre. The A-6 Intruder strike aircraft,

Far left: US Navy Avengers fly in echelon formation. The Avenger was the last specialized torpedo-bomber to serve aboard US Navy carriers and was to see a new lease of life postwar as an anti-submarine aircraft. (US Navy)

with a wing span 1ft less than the Avenger's, weighs nearly four times as much as the TBF-1 and can carry up to seven or eight times its warload. It proved to be highly effective in operations over Vietnam.

Grumman's factory floor space at the Bethpage plant had more than trebled since the beginning of 1942 to meet the demands of wartime production, especially of the F6F Hellcat. In the 1950s a new plant at Peconic River in eastern Long Island was opened for production of the F9F Cougar and F11F-1 Tiger, while later another plant at Stuart, Florida, built OV-1 Mohawks. On 29 September 1967 another new facility was opened at Savannah, Georgia, under the name of Grumman-Savannah, for building the Gulfstream II; later, production of the AA-1 and AA-5 range of light aircraft was transferred here from Cleveland under the Grumman American Aviation Corporation, and the plant is now the headquarters of Gulfstream Aerospace.

By 1969 Grumman had built more than 25,000 aircraft of all types, and during that year major changes in the company's corporate structure were announced. These resulted from the formation on 1 July 1969 of the Grumman Corporation as a small holding company with six wholly-owned subsidiaries, of which the most important was the Grumman Aerospace Corporation, which took over the activities and products of the original firm. The other subsidiaries were Grumman Allied Industries Inc.; the Grumman Data Systems Corporation; the Grumman Ecosystems Corporation, operational in January 1971; Grumman International Inc.; and the Monteuk Aero Corporation, which ceased operations in 1973. To these were added the Grumman American Aviation Corp. on 2 January 1973 and also the Grumman Export Sales Corp. and the Grumman Avio Systems Corp., this last being a joint venture with VFW-Fokker to manufacture and sell the latter's Aviobridge system of passenger loading gangways for airports. In addition, Grumman co-operated during 1973–74 with VFW-Fokker's subsidiary Rhein-Flugzeugbau GmbH in the design of the latter's two-seat Fanliner light aircraft powered by a Wankel-type engine driving a centrally mounted, ducted fan. Grumman has also played a leading part in the development and use of boron and graphite composite materials, which are used in the F-14 Tomcat's tailplane and undercarriage doors.

A notable Grumman achievement was the development of the Lunar Module (LM) for the Apollo spaceflight programme, the firm being selected in March 1963 from nine competing companies to carry out this programme. The first flight module, LM-1, flew unmanned on the Apollo 5 mission, and the first manned flight was with LM-3 on the Earth-orbiting Apollo 9 mission of 3 March 1969. Apollo 10, launched on 18 May that year, was a 'dress rehearsal' for the lunar mission: the Moon was orbited, and module LM-4, named *Snoopy* after the cartoon character, performed an eight-hour sequence of undocked activities in which astronauts Stafford and Cernan descended to within ten miles of the lunar surface and later rejoined the Command/Service Module. This led to that historic moment when, at 0356hrs. BST on 21 July 1969, Neil Armstrong stepped on to the Moon's surface from module LM-5, named *Eagle*, saying as he did so, 'That's one small step for man, one giant leap for mankind'. Grumman also developed the Orbiting Astronomical Observatory (OAO) to carry out various experiments and measurements in space. The last OAO in the series, launched on 31 August 1972, carried a 32in reflecting, ultra-violet telescope and three smaller X-ray telescopes; this was the heaviest scientific payload launched by the USA up to that time.

The author's very grateful thanks are due to Lois Lovisolo (Corporate Historian), H. J. 'Schoney' Schonenberg and Bill Barto of the Grumman History Center for their work in compiling the many photographs supplied by the Grumman Corporation for use in this book; indeed, without their efforts the book would not have been possible. Special thanks go also to J. M. G. Gradidge, Matt Rodina, T. C. Kosier of the Schweizer Aircraft Corporation and Frank V. Nixon Jr. of Volpar Inc. for their assistance with illustrations.

M. J. Hardy

The Early Grumman Biplanes

Leroy R. Grumman had been an associate of Grover C. Loening in the latter's firm, the Loening Aeronautical Engineering Co., which had produced a series of single-engined observation and utility amphibians such as the OL-1 to OL-9 aircraft for the US Navy and the related COA-1, OA-1, OA-2 and O-10 amphibian biplanes for the US Army Air Service during the 1920s. He left the Loening company to form the Grumman Aircraft Engineering Corporation, which was incorporated on 6 December 1929 with its headquarters at Bethpage, Long Island, New York – which has remained its home base ever since. The new concern started work with some Navy contracts to design floats for seaplane conversions of existing landplanes, including floats with the main wheels retracting into their sides. From these small beginnings grew a succession of US Navy fighters and military and commercial amphibians.

The FF-1 'Fifi'

Arising from its work building floats, the newly established Grumman company was awarded a Navy contract, dated 2 April 1931, to design and build a prototype two-seat fighter designated XFF-1. This machine would be noteworthy on two counts: it was the first fighter to be designed around the Wright R-1820 Cyclone nine-cylinder radial engine, and it was the first Navy fighter to have a retractable undercarriage, the two main wheels being raised in an upright position, by means of long screw jacks, into bays in the fuselage sides just ahead of the lower wing. Retracting the wheels was the observer's job, the latter being seated in tandem with the pilot under a long enclosed canopy with sliding sections. The Grumman G-2 or XFF-1 prototype, Bureau Number (BuNo) 8878, which first flew in December 1931, was also notable in having a structure entirely of light alloy, and although the big Cyclone

Below: The two-seat FF-1 was the first US Navy fighter to have a retractable undercarriage and this, together with the big Cyclone radial, resulted in the characteristically tubby Grumman fuselage shape. The 27 FF-1s built were known as 'Fifis' in service life, and they equipped VF-5B on the carrier *Lexington* from 1933. (Grumman)

radial and the upright position of the wheels resulted in a rather tubby fuselage – a hallmark of Grumman fighters of the 1930s – the XFF-1 was able to achieve no less than 195mph, even with the 616hp R-1820-E Cyclone initially fitted; with a 750hp R-1820-E Cyclone installed, it later achieved a speed of 201mph, higher than that of any single-seat fighter then in service. The armament consisted of two 0.30in fixed, forward-firing machine guns, and the second prototype, BuNo 8940, was completed as the XSF-1 two-seat scout.

The type's performance pleased the Navy sufficiently for it to place a production order in 1933 for 27 FF-1s (Grum-man G-5); these had a 700hp R-1820-78 Cyclone and, in addition to the nose armament, a 0.30in machine gun for the observer to fire from a dorsal position. First deliveries of the FF-1, which was to be known as the 'Fifi' in service, were made on 21 June 1933 to Fighter Squadron 5B (VF-5B) on board the carrier *Lexington*, which ship also housed the first SF-1 scout squadron, VS-3B. An order for 34 SF-1s (Grumman G-6) had been placed, these having a 700hp R-1820-84 Cyclone in a NACA cowling ring and provision for dual controls.

The 34th and last SF-1, BuNo 9493, was converted into the XSF-2 with a 650hp Pratt & Whitney R-1535-80 Twin

Above: The SF-1 was a two-seat scout version of the FF-1; 34 were built for the Navy, equipping VS-3B on board *Lexington*. In the SF-1 the observer was also responsible for over-water navigation and photo-graphy. (Grumman)

Left: The sole XSBF-1, the scout-bomber version of the SF-1, could carry a 500lb bomb under the fuselage and had a 700hp Pratt & Whitney R-1535-72 Twin Wasp Junior 14-cylinder, two-row radial. (Grumman)

Left: The CCF Goblin Is, of which '342' (constructor's number 145) is seen here, differed from the FF-1 chiefly in terms of equipment and had an 800hp Wright R-1820-F52 Cyclone engine. (Canada's National Aviation Museum)

Wasp Junior 14-cylinder radial, and a redesigned and streamlined forward fuselage; this engine was to power the later F2F-1 and F3F-1 fighters. One XSBF-1 scout bomber version of the SF-1, BuNo 9996, was delivered for Navy testing in February 1936, this having a 700hp R-1535-72 Twin Wasp Junior engine and provision for a 500lb bomb under the fuselage. By the end of 1936 both the FF-1 and SF-1 had been withdrawn from service with the Fleet and they then passed to various Naval Reserve units; 22 of the FF-1s were converted to have dual controls as FF-2s, the dorsal gun being deleted.

The Grumman GE-23 was the export version of the FF-1, and the Canadian Car & Foundry Co. Ltd., the largest manufacturer of railway rolling stock in the Dominion, acquired a licence to build it, producing a total of 57 aircraft in 1935–37. Of these, fifteen examples, serialled 334 to 348, went to the Royal Canadian Air Force as Goblin Is (one of these, 340, became the CCF demonstrator, registered CF-BLK), one was sold to Japan, and one was purchased by Nicaragua for that country's *Fuerza Aérea de la Guardia Aviacion*. The Nicaraguan machine was discovered in 1962 by Mr. J. R. Sirmons in a salvage dump in Managua, where it had lain for sixteen years. Mr. Sirmons restored it to its original condition after over three years' work, in the prewar US Navy colour scheme and with the registration N2803J. A Pratt & Whitney R-1340

Wasp was fitted in place of the original Cyclone, and N2803J was later acquired by Grumman, who painted it in the livery of VF-5 ('Red Rippers'), with the squadron commander's code letters 5-F-1 and Navy serial 9358, later 9351. The remaining 40 CCF-built GE-23s were acquired by the Spanish Republican Air Force through an agent in Turkey. They were known as Delfins (or Dolphins) to the Spaniards, bore the serials AD-001 to AD-034 and fought until the end of the Civil War in 1939 against generally superior Nationalist types such as the Messerschmitt Bf 109. The CCF-built GE-23s had an 800hp R-1820-F52 Cyclone powerplant and differed from the FF-1 chiefly in terms of equipment.

The F2F and F3F

The two-seat FF-1 proved sufficiently successful to justify a slightly smaller single-seat development of the same basic layout, and following flight tests with the XFF-1 the Navy ordered a prototype XF2F-1 (Grumman G-9) on 2 November 1932; this aircraft was serialled 9342 and first flew on 18 October 1933. It had a 625hp Pratt & Whitney XR-1535-44 Twin Wasp Junior engine and was the first Navy single-seater to be fitted with an enclosed cockpit. The XF2F-1 featured fabric-covered wings and an all-metal fuselage; two 0.30in machine guns were installed in the forward fuselage, while two 116lb bombs could be carried on underwing racks. It was followed by 55

Left: Bearing the code 5-F-1 of VF-5, BuNo 9672 was one of 55 F2F-1s built. The -1 was a slightly smaller, single-seat development of the FF-1, with a 700hp R-1535-72 Twin Wasp Junior engine, and was known to Navy men as the 'Flying Barrel'. (US Navy)

Left: The 54 F3F-1s differed from the F2F-1 in having an increased wing span and a slightly longer fuselage for better manoeuvrability. F3F-1s equipped VF-5B and VF-6B on board the carriers *Ranger* and *Saratoga*. (Grumman)

Below: Three F3F-2s, BuNos 0973 (the lead ship), 0977 and 0979 of Marine squadron VMF-2, fly in formation. (Grumman)

production F2F-1s which differed in having a 700hp R-1535-72 Twin Wasp Junior, and deliveries of these aircraft began in early 1935, the first examples equipping VF-2B – the famous 'Fighting Two' – on board *Lexington* and VF-3B on *Ranger*. Fighting Two kept their 'Flying Barrels', as the F2F-1s were known, until 1940, and VF-3B later became VF-7B on board USS *Yorktown* and later still VF-5 on the carrier *Wasp*. F2F-1s equipped VF-5 until they were replaced by F3F-3s in 1939, whereupon they were relegated to use as gunnery trainers. Some F2F-1s were used as station 'hacks' from 1942 onwards.

The last aircraft of the F2F-1 order was completed as the prototype XF3F-1 (Grumman G-11) with an increased wing span and a longer fuselage for improved manoeuvrability. The prototype, powered by a 700hp R-1535-72 radial, crashed on a test flight in May 1935, but a second prototype with the same Bureau Number, 9727, was ordered, differing only in detail from the first. Fifty-four production F3F-1s (Grumman G-19) were ordered on 24 August 1935; fitted with a 700hp R-1535-84 engine, and armed with one 0.30in and one 0.50in machine gun in the nose firing forward and with provision for carrying two 110lb bombs on underwing racks, the F3F-1s were delivered during 1936 to VF-5B on board *Ranger* and to VF-6B on *Lexington*'s sister-ship USS *Saratoga*. These two squadrons were re-designated VF-4 and VF-3 respectively in

July 1939, and the aircraft were later fitted with strengthened upper wings.

The prototype XF3F-2, BuNo 0452, which was test-flown at Anacostia in January 1937, was fitted with a 1,000hp Wright XR-1820-22 Cyclone, giving an improved performance, and had a rudder of revised shape. It was subsequently converted to F3F-1 standard, but in the meantime 81 F3F-2s (Grumman G-37) were ordered on 23 March 1937, these having a 950hp R-1820-22 Cyclone and a modified cockpit canopy. During 1938 they equipped VF-6 aboard *Enterprise* and also the Marine squadrons VMF-1 and VMF-2. The sixty-fifth F3F-2 was re-engined with an uprated R-1820 Cyclone as the XF3F-3, and was followed by 27 F3F-3s ordered on 21 June 1938 which differed only in detail from the F3F-2. The XF3F-2 was later fitted with a curved windscreen, redesigned wing leading edges and a revised engine cowling, becoming the XF3F-4 in this form. The F3F-3s were destined to be the last biplane fighters ordered for the Navy or the US Army Air Corps: they equipped VF-5 on USS *Yorktown* but were in front-line service for only just over a year, although some were used as station 'hacks' from 1942 onwards.

Two civil variants of the F3F series were also built after the last F3F-2s. NC1051, the Grumman G-32 *Gulfhawk III*, a two-seat F3F-2 airframe with its armament and military equipment removed and a 1,000hp Wright R-1820-G2

Below: NR1050, the Grumman G-22 *Gulfhawk II*, was a civil variant of the F3F-1 built as a fast personal transport for Major Al Williams of the Gulf Oil Corporation. (Grumman)

Cyclone fitted, was a fast personal transport for the use of Major 'Al' Williams of the Gulf Oil Corporation. It succeeded the same owner's *Gulfhawk II* (Grumman G-22), which was also based on the F3F. The G-32A, NC1326, which followed the G-32 on the production line, was a tandem two-seater with a 775hp R-1820-F52 Cyclone. It flew as a Grumman demonstrator, and was later used by Leroy Grumman as his personal aircraft. Both the G-32 and G-32A were impressed into USAAF service in November 1942 under the designation UC-103-GR; *Gulfhawk III* became 42-97044 and the G-32A was serialled 42-97045. The latter machine was disposed of in January 1945, later becoming N46110. It was acquired by Ben Bradley of Fort Lauderdale, Florida, who repainted it in prewar Navy markings to represent an F3F-2.

The First Amphibians

Meanwhile, as the first production FF-1s were nearing their roll-out and delivery dates, the prototype of the Grumman G-9 single-engined utility amphibian, designed for use aboard carriers and as a ship-to-shore communications aircraft, made its first flight on 4 May 1933. With the Navy designation XJF-1, the aircraft combined some of the major features of the FF-1 with those of the earlier Loening

amphibians such as the Navy OL series. Like the latter, the XJF-1 featured a central main float which, instead of being suspended by means of fuselage and wing struts, was faired directly into the fuselage, thus perpetuating the boot-shaped lines of the earlier Loening types; like them also, it had wing-tip floats. The pilot and observer were seated in tandem under an enclosed canopy with sliding sections, and the faired-in portion between the float and the fuselage provided space to carry a passenger or a stretcher case. The main wheels retracted into the sides of the float just ahead of the lower wings, in a manner similar to the FF-1.

The XJF-1 prototype, BuNo 9218, was powered by a 700hp R-1535-62 Twin Wasp Junior radial and was followed by 27 production JF-1s, deliveries of which began late in 1934, replacing the Loening OL-9 in Navy units. Two later went to the US Marine Corps. The JF-1s had a 950hp Pratt & Whitney R-1830-62 Twin Wasp engine, but the fourteen JF-2s for the US Coast Guard were powered by a 750hp Wright R-1820-102 Cyclone, and also differed from the JF-1s in having special equipment. Four JF-2s were later transferred from the Coast Guard to the Navy, and five JF-3s, fitted with a 750hp R-1820-80, were built for the Navy. Eight of an armed variant of the JF-2 were

Below: The XJF-1 single-engined utility amphibian prototype, BuNo 9218, was intended for ship-to-shore communications and carried on the traditional Loening configuration of a central main float faired into the lower fuselage. Power was provided by a 700hp R-1535-62 Twin Wasp Junior. (Grumman)

also supplied to the Argentine Navy, these having one 0.30in fixed, forward-firing machine gun and a similar weapon in the dorsal position, plus racks for light bombs under the wings.

In 1937 a development of the JF-1 designated J2F-1 (Grumman G-15) appeared, differing from the JF series chiefly in that the main float was larger, with its fairing extended rearwards, and the inter-aileron struts on each pair of wings were deleted. There was a cabin for two passengers in the lower part of the fuselage beneath the pilot and observer in their enclosed cockpit. There was no XJ2F-1, a total of 29 J2F-1s, fitted with a 750hp Wright R-1820-20 Cyclone, being ordered straight off the production line. These were followed by 21 J2F-2s for the Marine Corps, this armed variant having a 0.30in fixed, forward-firing machine gun, a similar dorsal gun for the observer and underwing racks for light bombs. Nine J2F-2As with the same armament and various equipment changes were built for Marine Corps squadron VMS-3 based at St. Thomas in the US Virgin Islands, which operated them on patrol duties over the Caribbean. They were followed by 20 J2F-3s, which differed from the -2 in having an 850hp R-1820-36 Cyclone, and 32 J2F-4s, which were also very similar to the -2 but were fitted with target-towing gear and had an 850hp R-1820-30 Cyclone. One J2F-4 was later transferred to the Marine Corps.

At the end of 1940 an order was placed for 144 J2F-5s, and at the same time the name Duck was officially confirmed for the J2F series. The J2F-5 had a long-chord cowling for its 850hp R-1820-50 Cyclone and certain aerodynamic improvements to give a better performance; this variant had provision for carrying a radio operator in addition to the pilot and observer. One J2F-5, BuNo 00660, was transferred to the USAAF in 1942 as an OA-12A-GR with the serial 42-7771, and in 1948 eight ex-Navy Ducks were procured by the US Air Force for delivery to the Colombian Air Force (*Fuerza Aérea Colombiano*). Five of these were former J2F-5s designated A-12-GR, and three were ex-J2F-6s designated A-12A-GR.

The J2F-5 was the last Grumman-built version, but after Pearl Harbor 330 more aircraft were ordered for production by the Columbia Aircraft Corporation at Valley Stream, Long Island. These were designated J2F-6, although more correctly this might have been JL-1, the letter 'L' being used to identify Columbia Aircraft since 1942. The J2F-6 had a 1,050hp R-1820-54 Cyclone in a long-chord cowling, provision for target-towing gear and underwing racks for carrying two 100lb bombs or 325lb depth charges; the machine-gun armament of earlier versions was deleted. Columbia delivered its last J2F-6 early in 1946, and altogether 653 examples of the J2F and JF series were built. Several J2F-6s were converted for civil use, and twelve were registered in the USA in the early 1960s. The Duck was never intended for aerobatics, but at the 1970 US National Air

Above: The J2F Duck series differed from the JF-1 and JF-2 chiefly in having a larger main float and no inter-aileron struts. This head-on view of a J2F-5 shows well the distinctive boot-shaped float/fuselage configuration. Note the small airscrew for a target-towing winch on the port side of the fuselage. (US Navy)

Races at Reno, Nevada, in September, Frank Tallman gave a spectacular display in his J2F Duck that included loops, Immelman turns, hammerhead stalls and slow and snap rolls.

An interesting and little-known operator of a war-surplus Duck was the Jungle Aviation and Rescue Service (JAARS), which was founded in 1946 to provide air transport and communications back-up for the widespread network of missionary outposts in the rain forests of South America. The missionaries carried the Gospel message to the Indian tribes by means of Biblical translations into the various Indian languages produced by the Summer Institute of Linguistics at Glendale, California, and the Wycliffe Bible Translators. A J2F-2 Duck declared surplus by a US Marine Corps Mission in Peru was acquired in 1946 as the first aircraft of the 'Jungle Air Force', and this Duck began operations flown by Lawrence Montgomery of the USAF Reserve, the first pilot and later Superintendent of the JAARS. By 1958, when the Service was based at Yarinacocha in Peru, it had grown to operate a fleet of some twenty aircraft, including a PBY-5A Catalina, Aeronca Sedan seaplanes, a Noorduyn Norseman and a Cessna 180 on floats, as well as a twin-engined Cessna T-50, a Stinson SR-10 Reliant and seven Helio Courier STOL aircraft, plus the J2F-2 Duck which was still in service. The J2F was large enough to carry a really useful load, yet compact enough to operate from the many smaller tributaries of the Amazon in Peru and Bolivia, and into the small airstrips, often with difficult approaches, on which the JAARS relied. This type of flying was especially demanding because of the difficulty and remoteness of the terrain, and the absence of almost any kind of navigational aid. Most navigation was achieved by dead reckoning, although rivers were used wherever possible, especially when weather conditions were marginal. If the weather clamped down completely, the seaplanes would simply land on the nearest convenient stretch of river and 'weather it out'. In spite of all the hazards the JAARS experienced only two accidents in its first twelve years of operation, neither involving serious injury.

Above: The 29 J2F-1s had a 750hp Wright R-1820-20 Cyclone, while the 21 J2F-2s for the Marine Corps, one of which is seen here, were very similar but were armed with machine guns and bomb racks. (Grumman)

From Goose to Albatross

Designed late in 1936, the G-21 Goose 6/7-seater for airline or executive use was the first of a range of twin-engined amphibian flying boats that would see widespread military and commercial usage and establish Grumman as one of the most successful manufacturers of this class of aircraft. It was of all-metal construction with a two-step hull, the design of which was actually based on the central float of the earlier J2F series; the main wheels retracted manually into the sides of the hull in a manner similar to the Duck, and the steerable tailwheel just aft of the second step also retracted. The engines comprised two 450hp Pratt & Whitney R-985-SB Wasp Junior nine-cylinder radials, and the G-21 first flew in prototype form in June 1937. The main production version for civil use was the G-21A, which differed from the G-21 in having a 500lb increase in loaded weight, to 8,000lb, and R-985-SB2 Wasp Juniors, giving 450hp for take-off. The hull was divided into six watertight compartments, with stowage space for an anchor and mooring gear, radio equipment and excess baggage provided in the nose; the two pilots, seated side by side, had dual controls, and access to the cabin was through a large hatch in the port side just aft of the wing.

The G-21's type certificate was issued on 29 September 1937, by which time ten G-21As has been ordered as luxury 'air yachts' by wealthy private owners such as financiers Wilton Lloyd Smith and Henry S. Morgan; Gar Wood, the speedboat racing 'king' of the 1930s; Boris Sergievsky, chief test pilot of the Sikorsky company (which had itself created many amphibious aircraft), who later owned one of the first production G-73 Mallards; and Lord Beaverbrook. The last-named in fact owned two: the first, G-AFCH, was registered to him on 26 October 1937 but sold abroad in the Dutch East Indies the

following July; it was replaced by G-AFKJ, which had its Certificate of Airworthiness issued on 4 January 1939. This was impressed into RAF service as HK822 in February 1941 and sank off Benghazi, Libya, on 9 December 1942 while serving with the Middle East Air Sea Rescue Flight.

For luxury executive use the cabin seated four or five people in roomy comfort in large reclining seats, and there was a pantry, a toilet and a large baggage compartment aft of the cabin. The single-spar wing was built in three pieces, a centre section and two outer panels; the forward portion was covered with 24ST metal sheet and the rear portion was fabric-covered, as were the rudder and elevators, while the split two-position flaps were vacuum-operated. Fuel tankage of 220 US gallons capacity was housed in the wing. The initial production G-21As had Hamilton-Standard two-blade, controllable-pitch propellers, constant-speed units by the same manufacturers being optional; later production aircraft had three-blade airscrews. The G-21B was a pure flying boat variant with the undercarriage deleted, and several of these were supplied to the Portuguese Naval Air Service (*Aeronautica Naval*). By early 1939 civil G-21As were in service with customers in Canada, Bolivia, Peru, Venezuela, New Guinea and the Dutch East Indies.

Below: The G-21 Goose prototype first flew in June 1937 and differed only slightly from the production G-21A, having two 450hp Pratt & Whitney R-985-SB Wasp Juniors and a loaded weight 500lb lighter. (Grumman)

The JRF Series

The G-21A's ruggedness and ample reserves of power soon made it attractive to military customers, and the first of these to place a production order was the US Army Air Corps, which in 1938 contracted for 26 G-21As designated OA-9 for use in the utility and liaison roles; the aircraft had more spartan interiors than the executive civil G-21A and were fitted with military versions of the Wasp Junior designated R-985-17. One of these OA-9s was still in service in 1948, when it was redesignated ZA-9-GR, the 'Z' prefix denoting 'obsolete'. In 1942 five Goose IAs originally destined for the Royal Navy and serialled FP505 to FP509 were transferred to the USAAF as OA-9-GRs, becoming A-9-GRs under the new postwar designation system. That year three civil G-21As were impressed into USAAF service as OA-13A-GRs and fitted with R-985-AN1 engines to the joint Army/Navy standard, while a US Navy JRF-4 and JRF-5 were also acquired by the USAAF in 1945 under the designation OA-13B-GR, these having R-985-AN6 engines.

In 1938 the US Navy ordered a single eight-seater version of the G-21A for evaluation as the XJ3F-1 and this, serialled 1384, had the maker's designation G-26 and was in effect the prototype for the JRF series. A Navy order for twenty of the latter (Grumman G-38) followed, of which the first ten were JRF-1 seven-seaters with R-985-AN6 Wasp Juniors, deliveries beginning late in 1939; two more civil G-21As were subsequently impressed by the Navy as JRF-1s. Five of the JRF-1s were later fitted with cameras for photography and with target-towing gear, thus becoming JRF-1As.

The next ten machines in the JRF series were seven JRF-2s for US Coast Guard air–sea rescue work (Grumman G-39), these being delivered in 1940, and three JRF-3s, also for the Coast Guard, which differed from the -2 in having de-icing equipment and an autopilot for rescue duties in northern waters. The JRF-4, ten of which were built for the Navy, was very similar to the JRF-1 but equipped for coastal anti-submarine patrols, racks for two 250lb bombs or depth charges being fitted under the wings just outboard of the nacelles; alternatively, cameras for photography and target-towing gear as on the JRF-1A could be fitted. Two more civil G-21As were impressed as JRF-4s and one of these became an OA-13B-GR in USAAF service in 1945. Several Navy JRF Geese were also used by the US Marine Corps.

Above: The G-21A Goose production version had 450hp R-985-SB2 Wasp Juniors, and those Geese delivered prewar served as luxury 'air yachts' or as executive transports; this one, belonging to the Texaco oil company, is seen taxiing up a slipway in Bayou County, Louisiana. (Grumman)

The first large-scale production version of the JRF series was the JRF-5, which could be distinguished from the -4 in having 450hp R-985-AN12 Wasp Juniors and certain minor improvements; it had provision for carrying cameras, and altogether 185 JRF-5s were built, deliveries beginning in 1941. Seven of these went to the Coast Guard as JRF-5Gs for rescue duties; one, an impressed civil G-21A, went to the USAAF as an OA-13B-GR; and five, serialled FP470 to FP474, were delivered to the RAF as Goose Is. Two more JRF-5s were ordered for delivery to the Cuban *Aviación Naval* (Naval Aviation), and a further seventeen JRF-5s were supplied to the Royal Canadian Air Force, which used them as navigational trainers as well as utility transports, serialled 382 to 397. The JRF-6B was ordered by the Navy for supply under Lend-Lease to Britain as a navigational trainer; compared with the JRF-5, this variant had a different electrical system and new radio equipment. Fifty JRF-6Bs were ordered for the RAF as Goose IAs, serialled FP475 to FP524 (although the last thirteen were not built). This batch replaced an earlier order for the same number of G-21As placed by the British Purchasing Commission in the USA in 1940; these aircraft, allocated the serials BW778 to BW827, were completed for the US Navy. Of another batch of ten Goose Is, FP738 to FP747, eight were retained by the US Navy and FP740 and FP742 were kept based at Miami. Most of the Goose Is and IAs were delivered to, and operated from, Piarco in Trinidad, although a few served in Great Britain with No. 24 Squadron and with the Air Transport Auxiliary.

After the war many JRF and other military versions of the Goose were disposed of as surplus, and they proved to be very popular with small bush and charter

Left: The US Coast Guard ordered seven JRF-2s for air–sea rescue, of which V174, seen here, was the first. The three JRF-3s were very similar but were fitted with de-icing equipment and an autopilot for use in northern waters. (Grumman)

Left: Ten JRF-5s went to the RAF as Goose Is, including MV993 seen here, while 37 (originally 50) JRF-6Bs were ordered by the US Navy for supply to Britain as Goose IAs. (Imperial War Museum)

operators and other airlines, especially in Canada and Alaska, and also in the Caribbean. A few were still in use in the early 1960s with such operators in Norway and Finland as well as North America, and also with small airlines serving island groups, such as Air Polynesie of Papéeté, Tahiti, in the Society Islands of French Polynesia, and Transportes Aereos de Cabo Verde, serving the Cape Verde Islands. The two largest airline operators of the Goose were Alaska Coastal-Ellis Airlines Inc. of Juneau, and Antilles Air Boats Inc. of Christiansted, St. Croix, in the US Virgin Islands. Alaska Coastal operated a network of domestic routes based on Juneau and Ketchikan and serving the coastal communities and islands in the south of the state, and by the time it merged with Alaska Airlines Inc. on 1 April 1968 it had thirteen Goose amphibians and one Turbo Goose, as well as four Super Catalinas, a Convair 240 and four Cessna 185 seaplanes, on its inventory. Antilles Air Boats was formed in February 1964 by Captain Charles F. Blair of Pan American, one of the world's most experienced flying boat pilots, and on the 4th of that month services began with a ten-passenger Goose between St. Croix's Christiansted harbour and St. Thomas in the US Virgin Islands. It was not long before the frequency of service between these points rivalled that of a good bus company, with two or even three flights an hour. Tortola in the British Virgin Islands, Fajardo and San Juan in Puerto Rico and St. Maarten, the Franco-Dutch island in the northernmost Leeward Islands group, were also served, and by 1979, the last full year of operations, over 120 services a day were being flown. Antilles Air Boats' fleet had by this time grown to eighteen Geese, two Grumman G-73 Mallards and three 'civilianized' HU-16B Albatross amphibians, as well as two Short Sandringhams acquired from Australia in 1974.

The Goose also served as an executive transport, again mainly in North America, and with several government and other official agencies. The Royal Canadian Mounted Police's Air Division, for example, had eleven aircraft in the mid-1950s, which included a Goose normally based at Victoria, British Columbia, operating among the islands and around coastal areas of that province. During the summer of 1950 this Goose completed a long patrol over the northern regions of Canada, leaving Ottawa on 9 June and taking in Manitoba, Saskatchewan, Alberta, the Yukon Territory, the Mackenzie River in the North West Territories and the western Arctic regions and flying along the northern shores of the Canadian mainland to Hudson's Bay, the eastern Arctic and back via Labrador and Quebec to Ottawa, where it landed again on 2 September after covering a total distance of 15,585 miles.

Several air arms also acquired examples of the Goose in the postwar years, including Argentina's Coast Guard force (*Prefectura Nacional Maritima*), the Peruvian Air Force (*Cuerpo de Aeronautica del Peru*, later *Fuerza Aérea del Peru*), and the French Navy (*Aéronavale*). The *Aéronavale* used the Goose in the Indo-China conflict against the Viet-Minh, twelve JRF-5s being handed over officially by the United States to *Escadrille 8S* at its home base, Cat-Lai, north of Saigon, on 13 March 1952; five more were acquired in 1954. This squadron had started operations late in 1945 with some captured Japanese seaplanes and an old prewar Loire 130 flying boat, but re-equipped with ex-RAF Supermarine Sea Otters in 1947; these were replaced at the end of 1950 by Catalinas, which were in turn succeeded early in 1951 − a year before the official handover − by the JRF-5s. The Grumman machines were used not merely for communications, but also for river and maritime reconnaissance, casualty evacuation and photo reconnaissance, and to provide some degree of close support for the ground forces, for which role twin 7.62mm machine guns were fitted firing through the entrance door and VHF radio equipment was installed to provide communications with troops on the ground. Racks for four 100lb bombs were added beneath the wings, and one JRF-5 was experimentally fitted with a fixed, forward-firing armament. Eight smaller bombs could be carried under each wing, as could rocket projectiles; two stretcher cases could be accommodated for the casevac role; and cameras could also be

Right: Goose N323 of Air Catalina (the operating name of Catalina Seaplanes Inc.) operates scheduled services from Long Beach and San Pedro in California to Catalina Island in Avalon Bay. This Goose has the McKinnon retractable floats modification. (Air-Britain)

installed. The aircraft operated all over Indo-China, from as far north as Cat-Bi near the Chinese border, and also from Laos and Cambodia. From 1 April 1952 to July 1954 the JRF-5s, often flying singly or in small detachments, notched up 3,800 sorties and 6,500 hours in Indo-China without incurring any losses, but, following the French defeat at Dien-Bien-Phu in May 1954 and the subsequent cease-fire and partitioning of Vietnam into North and South, eleven of *Escadrille 8S*'s JRF-5s were ferried back to Algeria. Their new base was on the naval side of Algiers' Maison Blanche airport, and their role in the Algerian conflict was to be not quite as dramatic as that in Indo-China, consisting essentially of maritime reconnaissance work (with particular reference to detecting arms smuggling into Algeria by sea) and some communications duties. The Goose finally left French Navy service

in 1961, but its little-documented career in Indo-China reflects an excellent record of adaptability and improvisation.

As part of a research programme into the use of hydrofoils, to make possible a truly open-ocean flying boat capable of operating in relatively high sea states, a US Navy JRF-5 Goose was fitted experimentally with a Gruenberg super-cavitating hydrofoil system by the Edo Corporation – well known as a manufacturer of seaplane floats – under a 1962 US Navy Bureau of Weapons contract. The aircraft featured a stainless steel main hydrofoil at and below its centre of gravity, attached by a pair of struts running up each side of the hull, and this hydrofoil was the main waterborne load-carrying surface. It had a very sharp leading edge and a blunt trailing edge, and it was supplemented by two protruding hydro-skis mounted one on each side of the bow, these being flat

Left: JRF-5G 37782 was fitted experimentally by the Edo Corporation with a Gruenberg hydrofoil system, with which it first flew in the summer of 1963. The main hydrofoil was fitted below the centre of gravity under the planing bottom, and was supplemented by two hydro-skis mounted on the bow. (Edo)

plates with chines designed to direct the spray downwards. As the waterborne speed increased, these hydro-skis contacted waves and so provided the angle of attack changes required by the main hydrofoil. The JRF-5 was first flown in this configuration in the summer of 1963 after water runs had been made at speeds of up to 110mph. Tests showed that, once the main hydrofoil was extended from the bottom of the hull, water handling characteristics were quite good. The JRF-5 was evaluated early in 1964 at the US Naval Air Test Center at Patuxent River, Maryland, and successfully completed its tests there, and plans were laid to test a new hydrofoil configuration on the aircraft. Edo were also awarded a similar Navy contract for the design, scale water-tank testing and scale manufacture of a similar super-cavitating hydrofoil configuration for the HU-16 Albatross.

McKinnon Modifications

By the 1960s the Goose was about the only 6/10-seater amphibian available in any numbers, and it seemed unlikely to be replaced, so ways were sought of extending its useful life by means of re-engining and modification programmes. McKinnon Enterprises Inc. of Sandy, Oregon (formerly the McKinnon-Hickman Co.), had in 1953 begun converting Grumman G-44A Widgeons into executive transports, and these conversions were successful enough to lead to a more ambitious four-engined modernization of the Goose known as the McKinnon G-21C which, fitted out to seat up to twelve people including the pilot, first flew on 25 January 1958. The first production G-21C conversion took to the air on 30 December 1958. The two Wasp Juniors were replaced by four 340hp Lycoming GSO-480-B2D6 'flat six' geared and supercharged engines driving Hartzell three-blade, constant-speed, reversible-pitch and feathering airscrews. The fuel tankage in the wings was increased from the 220 US gallons of the G-21A to 337 US gallons, and the other notable modification was the fitting of retractable wing-tip floats, float and undercarriage retraction, as well as that of the flaps, now being electrically operated, unlike the G-21A. Also featured were an

extended radar nose, a small dorsal fin, a one-piece windscreen and a new 24V electrical system. McKinnon also offered the retractable wing-tip float installation for the standard G-21A Goose whose owner did not desire the full four-engined conversion; these new floats gave an increased cruising speed and also better accessibility for loading or unloading the Goose on water. Similarly available was a conversion kit for increasing the maximum take-off weight of the standard G-21A Goose by 1,200lb, to 9,200lb.

In 1960 the G-21C was superseded by the G-21D, which differed in having its bow lengthened by 3ft to enable four passengers to be seated in a small cabin forward of the flight deck. Up to fourteen passengers could now be carried, plus the pilot, seven passengers being accommodated in the main cabin and four more in a small cabin aft of the main entrance door. The G-21D had a tailplane of increased span, an added rudder tab, and a reduced fuel capacity brought about by removing the centre-section tank. The aircraft received FAA Type Approval on 29 June 1960.

The first conversion of a G-21A Goose to turboprop power was carried out by Alaska Coastal-Ellis Airlines Inc. in its workshops at Juneau, and the Turbo Goose was first flown in this form in March 1966. Its Wasp Juniors were replaced by two 550shp Pratt & Whitney (UAC) PT6A-6 turboprops, and the conversion was managed by the Strato Engineering Corporation of Burbank, California, the parts being fabricated by Fairey Canada Ltd. and the actual installation being completed by the airline. Alaska Coastal considered converting all its Goose fleet to Turbo standard, but before any further work could be undertaken the company merged with Alaska Airlines Inc. on 1 April 1968. McKinnon Enterprises took up the Turbo Goose concept and marketed two similar conversions – still, rather confusingly, designated G-21C and G-21D, the former also being known for a time as the G-21E – that closely resembled the original Alaska Coastal modification but with two 550shp United Aircraft of Canada PT6A-20 turboprops driving Hartzell three-blade, constant-speed, feathering and

reversible-pitch airscrews. These engines were mounted 1ft 3in further inboard than the original Wasp Juniors and were canted outwards slightly to enable the propeller arcs to clear the bows. Fuel tankage in the wings was increased to 586 US gallons, and the Turbo G-21C had the retractable floats and other new features of the Lycoming-engined G-21C, plus larger cabin windows, a new instrument panel and an oxygen system. Besides the pilot, the Turbo G-21C could carry up to eleven passengers, seven in the main cabin and four more in a small cabin aft of the entrance door, and this version received FAA Type Approval in February 1967. The G-21D Turbo Goose was, except for its powerplant, very similar to the Lycoming-engined G-21D but had the longer bow with accommodation for four passengers, plus the further improvements added to the Turbo G-21C. This and the similarly powered G-21D superseded the Lycoming-engined versions. A Turbo Goose was flight-tested in the spring of 1969 with two 680shp PT6A-27 turboprops, these engines subsequently becoming standard for Turbo conversions.

For owners who did not require their aircraft to be converted to the full G-21C or G-21D Turbo Goose standards, McKinnon offered a simpler adaptation with PT6A-20 (and later PT6A-27) turboprops driving the same airscrews as those installed on the original Wasp Junior engine nacelles, and not moved inboard; any of the other new features of the Turbo G-21C and -D could also be incorporated at the customer's choice, and fuel capacity could be increased to 586 US gallons. The latest McKinnon conversion is the G-21G Turbo Goose, which differs from the G-21C chiefly in minor details, for example the inclusion of a rotating beacon on top of the fin and the application of a metallizing treatment to the wings. Optional 'extras' include picture windows for the cabin; a centre main fuel tank of larger capacity (bringing tankage up to 586 US gallons); a larger cabin, made possible by removing the bulkhead at station 26; dual landing lights in the wing leading edges; and electrical retraction of the undercarriage (this had previously been manual on both the Lycoming-engined and Turbo G-21C and -D). The G-21G, which received FAA Type Approval on 29 August 1969, has a maximum take-off weight of 12,500lb and its maximum operating speed is 245mph; range with full fuel tanks is now increased to 1,600 miles.

The only G-21A to come on to the British register since the pair owned prewar by Lord Beaverbrook has been G-ASXG, owned by the Grosvenor Estates, which administer the Duke of Westminster's landowning interests. This aircraft received its C of A on 16 October 1964 and was used for flights to Europe and to various Scottish and Irish lakes. G-ASXG started life with the Royal Canadian Air Force, serialled 926, and later became successively CF-BZY,

Above: G-21C Turbo Goose N121H has the standard bow and retractable floats; note also the extra dorsal fin area and one-piece windscreen. The G-21C was known for a time as the G-21E. (D. Goodwin, via J. M. G. Gradidge)

N36992 and N3692. As originally delivered it had R-985-AN6 Wasp Junior radials but featured the McKinnon retractable float installation and had a 9,200lb take-off weight. After three years' service it was converted to G-21C Turbo Goose standard, being re-engined by Marshalls of Cambridge (Engineering) Ltd. with two 550shp PT6A-20 turboprops, and in this form received its C of A on 19 July 1968. In 1972 it was withdrawn from use and cocooned at Leavesden in Hertfordshire.

Yet another re-engined version of the Goose was produced by Volpar Inc. of Van Nuys, California, who have devised and produced several turboprop conversions of the well-known Beech 18 light transport using AiResearch (formerly Garrett AiResearch) TPE 331 turboprops; known as the Turbo 18, Turboliner and Turboliner II, these modified versions had Volpar nosewheel undercarriages and 705shp TPE 331-1-101B turboprops. Using the nacelles developed for the Turbo 18 and Turboliner, Volpar later marketed the TPE 331 turboprop installation as Packaged Power, which was available with any of the different versions of this engine and with either over-engine or under-engine air intakes as required by the particular installation. The Goose was fitted with two 715shp AiResearch TPE 331-2U-203 engines in Packaged Power nacelles with intakes above the spinners; other types similarly re-engined with these Packaged Power

units included the De Havilland Dove and Beaver. McKinnon also investigated a conversion of the Goose with TPE 331 tubroprops under the designation G-21F, but this variant was not built.

The G-44 Widgeon

Meanwhile the success of the G-21A Goose had led to the similar but smaller G-44 Widgeon, which first flew in prototype form in July 1940. Seating four passengers in an executive interior, the G-44 was powered by two 200hp Ranger 6-440C-5 six-cylinder, inverted, in-line, air-cooled engines (military designation L-440-5). Like the G-21A, the G-44 was of all-metal construction, the two-step hull being divided into five watertight compartments and the single box spar wing having a fuel capacity of 106 US gallons. Wheel retraction was very similar to the G-21A but hydraulically operated, and the tailwheel also retracted. The outer wings were metal-covered to the rear of the spar and fabric-covered aft to the trailing edge, the centre section being wholly metal-covered; slotted flaps were fitted, and these and the ailerons were fabric-covered, as were the rudder and elevators. Just over twenty G-44s had been built for executive and private-owner use before deliveries of the first military version, the J4F-1, of which 25 had been ordered for the US Coast Guard, began in 1941. This was a three-seater variant for coastal anti-submarine patrol as well as utility use, and could carry one 200lb

Below: Devised by Volpar Inc., Goose N780 has two 840shp Garrett-AiResearch TPE 331-3 turboprops in Packaged Power nacelles developed by Volpar for their similarly re-engined Turbo 18 and Turboliner versions of the Beech 18. Note the dorsal fillet extending to the wing leading edge. (Volpar)

Left: The G-44 Widgeon first flew in July 1940 as a four-passenger executive amphibian; the first military versions were the 25 J4F-1s for the US Coast Guard, which could carry a 250lb depth charge on a rack under the starboard wing. (Grumman)

depth charge on a rack under the starboard wing just inboard of the nacelle. However, even with just the one external store and the crew reduced to two members, the J4F-1 was unable to climb on one engine, which restricted its use at any great distance from the coast. Nevertheless, a J4F-1 of Coast Guard Squadron 212 sank the German submarine *U-166* in 1942 in the Gulf of Mexico just off the Mississippi Delta. In 1942 fifteen civil G-44s were impressed into the USAAF as OA-14s, and in November 1944 a further example was acquired from the Corps of Engineers at Borinquen Field, Puerto Rico, to become an OA-14A-GR with the serial number 44-52997.

The J4F-1s were followed by 131 J4F-2 five-seat utility transports for the US Navy. Of these, fourteen were supplied to the Brazilian Air Force and sixteen more went to the Royal Navy as Gosling Is with the serials FP455 to FP469, plus JS996; later known as Widgeons, the British aircraft were used mainly for communications in the West Indies in 1943–45. One J4F-2 was assigned to the Foreign Commission in Miami, and this was also sometimes used as an instrument trainer. Twelve G-44s, built just before the second batch of J4F-1s, were supplied to the Portuguese Naval Air Service (*Aeronautica Naval*). After the J4F-2 a further 76 G-44As were built for civil use, this variant differing from the G-44 in having an improved hull shape, which resulted in better water handling characteristics. A total of 276 civil and military Widgeons were built by Grumman.

After the war Widgeons, both ex-military aircraft and G-44As, went into service with the smaller scheduled and

Below: The New Zealand airline NZ Tourist Air Travel had three of its five Widgeons, including ZK-BAY seen here, re-engined locally with two 260hp Continental IO-470-D 'flat six' engines. In this form they were known as Super Widgeons. (P. R. Keating)

charter airlines, chiefly in Alaska and Canada, and also with executive and private owners, mostly in the United States. The New Zealand airline NZ Tourist Air Travel Ltd. of Auckland, which in 1961 bought up another small Widgeon operator, Amphibian Airways of Invercargill in the South Island of New Zealand, finally operated five Widgeons on local services and sightseeing flights from Auckland and other parts of the country from 1954 until it was itself absorbed into Mount Cook Airlines in 1969. In 1962 three of the Widgeons had been re-engined locally with 260hp Continental IO-470-D 'flat six' powerplants in place of the Ranger engines, which by then had been out of production for some years; in this form the three amphibians were known by the airline as Super Widgeons. NZ Tourist Air Travel's Widgeons flew non-scheduled services to all the islands of the Hauraki Gulf on which Auckland is situated. Fishing parties were flown and ambulance flights made, as well as sightseeing trips to the lakes and sounds of the Southern Alps, and several local scheduled routes were also serviced. Mount Cook Airlines continued to use the Widgeons after taking over NZ Tourist Air Travel until finally retiring them in April 1975.

The first re-engined version had appeared in France, where Grumman had granted a licence for production of the Widgeon to SCAN (Société de Constructions Aéro Navales) of Port-Neuf and La Rochelle. SCAN built 40 Widgeons as the SCAN 30, and in place of the Ranger engines these had either two 220hp Mathis 8GB22 or 240hp Salmson 8 AS powerplants, both these being eight-cylinder, inverted-vee, air-cooled units; the Salmson was actually a French-built version of the well-known German Argus AS 10C. With Mathis engines the SCAN 30's cruising speed was 140mph and its alighting speed on water 56mph. The SCAN 30s were intended for the French Navy and for civil customers, but partly no doubt because the Navy was, as previously related, operating the JRF-5 Goose in Indo-China, most of the 40 French-built aircraft were later sold to the USA, where some were re-engined with 300hp Lycoming R-680-R3 nine-cylinder radials driving three-blade Hartzell airscrews and were known as the Gannet Super Widgeon. At least one example, registered N57LM, was re-engined with 220hp Continental W-670 radials, and at least two Grumman Widgeons were re-engined with Lycoming GO-435s. Most of the SCAN 30s were later converted by McKinnon Enterprises Inc. to their own *Super Widgeon* standard, along with a number of Grumman-built Widgeons.

The McKinnon Super Widgeon had the previous powerplants replaced by two 270hp Lycoming GO-480-B1D 'flat six' engines driving Hartzell three-blade, fully feathering airscrews. The hull and undercarriage were modified to allow an increase in maximum take-off weight to 5,500lb, and extra tanks in the outer wings increased fuel capacity from 108 to 154 US gallons. Other new features included picture windows, improved soundproofing of the cabin, the provision of an emergency escape hatch, and a more modern IFR instrument panel. A retractable float installation similar to that previously developed for the Goose was approved in 1960 as an 'optional extra'.

As part of an extensive research programme into the characteristics of a new generation of postwar flying boats, the Edo Corporation fitted a Widgeon with a series of six experimental hulls of high length-to-beam ratio in 1947–52. This Widgeon, nicknamed *Petulant Porpoise*, was at first fitted with a half-scale replica of the hull of the Martin XP5M-1 Marlin flying boat, and after this flew on 4 May 1948 the handling characteristics and performance of the full-size XP5M-1 hull were found to tally very closely with the Edo-modified Widgeon's test results. The last hull to be fitted to it was designed jointly by Convair and the Navy Bureau of Aeronautics, and had the highest length-to-beam ratio of any hull flown – 12.5:1, compared to the more traditional 5:1 of the PBY-5 Catalina and the 6:1 of the PBM-5 Mariner. This sort of hull, with its long afterbody, almost eliminates the conventional step and gives much greater stability in the water during landing and take-off. The Edo hulls on the Widgeon had windows in the bottom of the afterbody to enable water flow patterns to be observed and photographed during taxiing.

The G-73 Mallard

Grumman's first postwar amphibian, the G-73 Mallard, had a later manufacturer's designation than the G-64 or Albatross, although it first flew in prototype form in 1946, a year before the Albatross; three prototypes were built, and production deliveries began in 1947. It was unusual among the company's aircraft in not going into military service at all, the only Mallards to bear military markings being the two supplied as VIP transports to King Farouk of Egypt, which carried Egyptian Air Force roundels and the serials F7 and F8. Most Mallards were used as executive and corporate transports, although some served with the smaller airlines, mainly in Canada and Alaska. The standard accommodation was for two pilots and ten passengers, six in the forward compartment and four in the rear, although up to fourteen passengers could be seated in a high-density layout.

The Mallard was of all-metal, stressed-skin construction and was powered by two 600hp Pratt & Whitney R-1340-S3H-1 Wasp nine-cylinder radials driving Hamilton Standard Hydromatic three-blade, constant-speed airscrews. Fuel tanks in the wings housed 380 US gallons, while twenty US gallons of additional fuel could be carried in each float, this being fed to the main tanks by means of booster pumps. Both the split flaps and the under-carriage retraction were hydraulically operated. The Mallard featured a nose-wheel undercarriage instead of the tail-wheel arrangement of the Goose and Widgeon, the free-swivelling nosewheel retracting into the bow and the main wheels into the sides.

Sixty-one Mallards had been built when production ended in 1951 and, apart from King Farouk, among the wealthier private owners of Mallards were the French textile magnate and industrialist Marcel Boussac, who used to own the world-famous Maxim's restaurant in Paris; Mr. Daniel van Clief, of Esmont, Virginia, who, like Boussac, was a leading racehorse owner; and millionaire Sikorsky test pilot Boris Sergievsky, also President of the American Helicopter Corporation, who had been one of the first G-21A Goose owners back in 1937. Sergievsky made the first Atlantic flight with a Mallard in August 1947, 'just to see if it could do it', his aircraft, NC2940, arriving at Heathrow on 12 August. Several Mallards were owned by oil companies in Canada and elsewhere, and Shell operated

four in Indonesia in 1958. A number of airlines also operated Mallards, including Pacific Western Airlines Ltd. of Vancouver, British Columbia; BC Air Lines Ltd., which took over some of Pacific Western's Vancouver Island routes in 1959; Midwest Airlines Ltd. of Winnipeg; and Northern Consolidated Airlines Inc. of Anchorage, Alaska. In the South Pacific, Regie Aerienne Interinsulaire had begun operating in September 1950 as Air Tahiti with a Widgeon and, later, a Mallard from Papéeté on the island of Tahiti, the capital of French Polynesia, to other territories in the Society Islands group. It also operated monthly flights to Aitutaki in the Cook Islands but, as traffic grew, a larger type was needed and by 1956 the Mallard was replaced by a Catalina. Trans-Australian Airlines also used a Mallard for a time in the early 1960s, and in Japan four were owned by the Nitto Aviation Co. Ltd. and two by Japan Domestic Airlines, which absorbed Nitto Aviation in April 1964.

In 1969 one of Northern Consolidated's two Mallards, N2974, was acquired by Frakes Aviation Inc. of Angwin, California, for re-engining with two 715ehp PT6A-27 turboprops similar to those fitted to the Turbo Goose; in this form it became the Turbo Mallard, first flying as such in September 1969. This Mallard had previously been used to test the feasibility of the conversion in 1964, when the starboard R-1340 Wasp engine was removed and replaced by a PT6A-9

turboprop (the Wasp radial on the port side being retained), and after fifteen hours of flight tests with this mixed powerplant had proven the turboprop to be satisfactory, it was replaced by the Wasp and the Mallard resumed service with Northern Consolidated. The Turbo Mallard received its FAA Type Certificate in October 1970, and was made available to customers with either PT6A-27 or PT6A-34 turboprops, both of 715ehp. An automatic propeller feathering system was featured, and the standard wing and float tankage of the piston-engined Mallard could be supplemented by two optional 83 US gallon wing tanks, bringing the total fuel capacity up to 646 US gallons.

The Albatross

Design work on the G-64 Albatross amphibian started in 1944 to meet a US Navy requirement for a replacement for the JRF Goose, to be used as a utility transport and also as a trainer and for air–sea rescue duties. The G-64 was larger than the Mallard, and almost twice as large as the Goose, and the first of two prototypes, designated XJR2F-1 and carrying the Bureau Number 82853, completed its maiden flight on 24 October 1947. It was followed by the first Navy production version, with the interim designation PF-1, but the first 32 PF-1s ordered, now designated UF-1s, were diverted to the USAF as SA-16A-GR Albatrosses for air–sea rescue tasks,

Far left, top: J4F-2 Widgeon *Petulant Porpoise*, fitted with an experimental hull of slightly lower length-to-beam ratio than that of the replica XP5M-1 Marlin hull. (Edo)
Centre: Two G-73 Mallards were supplied as VIP transports to King Farouk of Egypt and carried the Egyptian Air Force serials F7 and F8; the latter machine is seen here. (Grumman)
Bottom: The Turbo Mallard, a conversion by Frakes Aviation of the piston-engined Mallard had two 715shp PT6A-27 or PT6A-34 turboprops similar to those installed in the Turbo Goose. N2966, seen here, was re-engined with PT6A-27s. (Matt Rodina Collection)

Below: Designed as a JRF-5 Goose replacement, the G-64 (or Albatross) was almost twice as large as the earlier design and was used mainly for air–sea rescue work. The first of two XJR2F-1 Albatross prototypes, BuNo 82853, is seen here on its maiden flight, 24 October 1947. (Grumman)

mostly with the Military Air Transport Service (MATS) Air Rescue Service. Twenty aircraft had been ordered before the PF-1/UF-1s were transferred, and the designation SA-16 followed on from OA-15, the last in the Observation Amphibian series (the Albatross was originally to have been designated OA-16). Eventually 170 SA-16A-GRs were built, these becoming HU-16As under the 1962 Tri-Service designation system. They had a crew of four to six, and could carry up to twelve stretcher cases in the rescue role, as did the Navy UF-1s. Both versions were powered by two 1,425hp Wright Cyclone R-1820-76, -76A or -76B nine-cylinder radials. A total of 104 UF-1s were built, these later becoming HU-16Cs, and 51 of these were later rebuilt to UF-2 standard with an increased wing span and other modifications. Six very similar UF1Gs for the US Coast Guard were also produced, to be supplemented later by 28 UF-1s transferred from the Navy; all 34 of these amphibians were subsequently modified to UF-2G standard. The UF-1L was a variant optimized for Arctic operations. One was built as such, and further air-frames were converted from UF-1s; all were redesignated LU-16C in 1962. Five UF-1s were completed as UF-1T crew trainers with dual controls, later becoming TU-16Cs.

The Albatross was of all-metal construction with a two-step hull, with which the fin was built integrally; the wings were built in three sections, a centre section permanently attached to the hull and two outer sections. The undercarriage was similar to that of the Mallard but had twin nosewheels; retraction was hydraulic. The engines drove Hamilton Standard three-blade, reversing airscrews, and the normal fuel capacity, in the wing centre section, was 675 US gallons. Drop tanks of 100, 150 or 300 US gallons capacity could be carried on a bomb rack under each wing outboard of the nacelles, and each wing-tip float could house a further 200 US gallons of fuel. The underwing racks could also carry, instead of bombs or drop tanks, a rescue boat or other packaged equipment, and weather radar was installed in a nose radome. JATO (jet-assisted take-off) could be effected with a single or double unit on each side of the fuselage attached to the cabin door, and there was stowage space for four of these JATO units under the cabin floor between the wheel wells. There was a separate oxygen system for crew and passengers, with twenty outlets for oxygen masks in the cabin.

The crew consisted of two pilots, a navigator and a radio and radar operator, plus, for the rescue or ambulance role, two medical attendants. Ten passengers could be carried instead of twelve stretcher cases, or alternatively 4,100lb of cargo or special equipment could be transported with the seats removed. The entrance door in the port side was split horizontally, the lower part being left shut to provide a higher freeboard in rough

Above: The Albatross first entered service with the USAF as the SA-16A-GR (later HU-16A) and was used mainly by the MATS Air Rescue organization. Like the Navy UF-1, it could accommodate up to twelve stretcher cases, and could carry two underwing drop tanks of 100, 150 or 300 US gallons capacity. (Grumman)

weather. A rescue platform could be attached to the bottom door sill from which a crewman secured by a safety belt could haul people on board from the water. There was a smaller emergency door in the starboard side, and both doors could be used for oblique photography. A hatch in the roof facilitated the loading of freight. A 'triphibian' variant of the SA-16A-GR, fitted with sprung skis under the hull and wing-tip floats to permit landings and take-offs from snow or ice as well as water, was developed in 1953. This ski installation was tested on SA-16A 48-588, and as a result the USAF ordered 127 conversion kits for modifying their Albatrosses.

In addition to the aircraft delivered to the USAF, SA-16A-GRs were ordered on USAF contracts for supply to various foreign air arms under the Mutual Defense Aid programme. Fourteen SA-16As went to the Brazilian Air Force (*Fôrca Aérea Brasileira*), fourteen to the Chilean Air Force (*Fuerza Aérea de Chile*), three to the Argentine Navy, some to the Italian Air Force (eight of these were still in service in 1979, equipping search and rescue squadrons), several to the Portuguese Air Force (*Fôrca Aérea Portuguesa*), some to the Chinese Nationalist Air Force (eight HU-16Bs were still in service in 1983, equipping a search and rescue squadron), and several to the Philippine Air Force (six HU-16Bs still equipping one squadron in 1983). Navy UF-1/HU-16Cs were supplied to the Indonesian

Republic Air Force (*Angkatan Udara Republik Indonesia*) from January 1958, equipping, with PBY-5A Catalinas, No. 5 Coastal Patrol Squadron, while some also went to the Indonesian Navy, where five were still in service in 1979. This variant also equipped the Federal German Navy's air arm (*Marinefliegertruppe*), which had five, these later being brought up to UF-2/HU-16D standard. In the same way, numbers of SA-16As in foreign service were also modified to the similar SA-16B/HU-16B standard, including the ten supplied to the Royal Canadian Air Force, which were designated CSR-110 by the RCAF. Serialled 9301 to 9310, these aircraft differed from other SA-16As in having 1,525hp Canadian-built Wright R-1820-82 Cyclones and a revised undercarriage.

The SA-16B-GR was much modified in order to achieve a higher speed, a longer range and an improved single-engine performance. The wing span was increased by 16ft 6in; a fixed, cambered leading edge of revised shape was incorporated; enlarged ailerons, a taller fin and rudder, and new high-pressure de-icing boots were fitted; and the radio antenna housings were modified to reduce drag. The SA-16B prototype first flew on 16 January 1956, and 118 SA-16A-GRs on order were completed to SA-16B standard, including two which went to the Coast Guard and later to the Spanish Air Force, and another pair which were transferred to the Thai Navy via the US Navy. Many

Above: The *Fuerza Aérea Argentina* had one SAR squadron – *Escuadron de Busqueda y Salvamento* – equipped with three HU-16B Albatrosses, of which 331-D2 is seen here. This unit also had six Aérospatiale Lama helicopters. (Air-Britain)

SA-16As were converted to SA-16B standard during IRAN (Inspection and Repair as Necessary) programmes in the manufacturer's workshops; the -B variant later became the HU-16B, and ten Navy UF-2s were also transferred to the USAF in 1960 as SA-16Bs, whilst 40 SA-16Bs were later turned over to the Coast Guard as UF-2Gs. The UF-2, sometimes known as the UF-2S, was the Navy equivalent of the SA-16B-GR, later becoming the HU-16D: 51 UF-1s were reconstructed to this standard and a further seventeen UF-2s were built initially as such. The UF-2G was the equivalent Coast Guard conversion of the UF-1G, 34 of the latter being modified to this standard and later supplemented by 40 transferred SA-16Bs; the UF-2G was redesignated HU-16E. A few HU-16Ds served for a time with the Japanese Maritime Self-Defence Force. By 1970 most Albatrosses had been withdrawn from US service, their rescue role having been taken over by helicopters, but a few HU-16Bs served with the Air National Guard as transports for US Army Special Forces.

An anti-submarine warfare version of the HU-16B for export under the MAP programme was developed as the Grumman G-111. This featured ASW search radar in an enlarged nose radome, a retractable MAD (magnetic anomaly detector) boom in the rear fuselage, a sonobuoy dispenser, ECM (electronic countermeasures) antennae in the wing tips, a searchlight under the starboard wing, and four underwing pylons for torpedoes, HVAR (high-velocity aircraft rockets) or depth bombs. Sixteen G-111s were supplied to the Royal Norwegian Air Force, where they equipped Nos. 330 and 333 Squadrons; seven more went to the Spanish Air Force (*Ejercito del Aire*), which designated them AD.1 and also AN.1, and where they equipped *Ala de Cooperacion Aeronaval* No. 61 at Jerez-Rota, while several more G-111s went to the Greek Air Force. In 1969 the Norwegian G-111s were transferred to Greece and Spain.

In Japan, Shin Meiwa (the former Kawanishi Aircraft Co.) completely rebuilt a UF-1 as a dynamically similar flying scale model of their big PX-S four-turboprop STOL military flying boat

then under development; in its new form the UF-1 became the UF-XS, and little of the original design remained. The hull was reconfigured to resemble that of the PX-S, with a high length-to-beam ratio, a deeper rear section, anti-spray strakes on the nose and other changes. The undercarriage was deleted. A T-tail and swept fin resembling that of the PX-S were fitted. Two 600hp Pratt & Whitney R-1340 Wasp radials were added outboard of the Wright Cyclones and, to operate the boundary layer control system for the flaps, ailerons, rudder and elevator that was to be a feature of the PX-S, two 1,000hp General Electric T58-GE-6 turbines were mounted in a dorsal fairing above and behind the flight deck of the UF-XS. Large leading-edge slats were fitted in place of the usual fixed slots and, for observation in flight, blister windows were added each side aft of the normal flight deck windows and two astrodomes aft of the wing. The UF-XS first flew in its rebuilt form on 20 December 1962 and completed its flight tests in September 1964.

Three standard 'civilianized' SA-16A Albatrosses each seating fifteen passengers were used by Trust Territory Air Service in Micronesia to fly certain scheduled inter-island services, such as those linking Guam, Truk and Ponape in the Caroline Islands. The first SA-16A entered service in the autumn of 1955, and the aircraft replaced the Catalinas previously used. TTAS was operated by Pan American under contract, having formerly been managed by Transocean Air Lines; it served the Trust Territory of the Pacific Islands, the former Japanese possessions of the Marianas, the Carolines and the Marshall Islands now administered by the USA under UN trusteeship. One of these SA-16s crashed at Palau on 20 July 1961, and TTAS ceased operations in May 1968 when it was succeeded by Air Micronesia. The company had also operated two Douglas DC-4s. Antilles Air Boats flew three 'civilianized' HU-16B Albatrosses on services in the Virgin Islands alongside its G-21A Goose fleet.

In September 1969 the Conroy Aircraft Corporation, in association with the Viscount International Corporation, began converting an HU-16A Albatross,

Right: This UF-2G was one of 37 SA-16Bs transferred to the Coast Guard to supplement the aircraft converted from UF-1Gs. (Grumman)

Right: The UF-XS was a UF-1 Albatross completely reconstructed by Shin Meiwa of Japan to serve as a dynamically similar flying scale model of its PX-S flying boat. The hull was rebuilt to resemble that of the PX-S, and a new tail unit was fitted. (Shin Meiwa)

N16CA, to their Turbo Albatross standard by fitting it with two 1,740ehp Rolls-Royce RDa.6 Dart 510 turboprops in Viscount 700-type nacelles, and driving Dowty-Rotol four-blade airscrews, in place of the existing Wright Cyclone radials. The Dart tailpipes exhausted over the wings. The Turbo Albatross first flew in this form on 25 February 1970, but only the prototype was converted before Conroy went out of business, and marketing plans for this variant had to be dropped.

The designation G-111 was later applied to an updated 28-passenger conversion of the UF-2/HU-16B Albatross for commercial use originated by Resorts International. The prototype conversion of a UF-2 to G-111 standard was completed by Grumman, and the aircraft first flew in this form on 13 February 1979; the G-111 received FAA certification on

29 April 1980. By January 1984 Grumman had completed and delivered twelve production G-111 conversions for Resorts International, which transferred five of these to its commuter airline associate Chalk's International Airline Inc. for operating scheduled services from Miami to Nassau and other localities in the Bahamas. The G-111s supplemented seven Mallards already operated by Chalk's, which has plans to use up to twelve G-111s. One G-111, registered PK-PAM, has gone to Pelita Air Service, the aviation division of Indonesia's state oil company, and Grumman, which has acquired 57 HU-16As and HU-16Bs for civil conversion to G-111s, believes there could be a market for about 200 such G-111 conversions in worldwide use.

The first stage in producing a G-111 conversion is the overall inspection and replacement of any parts necessary to

achieve a zero-time airframe. The flight deck is modernized, and 28 non-reclinable passenger seats at 32in pitch are installed in the cabin, together with two additional passenger cabin doors. A flight attendant can be carried, and there is a toilet at the rear of the cabin. The two 1,475hp Wright Cyclone R-1820-982-9HE3 radials are removed and overhauled, and new fire detection and autofeathering systems are installed. Grumman is also considering a turboprop G-111 with two Garrett TPE 331-15 engines driving Dowty-Rotol four-blade propellers, and a water-bomber variant of the Cyclone-engined G-111 has also been studied.

Grumman found, during their inspection of the first G-111 conversion, that a rear spar capstrip of 7075-16 light alloy had suffered deterioration, and it was replaced by a titanium capstrip. On subsequent G-111s, all four centre-section capstrips were made of titanium to give the airframe an unlimited service life. Other changes made in the conversion to G-111 standard are that the lower portion of the main cabin door now incorporates a dropdown ladder, and the port main passenger door and starboard emergency hatch now open outwards. The provision for carrying JATO units or underwing drop tanks, a feature of the military variants, is deleted, as is the provision for an autopilot, and an RCA Weatherscout 2 weather radar can be installed in the nose.

The civil G-111 can bring the seating capacity of a DC-3 to provide air services to island communities without the benefit of an airstrip.

A fire-fighting variant of the HU-16B Albatross has been produced recently by the Aero Union Corporation of Chico, California. This can carry 1,000 US gallons of water or chemical retardant in two side-by-side tanks in the fuselage, which can be filled from two retractable probes extended into the water under the fuselage when the Albatross is taking off and planing on its step. Alternatively, the tanks can be topped up on landing via a single filling point in the fuselage side. The tanks can be refilled from a lake within 10 seconds at a speed of 81mph.

Meanwhile the twelve HU-16B Albatrosses of the Greek Navy (which are actually flown by Air Force crews) are being updated to extend their service lives. The airframes are being modified by Grumman and Hellenic Aerospace Industries and, after inspection for fatigue and corrosion, titanium capstrips are being fitted in the centre-section spars in place of aluminium ones, as on the civil G-111. British mission avionics were installed in the Greek HU-16Bs; these include MEL Super Searcher radar, IFF equipment, GEC-Marconi LAPADS sonics processing equipment and AD.3400 radios. The latest military Albatross operator is the Royal Malaysian Air Force, which has acquired two HU-16Bs.

Above: The updated 28-passenger civil conversion of the UF-2/HU-16D completely refurbished to give a zero-time airframe, with a modernized flight deck and some other minor changes. This example is operated by Chalks International Airline Inc. (Grumman)

Feline Fighters I

The XF3F-1 was still undergoing its initial flight tests when design work began in 1935 on its successor, the first of the F4F series and the first of a long line of Grumman fighters bearing names associated with members of the cat family. In November that year the US Navy had initiated a design competition for a new carrier-based fighter, and the Brewster and Grumman entries were quickly selected for testing as prototypes. The former's XF2A-1 (Brewster Model 139) was a mid-wing monoplane with a 950hp Wright XR-1820-22 Cyclone and a retractable undercarriage, while Grumman's original submission, the XF4F-1, was an equal-span biplane which at first was backed by the Navy mainly as an insurance against the more advanced Brewster design's failure.

The F4F/FM Wildcat

A prototype contract for the XF4F-1 was awarded on 2 March 1936. Known as the Grumman G-16, it owed much to the XF3F-1 and was powered by a 900hp Wright XR-1670-2 14-cylinder, two-row radial, although a study utilizing an 875hp Pratt & Whitney R-1535-92 Twin Wasp Junior – the same 14-cylinder, two-row radial that had earlier powered the F2F-1 and F3F-1 biplane fighters – was also carried out. The armament of the XF4F-1 was to consist of two 0.5in Colt-Browning machine guns, or one 0.5in and one 0.3in gun, firing forward through the engine cowling, and the aircraft's gross weight was 4,500lb.

However, preliminary data on Brewster's XF2A-1 already showed it to be in many ways superior to the XF4F-1, while developments of the F3F series on the way promised to improve its performance to a point where the XF4F-1's advantage would be only marginal. An alternative mid-wing monoplane layout was therefore prepared using the same basic design (now known as the Grumman G-18), and it is said that Dick Hutton, who with Bill Schwendler was co-designer of the XF4F-1, simply deleted the biplane wings on an XF4F-1 general-arrangement drawing and made a pencil mark at the fuselage mid-section to indicate the new wing position. On 28 July 1936 a prototype of the resulting aircraft was ordered by the Navy as the XF4F-2, powered by a 1,050hp Pratt & Whitney R-1830-66 Twin Wasp radial. The aircraft's gross weight was 5,635lb, and its designed maximum speed was 290mph – which was 10mph faster than the Brewster XF2A-1, even though the Navy had in fact specified a top speed of 300mph. The armament comprised two 0.5in Colt-Browning machine guns firing forward through the fuselage decking and provision for two more of these weapons in the wings, plus two 100lb bombs beneath the wings. The manually retracted undercarriage was in essence similar to that of the F3F and earlier fighters.

Grumman's test pilot Robert L. Hall took the prototype XF4F-2, BuNo 0383, on its first flight from Bethpage on 2 September 1937, and flight testing proceeded for the next nine months. After completing the maker's trials the aircraft went to Naval Air Station Anacostia on 23 December 1937 for official evaluation. The test programme ran into some troubles: at Anacostia the deck arrester hook was found to be weak in simulated deck landings; engine crankshaft bearings failed on several occasions, leading to prolonged periods on the ground; and on 24 February 1938 a fire occurred in the rear fuselage while the XF4F-2 was flying at 10,000ft, although the machine landed safely. On 11 April 1938, during the course of a fly-off competition with the Brewster XF2A-1 and a third rival design, the Seversky NF-1, the XF4F-2's engine cut while the aircraft was conducting a simulated carrier deck approach and a forced landing had to be made, resulting in severe damage to the undercarriage, airscrew, engine cowling, starboard wing tip and tail unit. Repairs were completed at Bethpage within two weeks, and the XF4F-2 resumed official trials. Meanwhile, however, wind-tunnel tests with the Brewster XF2A-1 by the National Advisory Committee for Aeronautics (NACA) at Langley Field, Virginia, indicated that its maximum speed might be increased by 30mph by implementing a number of fairly minor design changes, and this, together with the XF4F-2's various mishaps, led the Navy to choose the Brewster design. An order for 54 F2A-1s was placed on 11 June 1938.

The XF4F-2 was still deemed to be sufficiently promising to justify a Navy development contract in October 1938 for a modified version designated XF4F-3 (Grumman G-36), and the XF4F-2 was redesigned and almost completely rebuilt to this standard. The -3 had a revised and slightly lengthened fuselage, its wing span was extended from 34ft to 38ft, the wing tips now being square-cut and the wing area increasing from 232 to 260ft², and the tailplane and the fin and rudder were likewise squared off. A new XR-1830-76 Twin Wasp radial with a maximum take-off rating of 1,200hp was fitted, with a two-stage supercharger, the F4F-3 being the first fighter to go into squadron

service with this particular piece of equipment. The supercharger gave 1,000hp up to 19,000ft, and 1,050hp at 11,000ft, the engine driving a three-blade, constant-speed Curtiss Electric air-screw. The XF4F-3 made its first flight, piloted by Bob Hall, on 12 February 1939, and a large airscrew spinner was initially fitted. The XR-1830-76 engine proved to be much heavier and more complex than the R-1830-66 fitted to the XF4F-2, and a number of cooling problems became evident, which were eventually solved by fitting wide 'cuffs' to the airscrew blades, modifying the engine cowling flaps and, after experimenting with various shapes, finally abandoning the spinner. The supercharger proved its worth: the XF4F-3 was able to attain a speed of 333.5mph at 21,000ft – faster than Britain's first production Hawker Hurricane Is – and climb and manoeuvrability were also good.

Other modifications to the XF4F-3 were introduced following further tests in the NACA's Langley Field wind tunnel, at the Naval Aircraft Factory in Philadelphia and at NAS Anacostia. Wing dihedral was slightly increased and the ailerons were reduced in area, the fin was increased in size at the base of the leading edge and, later, the tailplane was raised from the lower fuselage to the base of the fin. The armament of the XF4F-3 consisted of two 0.3in machine guns firing through the airscrew and two 0.5in guns

in the wings, and this same armament was fitted to the first two production F4F-3s, which flew in February and July 1940.

The Navy had placed an initial order for 54 F4F-3s on 8 August 1939, the third and subsequent aircraft having the fuselage guns removed and four 0.5in guns fitted in the wings. The engine was an R-1830-76 Twin Wasp, and the first production F4F-3 went to Pratt & Whitney after its official tests for use in engine development. The second production F4F-3 served with NACA at Langley Field for a time, testing various improvements to the engine cooling system, whilst the fifth and eighth aircraft were fitted with strengthened undercarriages and some armour protection for the pilot. Nos. 3 and 4 were completed in June 1940 as XF4F-5s, a Wright R-1820-40 Cyclone with a single-stage supercharger being substituted for the troublesome two-stage Twin Wasp fitted in the F4F-3. The two -5s were further modified in 1942–43, one having an R-1820-54 Cyclone with a turbo-supercharger and the second an XR-1820-48 with a two-stage supercharger. Several other snags persisted after F4F-3 production started, including a degree of longitudinal instability, a weak tailwheel and inadequate cockpit ventilation.

By December 1940 22 F4F-3s had been delivered, initially going to VF-4 on board the carrier *Ranger* and to VF-7 on *Wasp*. The next units to equip with the new aircraft were VF-42 and VF-71, and Marine Corps squadrons VMF-121, -211 and -221. The F4F-3 was officially named Wildcat on 1 October 1941, and altogether 369 examples of this variant were built. The Navy was sufficiently concerned about possible delivery delays with the two-stage Twin Wasp to have an F4F-3 fitted with an R-1830-90 Twin Wasp with a single-stage, two-speed supercharger as an insurance policy. This was the XF4F-6, which began trials at Anacostia in November 1940. A production order for 95 of these variants was placed, the designation being changed to F4F-3A before delivery, but the first 30 aircraft were released for shipment to Greece after the Italian invasion in November 1940. However, the Greek resistance collapsed in April 1941 in the face of the additional German assault, by which time the F4F-3As had only reached Gibraltar, and Britain later took them over for the Fleet Air Arm as Martlet IIIs. US F4F-3As equipped Navy VF-6 and Marine VMF-111 squadrons. A few F4F-3s, fitted with a camera installation, were designated F4F-3P, and BuNo 4038 was fitted with large twin floats by the Edo Corporation as the F4F-3S. For the latter, small auxiliary fins were fitted to the tailplane to compensate for the extra side area of the floats, and a ventral fin was later added. Inspired by the Mitsubishi 'Rufe' floatplane version of the Zero-Sen fighter, the F4F-3S first flew on 28 February 1943,

Far left: The Grumman G-18 or XF4F-2 prototype (BuNo 0383) is seen here in its initial form, with closely cowled R-1830-66 Twin Wasp radial, rounded fin and rudder tip and wing tips, and two 0.5in Colt-Browning machine guns in the cowling top. Just visible under the wing is a 100lb bomb. (Grumman)
Left: The XF4F-2 was rebuilt into the XF4F-3 prototype, with a more powerful engine, a revised fuselage shape, a wing of 4ft greater span with square cut tips, and tail surfaces also with square cut tips. An airscrew spinner was originally fitted. (Grumman)

but since the floats reduced the maximum speed to 241mph the performance loss was too great to make large-scale conversion worthwhile.

Meanwhile, at about the time the first production orders for F4F-3s were placed, the French Navy ordered 81 of an export version known as the Grumman G-36A, for use from their 18,000-ton carriers *Joffre* and *Painlevé* then under construction. These G-36As had 1,200hp Wright R-1820-G205A Cyclones with a single-stage, two-speed supercharger, and were to have had six 7.5mm Darne machine guns in the wings, a French gunsight, radio and instrumentation, and a throttle operating in the opposite direction to that of US aircraft. The first French G-36A made its maiden flight on 11 May 1940, but on the fall of France the order was taken over for the Fleet Air Arm, the aircraft being completed as Martlet Is with four 0.5in wing guns and the throttle modified to operate in the conventional direction. The first was delivered on 27 July 1940, ahead of the US Navy's F4F-3 deliveries, and the first seven at least were ferried across to Canada for transfer to Britain bearing civil registrations in the 'NX-G' sequence, NX-G3 being the third aircraft. The first six Martlet Is, AX824 to AX829, arrived at Prestwick during August 1940, and by the end of October the entire batch had been received. The aircraft had non-folding wings and lacked other items of equipment for carrier-based operations, and they were thus flown only from airfields. They first equipped No. 804 Squadron at Hatston in the Orkneys, replacing Gloster Sea Gladiators, and on Christmas Day 1940 two of the unit's new mounts, BJ515 and BJ562, flown by Lt. L. L. N. Carver RN and Sub. Lt. (A) Parke RNVR, shot down a Junkers Ju 88A out to attack ships of the Home Fleet anchored in Scapa Flow.

From March 1941 the first of 90 Martlet IIs began to supplement the Mk. Is. The new variant, which had the maker's designation G-36B, differed from the Mk. I in having folding wings (the first of any of the F4F series so equipped) and a single-stage, 1,200hp Pratt & Whitney R-1830-S3C4-G Twin Wasp, equivalent to the F4F-3A's R-1830-90.

The armament comprised six 0.5in machine guns in the wings. The Mk. II had catapult spools and a larger tailwheel, and these improvements, and in particular its folding wings, made it the first variant suitable for Royal Navy carrier operations. One hundred Mk. IIs had originally been ordered, but ten were relinquished in favour of F4F-3As, serialled AM954 to AM963; diverted from the US Navy contract, they supplemented the 30 aircraft originally destined for Greece. They were designated Martlet III and differed from the Mk. II chiefly in having non-folding wings. One of the ten was retained by Grumman for development. Of the Martlet IIs, 54 (AJ100 to AJ153) were shipped out to the Far East from late 1941, some being lost at sea en route, and the other 36 (AM964 to AM999) were retained in the United Kingdom.

The first seaborne Martlet unit was No. 802 Squadron, which embarked six Mk. IIs on board the Royal Navy's first escort

Top: F4F-3 4038 was fitted with large twin floats by the Edo Corporation as the F4F-3S, inspired by the Mitsubishi 'Rufe' seaplane version of the Zero-Sen. However, the floats made the aircraft too slow to make conversions worthwhile. (Grumman)
Above: An ex-French G-36A in non-standard livery as a Martlet I for the Fleet Air Arm, bearing the civil registration NXG2 for the purposes of ferrying the aircraft across to Canada. (Grumman)

carrier, HMS *Audacity*. An ex-German cargo liner which had started life as the Norddeutscher Lloyd line's *Hannover*, this vessel had been captured as a war prize and had served for a time as the cargo ship *Empire Audacity* before being converted to have a flight deck over the existing hull. The ship had neither a hangar nor a lift, and so her six aircraft had to be permanently parked on the flight deck, but despite these limitations No. 802 successfully pioneered what was to be one of the Martlet's most important roles – operating from escort carriers in defence of convoys. While escorting a Gibraltar-bound convoy in September 1941, 802's Martlets machine-gunned a U-boat, forcing it to submerge, and on 20 September shot down a Focke-Wulf Fw 200C Condor that had been shadowing the convoy. On *Audacity*'s second voyage in November that year, the Martlets destroyed no fewer than four Fw 200s. The air escort they provided kept the U-boats submerged and enabled them to be spotted in time to warn the convoy. *Audacity* was herself sunk by a U-boat on 21 December 1941 while escorting a homeward-bound convoy from Gibraltar, but her short life had proven beyond doubt the soundness of the escort carrier

concept. In one day alone 802's Martlets had flown for a total of 30 hours, and the last two aircraft to return to *Audacity* had to land in the dark while the ship was rolling 14 degrees.

Martlets from Nos. 881 and 882 Squadrons aboard HMS *Illustrious* took part in the Madagascar campaign during May 1942, carrying out tactical reconnaissance for the Army, encountering Vichy French Morane Saulnier MS.406 fighters in several sorties and shooting down three Potez 63 light bombers without loss. On the critical August 1942 convoy to the beleaguered island of Malta, HMS *Indomitable* had Martlets of No. 806 Squadron on board to provide fighter cover, and the aircraft also served in the North African landings in November that year, covering the troops going ashore. During this campaign a No. 882 Squadron Martlet from HMS *Victorious* flown by Lt. B. H. C. Nation landed on the French airfield at Blida near Algiers to accept its surrender, having first spotted a group of French officers on the ground signalling their wish to give themselves up. The Martlet IIIs originally ordered by Greece also served in a shore-based role in the Western Desert from September 1941 with the Royal Naval Fighter Unit.

Below: Martlet IIs at the Grumman plant awaiting delivery. The aircraft in the left background has the registration NX37174 painted above the starboard wing but as yet bears no serial number. (Grumman)

Blackburn Aircraft Ltd. played an important part in smoothing the entry of the Martlet and other US Navy aircraft into Fleet Air Arm service. In mid-1940 this company, because of its long experience with naval aircraft, was requested to carry out the necessary modifications to the Martlet to equip it to fit the Royal Navy's requirements, and it performed this task for all marks of the Martlet (later Wildcat), Hellcat, Avenger and Chance Vought Corsair that served with the FAA. After the first Martlet arrived in December 1940, Blackburn modified a total of 57 of these types – and also a single Curtiss SBW-1B Helldriver – into TI (Trial Installation) aircraft to test various new items of equipment and such devices as rocket projectile and camera installations, bomb carriers and RATOG (rocket-assisted take-off gear). Between the end of 1940 and 1945 over 400 modifications and TIs were undertaken, over 600 aircraft were modified by Blackburn under contract, and just over £1 million was spent on manufacturing and incorporating the new equipment.

It was realized before deliveries from the United States began that such things as US radio sets, gun sights, oxygen systems, batteries and accumulators would have to be replaced by their British equivalents, which might be of a different shape and size, but many other modifications proved to be necessary because there was practically no experience of operating American naval aircraft. Certain modifications, such as hinging the aerial mast on the Avenger and clipping the wing tips of the Corsair (to reduce the folded height) were necessary because of the more limited headroom in some British aircraft carriers. Apart from the basic task of bringing the aircraft up to full British standards in such things as radio and other equipment, Blackburn-devised 'mods' for the Martlet/Wildcat series included the introduction of catapult spools, and the associated airframe structural stiffening, devising an early but not wholly successful experimental UP (unrifled projectile) system for assisted take-offs (later superseded by RATOG in a Trial Installation) and fitting underwing bomb carriers and rocket rails for later marks of Martlet/Wildcat, the latter carrying three RPs under each wing on British rail-type launchers.

The US Navy F4F-3s did not see action until the Japanese attack on Pearl Harbor, when nine out of eleven of VMF-211's F4F-3s were destroyed or badly damaged on the ground at Ewa Marine Air Corps Station on the island of Oahu in a surprise attack by Mitsubishi Zero-Sens. A detachment of VMF-211 posted to Wake Island in mid-Pacific a few days previously lost seven aircraft on the ground in the Japanese attack of 8 December, but the five survivors fought a heroic defensive action for the next two weeks before they were finally destroyed, having made their first kill of a Japanese bomber on 9 December. Most of the Marine pilots had done no more than carry out a few familiarization flights in the F4F-3s, only two of which had self-sealing fuel tanks, and the 100lb bombs available on Wake Island did not fit their racks. More importantly, there were no shelters or revetments available for protection against bombing attacks, but the Wildcats nevertheless succeeded in repelling one seaborne attack, during which they sank a Japanese destroyer and damaged a transport with 100lb bombs. Captain Henry F. Floyd of VMF-211, who had shot down two Japanese bombers in his F4F-3 and also bombed the destroyer *Kisagara*, took part in the subsequent ground fighting after the last Wildcats were destroyed and was killed. He was awarded a posthumous Congressional Medal of Honor. America's supreme award for gallantry was also won by Lt. Edward H. 'Butch' O'Hare of VF-3 from USS *Lexington* for shooting down five Mitsubishi G4M1 'Betty' bombers and damaging a sixth in his F4F-3 over Rabaul, near New Guinea, on 20 February 1942. Wildcats from *Yorktown* and *Enterprise* took part in the first US carrier-based strike earlier that month against the Japanese Marshall and Gilbert Islands, and for the next three months or so provided the US Pacific Fleet with its main air defence capability. F4F-3s of VF-2 from *Yorktown* and VF-42 from *Lexington* took part in the Battle of the Coral Sea in May 1942, the first naval engagement ever to be fought without the opposing ships making visual contact, but when the Battle of Midway

took place the following month the F4F-3s had been largely replaced by F4F-4s, only VMF-221 still retaining the earlier mark.

The F4F-4, or Grumman G-36B, differed from the -3 chiefly in having manually folding wings, which swivelled about the forward spar on the stub centre section to lie aft along the fuselage sides, leading edge down. The XF4F-4 prototype, actually a conversion of the final F4F-3 of the initial order, had hydraulically folding wings; it first flew on 14 April 1941, but it was decided that the hydraulic folding mechanism did not justify its weight and complexity. The F4F-4, of which 1,169 were eventually built, also had six 0.5in M-2 Browning machine guns in the wings, provision for two 50 or 58 US gallon drop tanks as well as bombs under the stub wing centre section, armour protection for the pilot, and a 1,200hp R-1830-86 Twin Wasp driving a Curtiss Electric airscrew (this engine had also been fitted to the last production F4F-3s). The F4F-4A was a projected variant with an R-1830-90 Twin Wasp, while the F4F-4P, of which at least one was converted, featured a camera installation.

F4F-4s took part in the Coral Sea as well as the Midway battles, and in the Marines' attack on Guadalcanal, equipping VF-3, VF-5 and VF-42 from *York-town* and *Saratoga*, VF-6 and VF-10 from *Enterprise*, VF-8 and VF-72 from *Hornet*, and VF-71 from *Wasp*, while Marine squadrons VMF-112, -121, -212, -223

and 224 were all in action with F4F-4s — which by the end of 1942 equipped all US Navy carrier-based fighter squadrons. Wildcats also served in the North African landings of November 1942, equipping VF-41 on board the carrier *Ranger*, VGF-27, -28 and -30 on the escort carrier *Suwannee* and VGF-26 aboard *Sangamon*. Early combat experience had shown that the Wildcat was outclassed in terms of performance by the Mitsubishi Zero-Sen, which could out-turn it even though the Grumman machine was itself very manoeuvrable and could turn inside almost any other aircraft; it could also dive at 390–400mph. The CO of VF-3 Lt. Cdr. John S. Thach, evolved a tactic known as the 'Thach weave' during the Battle of Midway, in which Wildcats flew in pairs, criss-crossing back and forth so that each covered the other's tail, thus enabling pilots to use their superior firepower, armour plating and structural strength to the best advantage against the Zeros. One F4F-4 was experimentally fitted with electrically operated, full-span flaps, but it crashed when the electrical system malfunctioned and only one flap came down. Another Wildcat was used to test frangible wing tips, which were designed to break away from the wing at a predetermined high-*g* loading; this was a feature later incorporated in the F8F Bearcat. Several Wildcats were towed behind Douglas A-20 Havocs or Boeing B-17 Fortresses in experiments aimed at increasing the ferry range of single-engined fighters (a similar trial was made in Britain

Above: The F4F-4 Wildcat differed from the F4F-3 chiefly in having manually folding wings. It was the first US Navy variant with this feature, and also had six instead of four 0.5in guns. Two 50 or 58 US gallon drop tanks or a pair of bombs could be carried under the centre section. (Grumman)

in late 1944 using an FAA Wildcat and a Handley Page Halifax A.7).

The next production variant, after the experimental XF4F-5 and XF4F-6, was the F4F-7 for long-range photographic reconnaissance. This reverted to a fixed wing with 555 US gallons of fuel housed in it; total fuel capacity was 695 US gallons, to give a range of no less than 3,700 miles. The armament and armour were deleted, an autopilot was fitted, and a single camera was installed in the fuselage. The F4F-7 first flew 23 days after Pearl Harbor; over 100 were ordered, but only 21 were actually built, most of these later being converted to F4F-4s.

The Martlet IV for the Royal Navy, of which 220 were built under the US Navy designation F4F-4B, was similar to the F4F-4 but had a 1,200hp Wright GR-1820-G205A-3 Cyclone driving a Hamilton Standard Hydromatic airscrew, which gave it a slightly lower performance than the F4F-4, the maximum speed being only 296mph. The armament consisted of six 0.5in Browning M-55A machine guns in the wings, and the aircraft's gross weight was 7,904lb. Serial numbers were FN100 to FN319. The first Martlet IV unit was No. 892 Squadron, which took delivery of six aircraft at Norfolk, Virginia, on 15 July 1942 and

later served aboard the escort carriers *Battler* and *Archer*.

From the latter part of 1943 Wildcats began to be replaced on the large US carriers by the newer F6F-3 Hellcat, but they were still needed in large numbers for operating from the fleets of escort carriers in both British and American service. Production of the F4F-4 was thus turned over to the Eastern Aircraft Division of General Motors, which took its name from a group of five former automobile plants on the US eastern seaboard at Linden, Bloomfield and Trenton in New Jersey, Tarrytown in New York and Baltimore in Maryland, the headquarters being at Linden. Eastern was awarded a contract for 1,800 F4F-4s under the designation FM-1 on 18 April 1942, and the first aircraft, assembled from Grumman-supplied components, took off on its maiden flight on 31 August that year. Eventually 1,060 FM-1s were built, this version differing from the F4F-4 solely in having four 0.5in guns in the wings, with provision for two 100lb bombs or six 5in rocket projectiles. Another 312 FM-1s went to the Royal Navy as Martlet Vs (serial numbers JV325 to JV636), and in January 1944 the British name Martlet was dropped in favour of Wildcat, to conform with American usage. Eastern's production of

Below: The Martlet IV (later renamed Wildcat IV) for the Fleet Air Arm was similar to the F4F-4 but was powered by a Wright GR-1820-G205A-3 Cyclone driving a Hamilton Standard Hydromatic airscrew; FN114 seen here was one of 220 such aircraft supplied to Great Britain. (Imperial War Museum)

Left: The FM-1 Wildcat, built by the Eastern Aircraft Division of General Motors, differed from the F4F-4 solely in having four 0.5in guns, with provision for two 100lb bombs or six 5in rocket projectiles under the wings. (Grumman)

Wildcats and Avengers enabled Grumman to concentrate on the manufacture of the F6F Hellcat, the F7F Tigercat and the F8F Bearcat; Eastern produced its 1,000th Avenger on 5 December 1943 and its 2,500th Wildcat, an FM-2, on 11 April 1944. The last Grumman-built production version of the latter type was the F4F-7.

Royal Navy Wildcat IVs and Vs served for the most part aboard escort carriers and also merchant aircraft carriers, or MAC-ships, often operating in company with Fairey Swordfish, the latter using its rocket projectiles to attack U-boats while the Wildcat's machine gun fire kept the submarines from firing their own guns in defence. FM-1 Wildcats also served in an anti-submarine role from the many US Navy escort carriers. By mid-1944 some fifteen squadrons were flying Wildcat IVs and Vs from British escort carriers, taking part in the defence of Russian convoys, escorting Fairey Barracuda dive-bombing attacks on the German battleship *Tirpitz* and helping to provide cover for both the D-Day landings and the Allied invasion of south-west France. Wildcat IVs and Vs also flew from HMS *Illustrious* during the Salerno landings and from *Victorious* in the south-west Pacific.

The FM-2 Wildcat had a lighter airframe and a lighter and more powerful Wright R-1820-56 Cyclone than its predecessor, giving it a better performance from small escort carrier decks, and it could be distinguished by a taller fin and rudder, necessitated by the extra power, which was now 1,350hp for take-off. This was the first production US Navy Wildcat to have a Cyclone, the R-1820-56 having a single-stage, two-speed supercharger. The engine was installed by Grumman in two F4F-4 airframes which, redesignated XF4F-8, served as prototypes for the FM-2, the first flying on 8 November 1942. These aircraft were armed with four 0.5in guns and were equipped with slotted flaps (later replaced by standard split flaps), and the second XF4F-8 was later fitted with the taller fin and rudder of the FM-2. In early 1943 an initial order for 1,265 examples of the production FM-2 was placed with Eastern, which group eventually built no fewer than 4,127 FM-2s, plus 340 of an equivalent version, the Wildcat VI, for the Royal Navy. Wildcat production ended in August 1945, only some three months before that of its successor, the Hellcat. FM-2s usually had the R-1820-56 or -56A Cyclone, but some later production aircraft were fitted with the R-1820-56W or -56WA with water injection. The 2,401st and later FM-2s had a larger main fuel tank of 126 US gallons capacity instead of the 117 US

gallon tank of earlier aircraft, the reserve tank of previous versions being deleted on the FM-2. Two 58 US gallon drop tanks (or two 250lb bombs) could be carried under the centre section on universal racks, because in the FM-2 the oil coolers were moved from beneath the centre section to the cowling, which was revised in shape. The 3,301st and later FM-2s could carry six 5in rocket projectiles under the wings.

FM-2s served on board virtually all US Navy escort carriers, while the Wildcat VI entered service shortly after D-Day, the first operational squadron being No. 881, embarked on the escort carrier *Pursuer*. This FAA variant served chiefly in the Far East. The Martlet had been the first American naval aircraft in British service to shoot down a German bomber in the Second World War, and it was appropriate that the type scored the Fleet Air

Arm's last victory of the war – this time over German fighters, when 882's Wildcats shot down four Bf 109s during a sweep over Norway on 26 March 1945. Altogether 7,898 Wildcats were built, and this tubby little fighter, seemingly so hopelessly outclassed by the Zero-Sen in the early days of the Pacific war, gained a valuable new lease of life in the convoy escort role.

Some idea of the Wildcat's tubbiness can be gained from the fact that, after the war, a privately owned FM-2, registered N777A, was modified in the United States to enable seats for four passengers to be fitted in the fuselage just aft of the wing trailing edge. A small individual window was provided for each passenger, the deck arrester gear, armament and other military equipment, and also the radio mast, being deleted. This aircraft was still in use in 1956. Another civil-

Above: The FM-2 Wildcat had a lighter airframe than the FM-1, as well as the lighter and more powerful R-1830-56 Cyclone, and the taller fin and rudder was fitted to cater for the extra power. No fewer than 4,127 FM-2s were built by Eastern, plus 340 more as Wildcat VIs for the Royal Navy. (Grumman)

Below: Grumman's first twin-engined fighter, the G-34 or XF5F-1 Skyrocket, in its original form. The nose was later lengthened to bring it past the wing leading edge, the engine nacelles were lengthened to just aft of the trailing edge, airscrew spinners were fitted, and the cockpit height was reduced. (Grumman)

registered FM-2, N20HA, was in use at this time, having been modified into a crop sprayer, with the main wing fuel tankage replaced by two 30 US gallon wing-tip tanks, the spray mixture being distributed from a large drop tank under the starboard wing, fed from a wing tank. Another FM-2, YV-T-OTO, was registered postwar to a private owner in Venezuela, Señor Walter Idel.

The XF5F Skyrocket

Grumman's next fighter to fly after the XF4F-2 was the G-34 Skyrocket, designated XF5F-1 by the US Navy, which ordered a prototype on 30 June 1938. This single-seater was one of the first twin-engined shipboard fighters, with two 1,200hp Wright R-1820-40/42 Cyclones – which incorporated single-stage superchargers of the type fitted to the XF4F-5 – driving 'handed' airscrews. An unusual feature was that the tip of the nose was set back behind the wing leading edge. The undercarriage retracted backwards into the nacelles and the tailwheel was fixed. Folding wings were featured, as well as twin fins and rudders, and the multi-frame cockpit canopy, resembling that of the F4F-3, afforded the pilot a good rearward view. The designed maximum speed of the aircraft was 380mph at 16,500ft, and the initial rate of climb was 4,000ft/min.

The prototype XF5F-1, BuNo 1442, made its first flight on 1 April 1940. Flight testing brought about several improvements, including the lengthening of the nose and engine nacelles. It had

originally been intended to fit two 23mm cannon ahead of the cockpit, but instead four 0.5in machine guns were installed, in the redesigned nose. Simulated deck landing trials were conducted at the Naval Aircraft Factory at Philadelphia, but the Skyrocket was not ordered into production by the Navy as it was felt to be incompatible with existing carriers and not worth the cost. The aircraft did, however, provide useful design experience for the bigger, much heavier and more powerful F7F Tigercat. The XF5F-1 was not finally withdrawn from use and scrapped until December 1944.

From the XF5F-1 was developed the Grumman G-41, or XP-50, for the US Army Air Corps, which differed in having a tricycle undercarriage, the nosewheel leg retracting backwards into the longer, pointed nose that would resemble that of the F7F Tigercat. Power was provided by 1,200hp R-1820-67/69 Cyclones driving 'handed' airscrews and fitted with General Electric turbo-superchargers. The prototype XP-50 first flew on 18 February 1941 and was allocated the serial number 40-3057, but after only a few test flights it was lost on 14 March when one of the superchargers exploded in flight, damaging the hydraulic system and preventing the nosewheel from being lowered. Test pilot Bob Hall baled out, and the XP-50 crashed into Long Island Sound.

The Hellcat

In 1941 Grumman began work as a private venture on what was originally envisaged by the US Navy as a more

Below: The first prototype XF6F-1 Hellcat, BuNo 02981, first flew on 26 June 1942 powered by a Wright R-2600-10W Cyclone, as seen here. It was later converted into the second XF6F-3 with a Pratt & Whitney R-2800-10 Double Wasp, this engine being chosen to give more climb and speed against the Mitsubishi Zero-Sen. (Grumman)

Left: The XF6F-2 was originally to have had a turbo-supercharged Wright R-2600 Cyclone, but eventually flew in January 1944 with a turbo-supercharged R-2800-21 Double Wasp driving a four-blade airscrew, as seen here. The oil cooler intake is deeper than on production F6F-3s. (Grumman)

powerful development of the F4F Wildcat, with the new Wright R-2600 Cyclone radial. It embodied many of the lessons absorbed by European air combat experience, such as the importance of speed, rate of climb, firepower and good visibility for the pilot, and to these were added the need for ample fuel and ammunition capacity, which were of special significance for carrier-based fighters. The Navy ordered two prototypes, designated XF6F-1, on 30 June 1941. The design team, headed by Leroy R. Grumman and Bill Schwendler, had already been busy seeking the opinions of US Navy pilots about the salient features and qualities of the new aircraft, and the Hellcat, as it was to be known, came to resemble the Wildcat less and less as design work progressed. In particular, a slimmer fuselage was ensured by moving the main under-carriage gear to a new position within the wings, the wheels turning through 90 degrees as the gear retracted backwards. The wing was moved down to a lower, mid-set position, and only the oil cooler intake at the bottom of the engine cowling gave the Hellcat something of the Wildcat's portliness.

Initially the two XF6F-1 prototypes were to have been powered by the 2,000hp Wright R-2600-10W Cyclone 14-cylinder, two-row radial with water injection and, because fuel tankage and ammunition capacity had increased the gross weight by 60 per cent over the F4F, a generous wing area of 334ft^2 was provided to avoid too high a wing loading. To minimize drag in level flight, the wing was mounted at a minimum angle of incidence, but as a comparatively large angle of attack was necessary the thrust line of the engine was canted down 3 degrees, this giving the Hellcat a slight tail-down attitude in flight, and also improving the pilot's view. Design and prototype construction progressed very rapidly, and the prototype XF6F-1, BuNo 02981, was first flown on 26 June 1942.

It had been intended to complete the second prototype, BuNo 02982, as the XF6F-2 with a turbo-supercharged Wright R-2600 Cyclone, but early combat experience of the Mitsubishi Zero-Sen by Wildcat squadrons and the advice of some of the Navy's leading fighter pilots led to a decision to standardize on the Pratt & Whitney R-2800 Double Wasp 18-cylinder, two-row radial to give better climb and more speed. The second prototype was duly completed as the XF6F-3, powered by a 2,000hp R-2800-10 Double Wasp driving a three-blade Curtiss Electric airscrew with a spinner. The aircraft made its first flight on 30 July 1942, and was later fitted with a turbo-supercharged R-2800-21 Double Wasp driving a four-blade propeller, first flying with this engine in January 1944. The second prototype was afterwards converted to F6F-3 standard; the XF6F-1 was later modified into the second XF6F-3 and subsequently became the sole XF6F-4 when fitted with a 2,100hp R-2800-27 Double Wasp with two-speed supercharger, first flying in this form on 2 October 1942.

Early flight trials with the two proto-

types had revealed a few deficiencies (for example, excessive longitudinal stability), but nothing that could not be easily corrected, and the essential soundness of the design is shown by the speed with which the Hellcat went into production. The first F6F-3s were built on a pre-production line at Grumman's Bethpage works while the construction of a new plant dedicated to Hellcat production, begun in August 1942, went ahead. To avoid waiting while the Navy acquired the necessary priorities for the issue of steel for the plant, Grumman's president Leon A. Swirbul bought the material as scrap from New York's old Second Avenue elevated railway. The first production jigs were erected in October, and Hellcats started moving down the assembly line before the plant itself had been completed. Ten production aircraft were built in 1942, no fewer than 2,545 in 1943, 6,139 in 1944, and 3,578 in 1945. This very rapid production rate was greatly helped by avoiding any major design changes; indeed, only two basic sub-types, the F6F-3 and F6F-5, were built. Hellcat production by Canadian Vickers under the designation FV-1 was considered at one time but found to be unnecessary.

Production F6F-3s differed only slightly from the prototypes, chiefly in having a Hamilton Standard Hydromatic three-blade airscrew, with the spinner removed, instead of a Curtiss Electric propeller, and in having redesigned main undercarriage wheel fairings. The first production F6F-3 of the initial batch built at Bethpage flew on 4 October 1942; in December, following the complete failure of an F6F-3 fuselage during deck arrester trials, some structural strengthening was introduced to correct the weakness. Thenceforward, the Hellcat gained a reputation among its pilots for being exceptionally strong. The first production F6F-3s were delivered to VF-9 on board the carrier *Essex* on 16 January 1943, and the Hellcat was first flown operationally by VF-5 from *Yorktown* in Task Force 15 during a strike on Marcus Island, some way north of the main Caroline Islands group, on 31 August 1943. Thus, only twenty-six months had elapsed between the Navy's order for two prototype XF6F-1s and the Hellcat's operational début – a remarkable achievement.

Production F6F-3s were fitted with the 2,000hp R-2600-10 Double Wasp, and the 235 US gallon self-sealing fuel cells under the cockpit floor in that part of the wing passing through the fuselage could be supplemented by a 150 US gallon

Below: Production F6F-3 Hellcats differed only slightly from the XF6F-3 prototypes, chiefly in having a Hamilton Standard Hydromatic, three-blade airscrew with no spinner instead of a Curtiss Electric propeller, and in having redesigned undercarriage wheel fairings. This view shows Marine Corps F6F-3s at the newly captured airfield of Munda, New Georgia, in 1943. (US Navy)

ventral drop tank. Six 0.5in Colt-Browning machine guns, each with 400 rounds, lay in the wings, and later production F6F-3s had the gun fairings and lower cowl flaps removed, whilst a vertical instead of a forward-raked aerial mast was fitted behind the cockpit canopy. The three-spar wing was made to swivel at the forward spar and fold aft along the fuselage sides, leading edge down, and split flaps were incorporated. Later aircraft had the R-2800-10W Double Wasp with water injection, which boosted the emergency power rating to 2,200hp. Altogether 4,402 F6F-3s had been built when production of this variant ceased in April 1944 in favour of the F6F-5.

As F6F-3 deliveries increased, the re-equipment of Wildcat squadrons with the new type progressed rapidly. Being nearly 50mph faster than the F4F series and possessing a much better rate of climb, the Hellcat was much more nearly the equal of the Mitsubishi A6M Zero-Sen – so much so that, from the time it appeared in some numbers, the tide of air war in the Pacific turned increasingly in the favour of the United States. Hellcats were credited with 4,947 of the 6,477 enemy aircraft claimed as 'kills' by US Navy carrier-based pilots, while a further 209 were shot down by shore-based Navy and Marine Corps F6F units. Although the Zero-Sen still had the edge over the Hellcat in some respects, the two types were much more comparable in terms of manoeuvrability, and the the F6F's final ratio of 'kills' to losses was better than 19 to 1.

Two night fighter variants of the Hellcat were produced. The first, designated F6F-3E, carried AN/APS-4 radar in a pod on the starboard wing leading edge, was fitted with red lights for the instrument panels to reduce cockpit glare, and had the outer plexiglass windscreen removed to improve night-time vision for the pilot. Eighteen were built. The -3E was followed by the very similar F6F-3N, which featured the more advanced AN/APS-6 radar in the starboard wing pod. The prototype XF6F-3N first flew in July 1943, and 205 production aircraft were built. The -3N also had a radar altimeter, a redesigned instrument panel and new landing lights, as well as the R-2800-10W engine with water injection. F6F3N Hell-

cats flying from carriers made their operational début during the occupation of the Gilbert Islands in November 1943.

Early in 1943 the first of 252 F6F-3s were delivered under Lend-Lease to the Fleet Air Arm. The Royal Navy first called them Gannet Is, later renaming them Hellcat Is to conform to US usage. They first entered service with No. 800 Squadron on 1 July 1943, replacing the squadron's Sea Hurricanes. This unit embarked on the escort carrier *Emperor* that December, first seeing action in anti-shipping strikes off the Norwegian coast and later, in April 1944, helping to provide escort cover for the Fairey Barracudas on their way to dive-bomb the battleship *Tirpitz*. Hellcat Is of No. 1840 Squadron from the carrier *Furious* escorted another strike on the *Tirpitz* in August, but most Fleet Air Arm Hellcats, both the Mk. Is and the 930 F6F-5s supplied as Hellcat IIs, served in Far Eastern waters with the British Pacific Fleet, where they equipped squadrons serving aboard the fleet carriers *Indomitable* and *Indefatigable* and a number of escort carriers, including *Emperor, Khedive* and *Empress*. Hellcats of 1830 and 1840 Naval Air Squadrons from *Indomitable* played a major part in the FAA's first action on a large scale against the Japanese, the attack on the oil refineries at Pangkalan Brandon and Palembang in Sumatra in January 1945; 1844's Hellcats saw action over the Sakashima Islands during March and April 1945 and over Taiwan (Formosa) during May, while 800's aircraft flew escort sorties during the capture of Rangoon on 2 May.

As part of the quest for greater speed, a specially streamlined variant of the F6F-3 attained 410mph at 21,000ft in level flight, and this aircraft led to the F6F-5, which incorporated some of these modifications, as well as improvements made during F6F-3 production and some features of the F6F-3N. The F6F-5 first flew on 4 April 1944. It had the R-2800-10W Double Wasp with water injection in a redesigned and closer fitting engine cowling, a flat-fronted windscreen and red instrument panel lighting similar to the F6F-3N's, spring tab ailerons, extra armour protection, a stronger tail assembly and a special smooth finish. Many F6F-5s

Right: The F6F-3N Hellcat night fighter, of which 205 were built, had AN/APS-6 radar in a starboard wing pod, as well as a radar altimeter, a redesigned instrument panel and an R-2800-10W Double Wasp with water injection. (Grumman)

Right: The F6F-5 incorporated progressive improvements made during F6F-3 production, together with some features of the F6F-3N, as well as extra armour for the pilot, a stronger tail and a special smooth finish. These two F6F-5s each have a 137 Imp. gallon ventral drop tank and underwing racks for two 500lb or 1,000lb bombs. (Grumman)

had the windows aft of the sliding canopy removed, and a few late production aircraft had two 20mm cannon in the wings plus four 0.5in machine guns. One of these F6F-5s was fitted experimentally with a radome on each outer wing near the tip. The -5 could also carry two 500lb or 1,000lb bombs on racks beneath the centre section, plus six 5in rocket projectiles under the wings. Royal Navy Hellcats could carry up to eight 60lb rocket projectiles under the wings, at first using the British rail-type launchers fitted by Blackburn and later stiffened US Mk. V zero-length launchers with British modifications to the wiring and sighting systems. A total of 6,118 F6F-5s were built, plus 1,529 F6F-5N night fighters which, like the F6F-3N, had AN/APS-6 radar in the starboard wing pod as well as the other changes made to the -3N for the night-fighting role. Some F6F-5s were later converted to -5N standard.

The Hellcat NF.II was equivalent to

the F6F-5N, and 75 were delivered to the Fleet Air Arm. They equipped two squadrons, No. 892, the first, being formed at Eglinton in Northern Ireland in April 1945, followed by No. 891. The NF.IIs were just too late to see operational service before VJ-Day, although 892 served for a short time aboard the carrier *Ocean* in the early postwar months. The F6F-5N was used extensively by US Navy units in the Pacific, and enabled an effective defence against night attacks to be provided without recourse to the longer runways that twin-engined night fighters would have needed. Some F6F-5s were fitted with a camera installation in the rear fuselage, becoming F6F-5Ps; the British equivalent was the Hellcat FR.II, which was fitted by Blackburn with two oblique F24 cameras and one vertically mounted F24 in the rear fuselage just aft of the pilot. Flying from the escort carrier *Empress*, No. 888 Squadron used its Hellcat FR.IIs for photo-reconnaissance sorties over Malaya during February and March 1945, photographing the Kra Isthmus and Penang to gain information about landing beaches suitable for the

planned amphibious assault on Malaya. When VJ-Day arrived, the Fleet Air Arm had fourteen Hellcat squadrons, but they were rapidly run down, the last two, 892 and 888, being disbanded in April and August 1946 respectively. The aircraft were returned to the USA. Only one Hellcat II, KE209, survived: it was flown by Capt. J. A. Ivors, CO of RNAS Lossiemouth, Scotland, as late as 1953 and is now in the Fleet Air Arm Museum at Yeovilton.

Two F6F-5 airframes were fitted with the R-2800-18W Double Wasp of 2,100hp (2,450hp with water injection), driving a Hamilton Standard four-blade propeller. This powerplant was a re-designed version of the R-2800, with better cooling and certain important parts strengthened. The two re-engined aircraft were designated XF6F-6, the first making its maiden flight on 6 July 1944. The fastest Hellcat variant, the XF6F-6 achieved a speed of 417mph at 22,000ft, but the production of Hellcats ceased in November 1945, before the XF6F-6 test programme had been completed. Altogether, 12,274 Hellcats were built.

Below: Two F6F-5s were re-engined with the R-2800-18W Double Wasp giving 2,450hp with water injection and driving a Hamilton Standard, four-blade propeller. In this form they became XF6F-6s, which, with a top speed of 417mph, were the fastest variants of any of the Hellcats. (Grumman)

F6F-5s and F6F-5Ns served for a number of years after the war with US Navy and Reserve units, and some Hellcats, both F6F-5s and F6F-5Ns, were converted into F6F-5K radio-controlled target drones for missile tests. A few of these were used operationally during the Korean War by Guided Missile Unit 90, embarked on the carrier USS *Boxer*. The F6F-5K carried a 2,000lb bomb load and was controlled, from a catapult take-off from the carrier, by a Douglas AD-2D Skyraider drone director. These F6F-5Ks made six attacks on North Korean targets, the first on 28 August 1952, and some of the drones were fitted with television cameras to assist in guidance to the target. A few F6F-5s were also converted into F6F-5D drone director ships.

By about the time the F6F-5Ks went into action, Grumman had completed its only venture into the missile field, the Rigel long-range surface-to-surface mis-

sile for the Navy's Bureau of Aeronautics. Powered by a Marquardt integral ramjet, it never got past the prototype stage. As part of the XF10F-1 Jaguar fighter programme, a Hellcat was specially modified by the National Aeronautics and Space Administration (NASA) into a variable-stability aircraft to simulate the Jaguar's variable-sweep flight characteristics before the new aircraft flew. A war-surplus F6F-3 Hellcat was converted for civil use in the crop-spraying role, with the registration N4965V. The spraying liquid was carried in large underwing drop tanks, and spraying bars were not fitted. After the war a small number of F6F-5s were supplied to Uruguay for that country's naval air arm, the *Aviación Naval*, where they equipped one fighter-bomber squadron and remained in service until 1961, and Hellcats also equipped squadrons of the French Navy (*Aéronautique Navale*) in the postwar years.

Avenger and Guardian

Perhaps rather surprisingly, for a company specializing in naval aircraft, Grumman produced only two torpedo-bomber designs in the classical mould, the Avenger and the Guardian. The Avenger, despite its disastrous operational début during the Battle of Midway, went on to become the last dedicated torpedo-bomber to serve on board US Navy carriers – and was arguably the most important Allied type of the war in its class – and its large internal volume and carrying capacity enabled it to enjoy a new lease of life postwar in the anti-submarine search/strike and associated roles, in which it served as a very useful stop-gap until such aircraft as the Fairey Gannet and Grumman S2F-1 Tracker entered squadron service.

The TBF/TBM Avenger

When in 1940 the US Navy began an ambitious programme to expand its carrier forces, it needed a new torpedo-bomber to replace the obsolescent Douglas TBD-1 Devastator, deliveries of 129 of which had begun in October 1937 and which, although pleasant to fly, lacked an adequate performance owing, for the most part, to its very thick wing. Grumman was awarded a Navy contract on 8 April 1940 for two prototypes of a carrier-based TBD-1 replacement designated XTBF-1, which was its first torpedo-bomber design. The Navy specification stressed robustness, the ability to withstand heavy battle damage, and ease of production and maintenance as desirable features. The Grumman design team, under Bill T. Schwendler, decided to rely heavily on their experience with the F4F-3 Wildcat in the new project, and the XTBF-1 grew to have a strong family resemblance to this and to the later F6F Hellcat. Like the F4F, it had mid-set wings that folded along the fuselage sides, leading edge down, but it was unusual among its contemporaries in having an internal weapons bay, with hydraulically operated doors, which could take a 22in torpedo, four 500lb bombs or one 2,000lb bomb, or such loads as mines or depth charges. This weapons bay was to be the means of prolonging the Avenger's life well into the postwar era by enabling it to carry such equipment as the APS-20 radar system with its big ventral radome, or tanks for fire-bombing chemicals.

The crew of three consisted of the pilot, a navigator/gunner and a radio operator/gunner, and the armament comprised one fixed, forward-firing 0.5in machine-gun in the starboard side of the engine cowling (operated by the pilot), a flexibly mounted 0.3in Browning machine gun in the ventral gun position aft of the weapons bay (fired by the navigator), and a 0.5in machine gun offset to port in the Grumman-designed, power-operated dorsal turret at the end of the cockpit enclosure (fired by the radio operator). The XTBF-1 was the first US single-engined aircraft with a turret, and it is worth noting that Grumman had originally considered using a Boulton Paul turret of British design in the dorsal position, but this was rejected as being too vulnerable to battle damage. The powerplant selected for the XTBF-1 and TBF-1 was the 1,700hp Wright R 2600-8 Cyclone 14-cylinder, two-row radial, driving a Curtiss Electric three-blade airscrew. The main wheels retracted outwards into the outer wings and the tail-wheel was mounted further forward than usual, just aft of the ventral gun position. A retractable 'sting' type arrester hook was stowed in the extreme rear fuselage, beneath the rudder.

The first prototype XTBF-1, BuNo 2539, made its first flight on 1 August 1941 with Bob Hall at the controls, and the maker's trials proved to be entirely satisfactory, the only external change

found necessary being the addition of a dorsal fillet for improved directional stability. The first prototype crashed on 28 November 1941 as the result of a fire in the bomb bay before this modification could be carried out, both crew members surviving the accident. The second prototype, BuNo 2540, made its first flight on 20 December, however, so there was little interruption in the test programme. This and production TBF-1s featured the dorsal fillet. An initial order for 286 TBF-1s was placed three days after the second prototype's maiden flight, and the first production aircraft was handed over to the US Navy on 30 January 1942. Production built up at a rapid rate, a total of 145 Avengers (as the type was now named) being delivered by the end of June 1942. Grumman had built 2,293 TBF-1s, including prototypes, by the time it ended Avenger production in December 1943 in favour of the Eastern Aircraft Division of General Motors. Grumman-built aircraft were mainly TBF-1s and TBF-1Cs, the latter having two 0.5in machine guns, one in each wing, in place of the single fixed gun in the engine cowling. This variant could also accommodate an auxiliary ferry tank in the bomb bay, increasing fuel capacity from 395 to 726 US gallons. Both TBF-1s and TBF-1Cs were later modified into a

number of special variants, such as the TBF-1D, -1E, -1J and -1L.

The first unit to be equipped with TBF-1s was VT-8 (Torpedo Squadron Eight), whose pilots, after working up their Avengers at Norfolk Naval Air Station, Virginia, in May 1942, flew the first six to Pearl Harbor to embark on the carrier *Hornet*, which had already taken on board the remainder of VT-8 and its TBD-1 Devastators. The six Avengers flew from Midway to attack the Japanese fleet at 07.10hrs on 4 June 1942, but five of them were shot down and the sixth flew back to Midway badly damaged, with one wheel down, the bomb bay doors open, one gunner dead and the other wounded, and with only the elevator trim tab for longitudinal control. No Avenger had scored a torpedo hit, and VT-8 was decimated, also losing all its TBD-1s. (In all, 38 out of 42 Devastators, from three squadrons, failed to return.) This unhappy début was followed by better results in later operations: Avengers from VT-3, VT-7 and VT-8 on board *Enterprise*, *Wasp* and *Saratoga* as part of Task Force 61, covered the amphibious assault on Guadalcanal in the Solomon Islands on 7 August 1942, and on 24–25 August these three units helped to sink the Japanese carrier *Ryujo* off the eastern Solomons. By this time Avengers

Above: The second prototype XTBF-1 Avenger, BuNo 2540, seen on the day of its first flight, 20 December 1941. This aircraft differed from the first prototype in having the dorsal fin of production TBF-1s. (Grumman)

had completely replaced the TBD-1 Devastators. TBFs also took part in the battle of the Santa Cruz Islands to the east of the Solomons, on 26–27 October.

Avengers were used by the Marine Corps, whose first TBF-1 squadron, VMSB-131 (later redesignated VMTB-131), based at Henderson Field, took part in operations against the offensive launched by the Japanese on Guadalcanal on 11 November 1942. Two days later, four of this unit's Avengers scored a torpedo hit on the Japanese battleship *Hiei* which, after repeated hits by US cruisers and destroyers and another torpedo hit by an Avenger of VT-10, was eventually scuttled five miles NNW of Savo Island. Marine Corps TBF and TBM Avengers, however, were flown mainly against land targets, using bombs and rocket projectiles, or on anti-submarine patrols, armed with depth charges and rockets. Navy Avengers also took part in the Allied landings in North Africa from 8 November 1942, 27 TBF-1s of VGS-26, VGS-27 and VGS-29 from the escort carriers *Sangamon*, *Suwannee* and *Santee* providing supporting cover.

Several special variants were produced in 1944–45 by modifying TBF-1s and TBF-1Cs. The TBF-1CP and TBF-1P were the TBF-1C and TBF-1 fitted with a trimetrogen camera installation, and the TBF-1CD and TBF-1D were -1Cs and -1s fitted with centimetric radar in a radome on the starboard wing leading edge. The TBF-1E was a TBF-1 with special electronics equipment; the TBF-1J was a variant specially equipped for bad-weather operations; and the TBF-1L was a TBF-1 fitted with a retractable search-light in the bomb bay to illuminate a target during a night attack by other aircraft. The designation TBF-1B was

Below: An early production TBF-1 with its armament not yet fitted in the dorsal turret and ventral gun position. The dorsal turret was designed by Grumman and was the first to be fitted to a single-engined aircraft of US design. (Grumman)

applied, for contractual purposes, to the 402 Tarpon Is (later Avenger Is) delivered under Lend-Lease to Britain for service with the Fleet Air Arm. Many TBF-1s, -1Cs and other TBF-1 variants were fitted with 3in rocket projectiles, up to four being carried below each wing, at first on rail-type launchers but more usually on zero-length launchers. The XTBF-2 was the twenty-first production TBF-1, BuNo 00393, fitted with a 1,900hp Wright XR-2600-10 Cyclone; it first flew in this configuration on 21 May 1942, but the variant did not go into production. The two XTBF-3s, 24141 and 24341, were TBF-1s fitted with the 1,900hp R-2600-20 Cyclone and serving as prototypes for

the proposed TBF-3 production version by Grumman, which was supplanted by the very similar TBM-3 built by Eastern.

The first contract with the Eastern Aircraft Division of General Motors for the production of TBF-1 Avengers, redesignated TBM-1s, was placed on 23 March 1942, and the first Eastern TBM-1, assembled from parts supplied by Grumman, flew on 11 November that year. Eastern built 550 TBM-1s and 2,336 TBM-1Cs, corresponding respectively to the TBF-1 and TBF-1C, and the 1,000th Eastern Avenger was produced on 5 December 1943. The Eastern programme enabled Grumman to close down its Avenger line that same month, and henceforth it concentrated on the Hellcat, the F7F Tigercat and the F8F Bearcat. The TBM-1CP, -1D, -1E, -1J, -1L and -1P were modifications of the TBM-1 and -1C corresponding to the TBF aircraft bearing the same suffixes. The sole TBM-2, BuNo 24580, was a TBM-1 re-engined with a 1,900hp Wright XR-2600-10 Cyclone and corresponding to the XTBF-2. A total of 334 TBM-1s and -1Cs were supplied to the Fleet Air Arm as Avenger IIs, allocated the serial numbers JZ301 to JZ634.

The Fleet Air Arm called its TBF-1s Tarpon Is until January 1944, when the name was changed to Avenger I. The first Tarpon squadron was No. 832, previously equipped with Fairey Albacore biplanes, and this unit took delivery of its aircraft at Norfolk Naval Air Station, Virginia, on 1 January 1943. Unusually for a British squadron, it embarked on board a US carrier, *Saratoga*, that April and first saw action on 27 June during the landings on the Middle Solomon Islands in the Coral Sea, also bombing enemy shore positions during the landings on New Georgia. The unit's aircraft later flew from HMS *Victorious* and *Illustrious* and, in the Indian Ocean, from the escort carrier *Begum*. By the end of 1943 eight Tarpon/Avenger squadrons had been formed, taking delivery of their aircraft at the Naval Air Stations of Norfolk, Quonset and Squantam, and embarking on escort carriers bound for the United Kingdom. Six more FAA Avenger squadrons were formed in 1944 and one in

February 1945, making a total of fifteen first-line units equipped with the type at the war's end. The Avengers were generally armed with bombs or depth charges, or mines, rather than torpedoes or rocket projectiles, and they operated from escort carriers in the Battle of the Atlantic (sometimes escorting the Russian convoys) and from shore bases on antisubmarine patrols, using both Royal Navy air stations or, under Coastal Command control, RAF airfields.

Blackburn Aircraft Ltd. was responsible for the modifications necessary to equip the Avenger for Fleet Air Arm service, as it had been for the Wildcat and Hellcat. Two of the most important 'mods' were the rearrangement of the second cockpit to accommodate the navigator immediately behind the pilot (which necessitated moving a considerable amount of equipment, including most of the radio gear) and the fitting of an F24 camera in the ventral gun position, after it was found that this gun could safely be removed since fighter attacks rarely came from below; it was also found necessary to hinge the Avenger's aerial mast because of the restricted height of British carriers' hangars.

Some Avenger IIs and IIIs were fitted with underwing launchers and aiming equipment for the newer and larger rocket projectiles coming into service at the war's end. Among these was the 1,050lb rocket known as 'Uncle Tom', which corresponded to the US 'Tiny Tim'. An Avenger was chosen for the Trial Installa-

Left: Avenger I FN795/ 'C2Y' was one of 402 TBF-1Bs supplied to Britain as Tarpon Is, the name being that of a large game-fish common in US south coast waters. In January 1944 the name Avenger was adopted by the Fleet Air Arm to conform to US usage. (US Official)

tion of this weapon because of its 15-degree angle of depression over the nose, one 'Uncle Tom' being carried under each wing. Development of 'Uncle Tom' continued for some time after the war, and it was fired from an Avenger, along with a number of other weapons on show, at a School of Air Support display held at Old Sarum, Wiltshire, for British Service officers and guests in May 1947, but it did not go into production and was never used operationally. One Avenger was experimentally fitted with the Frazer Nash FN.95 remotely controlled barbette turret housing two 0.5in machine guns that had been designed for, but never installed in, the Fairey Spearfish torpedo bomber. On the Avenger, this barbette occupied the place of the dorsal turret.

The Avenger III, of which 222 were supplied to the Fleet Air Arm from 1944, serialled JZ635 to JZ746 and KE430 to KE539, corresponded to the Eastern-built TBM-3 and TBM-3E, the latter being distinguished in FAA service by its Sea Blue ('midnight blue') finish and centimetric radar in a radome under the starboard wing; Avenger IIIs also had a GEC Mk. IV autopilot. On 19 May 1944 24 Avengers from 832 and 845 Naval Air Squadrons on board HMS *Illustrious* joined with SBD Dauntless dive-bombers from the US carrier *Saratoga* in a very successful raid on the Japanese naval dockyard and aviation fuel stores at Surabaya, Java. Avengers later operated with the Eastern Fleet based at Colombo, Ceylon, and with the British Pacific Fleet from its bases in Australia. On 24 and 29 January 1945 a total of 48 Avengers from Nos. 820, 849, 854 and 857 Squadrons flying from, respectively, *Indefatigable*, *Victorious*, *Illustrious* and *Indomitable*, and escorted by Corsairs, Hellcats and Fairey Fireflies, attacked the Japanese oil refineries at Songei Gerong and Pladjoe, Palembang, Sumatra, which were the sources of much of the oil for the Japanese Navy and of aviation spirit for its Air Force. Both refineries were completely destroyed in this, the Fleet Air Arm's first really large-scale action against the Japanese, and the loss of these oil supplies accentuated the critical fuel shortages which the enemy was already suffering.

Avengers from Nos. 848 and 828

Squadrons, the latter from HMS *Implacable*, were the first FAA aircraft to bomb Japan itself when they attacked Yakushima airfield on 24 July 1945, and Avenger units continued bombing raids on Japan right up to VJ-Day on 15 August. With the coming of peace, the Avenger squadrons were rapidly run down, the last two, 820 and 828, being disbanded in March 1946 and on 3 June 1946 respectively. Instead of being returned to the United States like other Lend-Lease aircraft, many Royal Navy Avengers were simply pushed overboard from the carriers as the US Navy did not need them and neither, at the time, did the postwar Fleet Air Arm. This casual disposal was to be regretted a few years later when it became necessary to acquire Avenger AS.4s as interim equipment for FAA squadrons pending deliveries of the Fairey Gannet.

From the summer of 1943 the Royal New Zealand Air Force took delivery of six TBF-1s, serialled NZ2501 to NZ2506, and 42 TBF-1Cs, serialled NZ2507 to NZ2548. The aircraft equipped Nos. 30 and 31 Dive-Bomber Squadrons, formed respectively in September and December 1943, and these units both did a tour of operations in the Solomon Islands, but in 1944 they were disbanded as the result of a change in RNZAF policy. Nine of the Avengers were turned over to the Royal Navy in September 1945, and sixteen more to the US Navy the following month, but some continued in service in New Zealand for a long time as target-tugs, equipping the RNZAF Target Tug Flight at Ohakea and later the General and Utility Flight at Hobsonville, the last two RNZAF Avengers, TBF-1 NZ2504 and TBF-1C NZ2527, not being finally retired until 1960. They had their dorsal turrets removed and their ventral guns deleted. A few RNZAF Avengers were also used for aerial top-dressing trials in New Zealand.

Meanwhile in 1944 the TBM-1 variants were succeeded in production at Eastern by the TBM-3 series, of which 4,657 were built as TBM-3s proper and a large family of special variants produced by means of conversions. The grand total of Avengers built was 9,839. Four TBM-1Cs were re-engined with the 1,900hp Wright R-

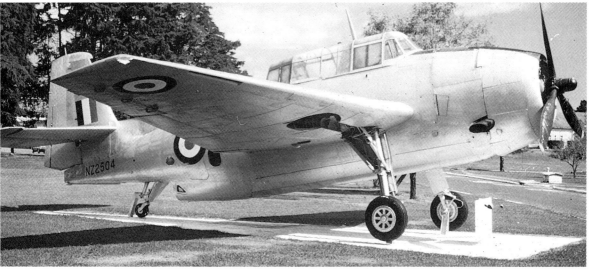

2600-20 Cyclone to become XTBM-3s, and this more powerful engine, already fitted in the two Grumman-built XTBF-3s, was the main difference between the TBM-3 and TBM-1. The TBM-3 also had the TBM-1C's armament and provision for carrying rocket projec-tiles on zero-length launchers under the outer wings, or two 58 US gallon drop tanks, while the auxiliary ferry tank in the bomb bay could also be jettisoned. TBF and TBM Avengers could be equipped to lay a smoke screen, produced from a tank installed in the bomb bay, where target towing gear could also be fitted if required. The TBM-3D, TBM-3J, TBM-3L and TBM-3P corresponded to the earlier TBM-1D, -1J, -1L and -1P variants, while the TBM-3H had special surface-search radar. Some TBM-3Ds were flown with the turret removed, the canopy being lengthened to cover the space left by the turret, and a small number of TBM-3Ds were also fitted with a powerful searchlight mounted under the port wing centre section. The TBM-3E, like the TBM-1E, was fitted with centimetric anti-submarine radar in a small cylindrical radome under the starboard wing but, unlike the TBM-1E and TBF-1E, also incorporated some lightening and strengthening of the airframe, the overall length of the aircraft being increased by almost 1ft. With updated electronics the TBM-3E became the TBM-3E2, and these two variants were among the most important operational versions of the Avenger with the US Navy in the early postwar period. Three prototype XTBM-4s were built, serialled 97673 to 97675, and this variant, which was about to enter production when the war ended, was similar to the TBM-3E but had reinforced wing centre-section panels and an improved wing-folding mechanism. Orders for 2,141 production TBM-4s were cancelled after VJ-Day, and 70 of these, serialled KE540 to KE609, were allocated to the Royal Navy as Avenger IVs but were never delivered. This particular mark number would be applied to the TBM-3Es supplied to the FAA from 1953.

From late 1943 carrier-based TBF and TBM Avengers were operating in some strength in the US 'island-hopping' campaign across the Pacific. During the battle of the Philippine Sea on 19–24 June 1944, a large force of Avengers bombed airfields on Guam to neutralize enemy air opposition prior to the attack on the Japanese carrier force and escorting ships on 20 June made by Avengers, SBD Dauntlesses and SB2C Helldivers, with Hellcats flying escort, which helped to sink the carrier *Hiyo* and to damage the carriers *Chiyoda* and *Zuikaku*. On 24 October 1944 Avengers from Fast Carrier Force TF.38, supporting the amphibious landings in Leyte Gulf in the Philippines, played a major part in sinking the Japanese battleship *Musashi*, scoring nineteen torpedo hits. This great vessel was, with her sister-ship *Yamato*, the largest and most powerful battleship ever built, with a main armament of nine 18.1in guns. During 25–26 October, in the naval battle off Cape Engaño on the northernmost tip of the Philippines, Avengers helped to sink the carriers *Chitose*, *Chiyoda*, *Zuiho* and *Zuikaku*.

As fighting in the Philippines progressed, the Japanese resorted increasingly to night air attacks, and to counter these several specialized Night Air Groups were formed. F6F-3N and F6F-5N Hellcats operated in conjunction with TBM-1D and TBM-3D Avengers, whose centimetric radar in the starboard leading edge pod assisted the Hellcats' own radar in detecting the Japanese bombers. Task Force 55 helped to protect US warships from 'kamikaze' attacks during the Okinawa landings of April 1945, and on 7 April Avengers from its squadrons took part in sinking the battleship *Yamato*, putting ten torpedoes into her. The 68,000-ton ship was overwhelmed by superior US forces in two hours.

In August 1944 the Marine Corps reached agreement with the US Navy to use a number of escort carriers purely for Marine squadrons. The first of these carriers, USS *Block Island*, embarked the Avengers of VMTB-233 in March 1945, this unit providing close support for the Okinawa landings and also flying air strikes over the Ryukyu Islands. Three more carriers, *Gilbert Islands*, *Vella Gulf* and *Cape Gloucester*, later embarked, respectively, VMTB-143, VMTB-234 and VMTB-132 with their Avengers.

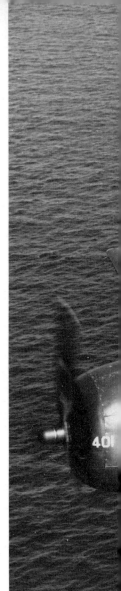

The Avenger Postwar

With the ending of the Second World War many Navy and Marine Corps Avenger squadrons were disbanded, and large numbers of carriers were decommissioned. During the closing months of the conflict a new generation of single-seat attack aeroplanes, exemplified by the Douglas AD Skyraider and Martin AM Mauler, had begun to appear, and these started to replace the more traditional, multi-seat torpedo-bombers and dive-bombers like the Avenger and Dauntless, both the Torpedo-Bomber (TB) and Scout Bomber (SB) classifications being discontinued in 1946. However, far from being phased out rapidly, the Avenger was given a new lease of life thanks to its large internal weapons bay, which enabled it to carry the big APS-20 ventral radar or other electronics apparatus, whilst removing the dorsal turret and reworking the interior provided the necessary work-space for a radar operator.

Several postwar Avenger variants featuring a big ventral radome were developed. One was the TBM-3Q for the electronic countermeasures (ECM) role, which had a radar operator's position behind the pilot under what was now the metal-covered rear part of the cockpit canopy, the dorsal turret having been removed. The rear fuselage undersides were rebuilt so as to eliminate the bomb doors and the ventral

Above: Two TBM-3Es, 53688 (foreground) and 53800, from the Naval Air Station at San Diego, California, March 1950. The TBM-3E, like the TBM-1E, carried its centimetric radar in a small pod on the starboard wing, but mounted beneath it and further inboard than the radome of the TBM-3D; unlike the -1E, however, the -3E had a lightened and strengthened airframe. (Grumman)

gun position, while to counter the additional side area of the ventral radome, auxiliary fins were fitted at the end of each horizontal stabilizer, projecting above and below. The TBM-3W anti-submarine search variant – with updated electronics it became the TBM-3W2 – was very similar externally to the TBM-3Q, with APS-20 radar in a big ventral radome, a radar operator's position under the metal-covered part of the canopy, auxiliary fins and the ventral gun position deleted. The -3W variant was converted from either a TBM-3 or a -3E, and it operated in a pair with the TBM-3S ASW strike variant as a hunter-killer team; with updated electronics the -3S became the TBM-3S2. These strike variants, likewise converted from TBM-3s and -3Es, retained the bomb-bay doors and ventral gun position of the TBM-3 and, not carrying the big ventral radome, did not need the auxiliary fins on the tail-plane. The dorsal turret was deleted and replaced by a transparent cover, some of the centre portions of the canopy being replaced with metal components. Centimetric radar like that fitted in the TBM-3E was carried in a cylindrical pod under the starboard wing, and four rocket projectiles could also be carried under each wing. Royal Canadian Navy TBM-3S Avengers retained the same cockpit transparencies as the TBM-3 with the dorsal turret removed – a feature, in fact, of many wartime TBM-3s. The TBM-3W and TBM-3S remained in first-line service

with US Navy units until June 1954, when their successor, the S2F-1 Tracker, began to replace them in the squadrons.

Other postwar variants of the Avenger included the TBM-3R seven-passenger transport for COD (carrier on-board delivery) flights; these modified TMB-5s could also carry cargo and had attachment points for carrying a litter or stretcher cases. The -3R had the rear part of the cockpit covered in metal, the dorsal turret being removed and the rearmost window in each side, just forward of where the turret would have been, serving as an entrance hatch for the passengers. The acronym 'COD' for the TBM-3R's ship-to-shore utility flights led to the nicknames 'Codfish Line' or 'COD Turkey'. The TBM-3M and the updated TBM-3M2 were specially equipped to launch missiles, while the TBM-3N was a postwar variant modified for night attacks. The TBM-3U was a postwar utility conversion of the TBM-3 or -3E that could be used for target-towing, and some of these aircraft continued to serve the US Navy after the Avenger had been withdrawn from first-line operational service.

Several foreign naval air arms also operated postwar variants of the Avenger. A total of 115, for example, were supplied to the Royal Canadian Navy during 1950–52 in the TBM-3E, TBM-3S and TBM-3W versions, these operating from shore bases with Nos. 880 and 881 Squadrons, and also from the light fleet

Above: The TBM-3R was a seven-passenger transport variant for COD use, with the dorsal turret removed and the rear part of the cockpit canopy faired over. TBM-3E 91633, seen here, retains the TBM-3E's underwing radome. (Grumman)

Right: A Dutch Navy TBM-3W2 in the later colour scheme of Dark Sea Grey and Light Sea Grey with black lettering and serial numbers. (Afdeling Maritieme Historie)

carrier HMCS *Magnificent*. One RCN TBM-3E, still retaining its US Navy serial 53078, was specially modified by the Fairey Aviation Company of Canada Ltd. to have an MAD (magnetic anomaly detector) boom under the rudder and a raised rear cockpit in place of the dorsal turret. Twenty-five ex-RCN TBM-3 Avengers were later acquired by Wheeler Airlines Ltd. of Montreal and St. Jovite Station, Quebec, a leading Canadian bush and charter operator, which modified them for crop spraying using insecticides, and for forest spraying. Seven of these TBM-3Es were still in service with Wheeler in 1961. The Uruguayan Naval

Aviation Service (*Servicio Aeronautica de la Marina*, later known as the *Aviación Naval*), purchased about a dozen TBM-1C Avengers in the 1950s, and a few of these were still thought to be surviving in the late 1960s. Japan, against whose wartime Navy the Avenger struck so many telling blows, acquired ten TBM-3Ws and ten TBM-3Ss as part of the initial equipment of its newly formed Maritime Self Defence Force (*Kaijo Jieitai*) in 1954–55. They operated from the Omura base at Sasebo, and were later replaced by S-2A Trackers and P-2H Neptunes.

The Royal Netherlands Naval Air Service operated the TBM-3W2 and

Above: The TBM-3W, for anti-submarine search, had APS-20 radar in the big ventral radome, auxiliary fins on the tailplane to counter its side area, the fuselage undersides rebuilt to eliminate the ventral gun position and bomb doors, and a radar operator's position under the faired-in rear canopy. With updated electronics, the -3W became the TBM-3W2. BuNo 69476, shown, is a TBM-3W. (Grumman)

TBM-3S2 hunter/killer variants, taking delivery of 60 during 1953–54. These equipped two squadrons embarked on the carrier *Karel Doorman*, each Avenger unit forming, with a squadron of Hawker Sea Fury FB.51s, an air group dedicated to the Dutch NATO anti-submarine and convoy escort commitments. France's *Aéronautique Navale* (*Aéronavale*) also acquired several dozen TBM-3E, TBM-3W2 and TBM-3S2 Avengers in the early 1950s, and these operated both from shore bases and from the light carriers *Bois Belleau* and *Lafayette* (both ex-US Navy vessels) and the light fleet carrier *Arromanches*, formerly HMS *Colossus*. Flotilles equipped with these Avengers included No. 2S at Lann-Bihoué near Lorient, No. 3S at Cuers, No. 10S at St. Raphael, No. 15S and No. 6F at Lartigue, near Oran in Algeria, No. 4F at Karouba and No. 9F at Aspretto. During the Suez operations of 1956 some of these Avengers flew on anti-submarine patrols, having multiple white stripes hastily applied to their wings and rear fuselages for recognition purposes. The last Avengers were not finally retired from *Aéronavale* service until 1 April 1965.

Due not least to changing official requirements, the much more advanced Fairey Gannet, which combined a search and strike capability in one airframe, was late in entering service, and so it was decided to purchase 100 TBM-3Es, designated Avenger AS.4, for the Royal Navy as stop-gap aircraft under the MDAP (Mutual Defense Assistance Program). The Fleet Air Arm chose the TBM-3E rather than the TBM-3W, since deliveries of the Douglas AD-4W Skyraider for the early warning and search role were beginning, and the first Avenger AS.4s arrived at Glasgow on board the carrier *Perseus* on 30 March 1953. They equipped their first squadron, No. 815, in May that year, replacing Fairey Barracudas, and this unit later embarked on board *Illustrious*. The second Avenger AS.4 unit was No. 824 Squadron, which had previously been equipped with Fireflies, and the third was No. 814, followed by Nos. 820 and 831. The first batch of unmodified TBM-3Es shipped over were followed at the end of 1953 by about 80 Avenger AS.4s fully modified to British requirements. As they

began to be replaced in first-line squadrons by Fairey Gannets from 1955–56, the Avenger AS.4s themselves replaced Fireflies in the RNVR, equipping No. 1830 (Scottish Air Division) Squadron at Abbotsinch, 1841 (Northern Air Division) at Stretton and 1844 (Midland Air Division) at Bramcote, with which the aircraft served until these RNVR air units were disbanded as the result of the 1957 Defence White Paper. By this time the other first-line units had lost their Avenger AS.4s, although a few continued to serve with No. 831 until as late as 1962. Altogether about 500 of the post-war Avenger variants saw service with the US Navy and the naval air arms of Canada, France, Great Britain, Japan and the Netherlands.

Fighting Forest Fires

The Avenger's large internal volume also made it readily adaptable to carrying a crop-dusting hopper for aerial agriculture, or a tank full of retardant chemicals for fighting forest fires. Some TBM-3s with an enlarged ventral tank occupying the bomb bay could carry up to 6,000lb of such chemicals, or three times the aircraft's war load. The first TBM Avenger to be used for fire-fighting in California was owned by the late Paul Mantz, who modified it for this role and flew it in tests in 1954 to determine its suitability for the job. By 1964 there were 125 TBM-3s on the US civil register, of which 76 were active, most of these being used to combat forest fires and for aerial agriculture work. It is in the western states of the USA, and particularly in California, with their hundreds of thousands of square miles of virgin timber, that forest fires are such a scourge. The old trees which die during the long cold winters ignite readily when the hot, dry months of spring and summer come, and lightning strikes and fires caused by careless campers or tourists can bring about sizeable conflagrations, so that from May to October the task of fighting brush and timber fires is almost continuous.

At first, up to the late 1950s, modified Boeing Stearman PT-17 and Naval Aircraft Factory N3N-3 trainer biplanes had begun to be used widely for fire-fighting in California, but as techniques developed larger war-surplus types such as the B-25 Mitchell and the F7F Tigercat, first used in this role in Oregon in 1958, began to appear. The TBM Avenger was the most widely used fire-fighting aircraft, and remained so until 1974, no fewer than 68 making contract flights as fire-bombers for the US Forest Service and various state agencies at one period. The Forest Service, however, had always preferred to employ multi-engined aeroplanes, and to contract for their use, which left Avengers and other single-engined types chiefly in the hands of state agencies; moreover, by 1971 a disturbing number of TBM Avengers had been lost in accidents, and in 1973 the type was withdrawn at short notice from the fire-fighting role. To fill the gap caused by its departure, the California Division of Forestry leased fifty Grumman S-2A Trackers from the US Navy for conversion to the fire-fighting role, sub-leasing them out to the various operators, and this type has now replaced the Avenger as the most numerous such aircraft in California.

Among the fire-fighting operators who have used TBM Avengers are Aerial Applicators Inc. of Salt Lake City, Utah (four TBM-3s); the Aero Union Corp. of Chico, California (one TBM-3); Air Tankers Inc. of Buckeye, Arizona (four TBM-3s, all later sold to the Canadian operator Norfolk Aerial Spraying Ltd.; Evergreen Air and Evergreen Helicopters Inc. (formerly Johnson Flying Service) of Missoula, Montana (seven TBM-3s, all later sold to a Canadian affiliate, Evergreen Air Service Ltd.); Hemet Valley Flying Service of Hemet-Ryan, California

(eleven TBM-3s, of which three were later sold to Evergreen Air Service of New Brunswick, in eastern Canada); Reeder Flying Service of Twin Falls, Idaho (ten TBM-3s); Sis-Q Flying Service of Santa Rosa, California (five TBM-3s, all later sold to Evergreen Air Service of Canada for combating spruce budworm in New Brunswick); and TBM Air Tankers Inc. of Tulare, California (three TBM-3s). Fire-fighting Avengers were usually flown as single-seaters with the cockpit canopy aft of the pilot faired over in a manner similar to the TBM-3W, and they often had enlarged ventral tanks projecting outside the bomb bay, although one TBM-3 used in Alaska by the US Department of the Interior as a fire-fighter, and registered N9598C, carried its fire-retardant chemicals in two large, underwing tanks.

Canada, with its vast forest regions, has also found aircraft of many types indispensable in the fire-fighting role, using them in prewar days to spot and patrol for fires, and to ferry in crews and supplies to fight them on the ground; bombing fires from the air was a later development. Among the first tentative steps in this direction was the dropping of paper bags full of water from a G-21A Goose in 1956 over British Columbia forests. In January 1958 the Royal Canadian Navy disposed of an initial batch of thirteen of its now-surplus TBM-3s to civil operators, and by 1959 four of these were in use by Skyway Air Services Ltd., of Langley and Abbotsford, British Columbia, while another user of Avengers was Wheeler Airlines Ltd., mentioned earlier. Skyway Air Services was a bush and charter operator

Left: About 70 TBM-3 Avengers were used for fighting forest fires in the US western states, operating under contract to the US Forest Service and various state agencies. Among them was TBM-3 N5168V (formerly BuNo 53592), of the Hemet Valley Flying Service, fitted with a large ventral tank for fire-retardant chemicals. (R. Bulinski)

Left: Another TBM-3 used for forest fire fighting was N6827C, formerly BuNo 91110 and operated by TBM Air Tankers Inc. of Tulare, California. (R. Bulinski)

that did a good deal of aerial agriculture work and flying training, and late in 1969 the company decided to concentrate on the latter activity, selling off its aerial agriculture and fire-fighting fleets to Les Kerr, who formed a new company known as Conair Aviation Ltd., with thirteen TBM-3E Avengers, five Boeing-Stearman A75N1 biplanes and a Harvard. Although the TBM-3Es could carry 500 gallons of chemicals, they were rather deficient in the speed and range needed to reach fires far from base, and larger types with bigger payloads, such as the Douglas A-26 Invader and DC-6B, began to supplement them. Later two ex-RCN/ Canadian Armed Forces CS2F-1 Trackers were acquired and, although now used only for certain types of forest fire-fighting in British Columbia, the surviving Conair Avengers are still active in spraying the spruce budworm in the Quebec and New Brunswick forests.

The AF-2 Guardian

In 1944 consideration started to be given to a replacement for the Avenger in US Navy service, and that year two projects were schemed to meet this requirement. One was a twin-engined type owing something to the F7F-1 and -2 Tigercat and fitted with the same powerplants, 1,900hp Pratt & Whitney R-2800-22 Double Wasps. Two prototypes, BuNos 84055 and 84056, were ordered, at first designated XTSF-1 and later XTB2F-1, but they were cancelled in January 1945 in favour of the second project, the Grumman G-70, three prototypes of

which were ordered the following month as the XTB3F-1. Like the Avenger, this was a mid-wing design but rather larger, with the crew of two seated side by side. Power was provided by one 2,300hp R-2800-46 Double Dasp plus, unusually, a 1,560lb static thrust Westinghouse 19XB-2B turbojet in the rear fuselage. The latter conferred a high-speed escape capability after attacking the target, the XTB3F-1 relying on this instead of defensive armament. The turbojet, which had the US Navy designation J30-WE and comprised a ten-stage, axial-flow compressor and a single-stage turbine, exhausted under the tail unit. Two torpedoes or up to 4,000lb of bombs could be carried in the weapons bay, and there was a 20mm cannon in each wing for strafing attacks on ships or submarines.

The first prototype XTB3F-1 conducted its maiden flight on 19 December 1945 but the test programme showed that the performance benefits of the Westinghouse jet in the tail were not sufficient to justify its retention, and it was removed for production aircraft; the engine itself went out of production in 1948. The first and second prototypes, serialled 90504 and 90505, were later used as test-beds for the Westinghouse 24C-4B (or J34-WE), an enlarged version of the 19XB, and the Allis-Chalmers J36, these being mounted in the rear fuselage like the original Westinghouse powerplant.

The removal of the turbojet enabled a heavier load to be carried (the 19XB-2B had a dry weight of 692lb), and the third prototype, BuNo 90506, was rebuilt into

Left: Designed to succeed the Avenger, the XTB3F-1 Guardian had a 1,560lb s.t. Westinghouse 19XB-2B turbojet in the rear fuselage to supplement the R-2800-46 Double Wasp in the nose. This is one of the three XTB3F-1 prototypes, *Fertile Myrtle*. (Grumman)

Left: The XTB3F-1 went into production as the AF-2W search variant and the AF-2S strike aircraft, the two types operating together as a hunter/killer team. The AF-2S (shown) had an APS-30 radar pod under the starboard wing and a searchlight under the port wing. (Grumman)

the XTB3F-1S anti-submarine search aircraft with a big ventral radome like that of the TBM-3W Avenger; it was later designated XAF-1. Production aircraft, which had the maker's designation G-82, were ordered in two variants. The AF-2W, for search, was very similar to the XTB3F-1S with the same ventral radome; the AF-2S, for strike, had a smaller APS-30 radar in a radome under the starboard wing, to pinpoint the target after it had been detected by the AF-2W, and a searchlight under the port wing. The AF-2S had a crew of three, and could carry a 2,000lb torpedo, two 2,000lb bombs or two 1,600lb depth charges in its weapons bay, while the AF-2W differed from the XTB3F-1S chiefly in having two radar operators in the fuselage behind the pilots. The two variants operated together as a hunter/killer team, and both differed from the prototypes in having a 2,400hp R-2800-48W Double Wasp.

The production AF-2, named Guardian,

first flew on 17 November 1949. A total of 190 AF-2S and 156 AF-2W Guardians were built, even though large numbers of TBM-3S and TBM-3W Avenger conversions were produced at the same time. The first AF-2 deliveries were made to VS-25 in October 1950, and deliveries continued until 1953. That year the AF-3S, of which 25 were built, entered service, this variant having a retractable MAD boom under the tail, and possessing both search and strike capability. It could carry up to 8,000lb of weapons both internally and externally.

The Guardian remained in service until it began to be replaced by S2F-1 Trackers. Two Guardians, AF-2S 126792 and AF-2W 123100, were later converted into forest fire-bombers by the Aero Union Corporation, registered N9995Z and N3144G respectively. Both have now been withdrawn from service; N9995Z has been stored, but its companion has been repainted in USN markings.

Feline Fighters II

Grumman's first twin-engined shipboard fighter, the XF5F-1, had not gone into production partly because of its incompatibility with existing carriers, but the aircraft, together with its US Army Air Corps development the XP-50, nevertheless provided useful design experience for the new XF7F-1 (Grumman G-51). Known as the Tigercat, a prototype of the XF7F was ordered on 30 June 1941 – the same day as the two XF6F-1 Hellcats were ordered. Like the latter, the Tigercat was to incorporate the lessons of European air combat experience to that date, with particular emphasis on the need for high speed, heavy firepower and a good rate of climb, and on the importance of armour protection and self-sealing fuel tanks. It was altogether bolder in concept than the

XF5F-1, being a much bigger, heavier and more powerful aircraft, intended to operate from the three *Midway* Class carriers (CVB-41 to CVB-43) ordered in 1942–43. These were the longest and heaviest ships yet built for the US Navy, with an overall length of 986ft and a displacement of some 45,000 tons. The size of these ships was reflected in that of the XF7F-1 itself, which was the heaviest carrier-borne fighter aircraft attempted to date. It had nearly four times the horsepower of the F4F-3 Wildcat then in service with Navy squadrons, and nearly four times the loaded weight.

The F7F Tigercat
The single-seat XF7F-1 was powered by two 2,100hp Pratt & Whitney R-2800-22W Double Wasp radials, the large

diameter of these engines and the rather short-span wings with their square-cut tips giving the aircraft a very racy appearance. The wings folded upwards just outboard of the nacelles, and early production F7F-1s had large airscrew spinners. The Tigercat was the first carrier-borne fighter to have a nosewheel undercarriage, the gear retracting backwards into the long, pointed nose that resembled the earlier XP-50's. The armament was formidable, consisting of four 20mm M-2 cannon in the wing roots with 200 rounds per gun, and four 0.5in machine guns in the nose each with 300 rounds. Two 1,000lb bombs could be carried on underwing strong points, or six rocket projectiles on zero-length launchers; alternatively, a 21in torpedo could be accommodated beneath the fuselage. The first of two XF7F-1 prototypes, BuNos 03549 and 03550, made its first flight in December 1943, by which time 500 had been ordered for Marine Corps squadrons operating from shore bases in support of Pacific island amphibious operations.

Deliveries of the F7F-1, a day fighter, started in October 1944, but a combination of changing requirements and opera-

tional problems – together with the fact that the war was ending – led to only 34 examples of this variant being built. A fuselage fuel tank was removed to make way for an observer in the two-seat F7F-2N night fighter. Sixty-six were built, including the XF7F-2 prototype, BuNo 80261. As well as the second crew member, this version had nose radar in place of the machine guns. Two F7F-2Ns were evaluated in Britain in 1945 for possible use by the Fleet Air Arm. They bore the serials TT346 and TT349, but retained their US Navy 'midnight blue' scheme and white 'star and bar' markings, the British serials being in white just ahead of the tailplane.

The major postwar production variant was the F7F-3: 189 examples were built, although a further 1,386 were cancelled after VJ-Day. This was a single-seater similar to the -1 but with a taller fin and rudder, better armour protection and 2,100hp R-2800-34W Double Wasps which, like the R-2800-22Ws in the -1 and -2N, each gave 2,400hp with water injection. Some of these Tigercats were fitted with a camera installation as F7F-3Ps, and the F7F-3E was a variant of the -3 with special electronic equipment. The 60 F7F-3N two-seat night fighters that followed the F7F-3s were similar to the -2N, with an observer's position and the nose guns replaced by radar in a lengthened nose with a blunter tip and a slight bulge beneath. This sub-type, and the very similar F7F-4N (of which thirteen were built), had a taller fin and rudder like the F7F-3. The -4N was also strengthened, with an improved nose radar and a modified undercarriage; this variant was cleared for carrier operations, and had a deck arrester hook, the only version of the Tigercat with this feature. The -3N and -4N could also carry a 300 US gallon drop tank under the fuselage. The Tigercat was just too late to see operational service in the war, and although it served postwar with a few shore-based Marine Corps squadrons, it was fairly soon replaced by jets. Even so, a total of 364 had been built when production ended in 1946, the last delivery being made in December that year.

The use of the Tigercat for forest-fire bombing was pioneered in Oregon in

Far left: Owing something to the earlier XF5F-1 Skyrocket, the XF7F-1 twin-engined fighter, the prototype of which is seen here, was designed to operate from the *Midway* Class carriers. (Grumman)

Left: The 66 F7F-2N night fighters were equipped with radar in place of the nose-mounted machine guns and featured a second cockpit over the wing for the observer. The Tigercat was just too late to see operational service in the Second World War. (Grumman)

Left: The F7F-3 was the major production version of the Tigercat. A single-seater similar to the -1, it had R-2800-34W Double Wasps and a taller fin and rudder. This F7F-3N night fighter carries a 21in torpedo under the fuselage. (Grumman)

Left: F7F-3 Tigercat N7654C seen here, formerly BuNo 80373, was operated as a forest fire bomber by TBM Air Tankers Inc. of Tulare, California. During the 1960s and 1970s several F7F-3s and -3Ns, fitted with a big ventral tank under the fuselage, were used in this role in California and Oregon. (P. Kirkup)

1958 by Kreitzberg Aviation of Salem, and the aircraft was one of the first twin-engined war-surplus types used in this role. It was fitted with tankage for 750 to 800 US gallons of fire retardant slurry, and by 1964 there were thirteen F7F-3s and F7F-3Ns on the US civil register, of which seven were active, mostly as fire-fighters. By 1977 Sis-Q Flying Services of Santa Rosa, California, had four F7F-3 fire-fighters on strength, and TBM Air Tankers Inc. of Tulare, California, had two F7F-3s. With a big ventral tank under the fuselage holding 833 US gallons or 7,500lb of fire retardant, the F7F-3's gross weight had risen from 25,720lb in military form to 27,996lb. One F7F-3 on the 1964 US civil register was actually modified into a twin-float seaplane, but it is not certain if it flew in this form.

The F8F Bearcat

Meanwhile in 1943 the Navy decided that it needed a lightweight development of the F6F Hellcat to operate from the smallest carriers, primarily as an interceptor, for which an outstanding performance, especially in the climb, was mandatory. In response, Grumman began work on the G-58, to be known as the F8F Bearcat, and the Navy ordered two XF8F-1 prototypes on 27 November 1943. The company strove for the smallest possible airframe that would accommodate a 2,100hp R-2800-22W Double Wasp radial and a specified amount of fuel. With a span 7ft less, and a length 3ft 4in less, than that of the F6F, the F8F-1 was one of the fastest piston-engined fighters of the war, even though its loaded weight was about the same as the Hellcat's. It was similar in appearance to the latter except for its 'teardrop' cockpit canopy and inward-retracting undercarriage, and an unusual feature of the original design – and one that was eventually abandoned – was the provision of break points, coupled with explosive bolts, in the wings: if a Bearcat were handled too violently in rolling manoeuvres, these would enable both wing tips to fail simultaneously at selected points, thereby preserving symmetry and hence control.

The first of two XF8F-1 prototypes (which were serialled 90460 and 90461) made its maiden flight on 21 August 1944 fitted with an R-2800-22W Double Wasp, a mere nine months after the aircraft had been ordered. It soon lived up to expectations by achieving a top speed of 424mph and an initial rate of climb of no less than 4,800ft/min. An armament of four 0.5in Browning machine guns was installed in the wings, and underwing pylons for two 1,000lb bombs or drop tanks and zero-length launchers for four 5in rockets were provided for. The prototypes' performance was sufficiently promising for contracts to be placed with Grumman for 2,023 F8F-1s on 6 October 1944, and a further 1,876 machines were ordered in February 1945 from the

Left: The F8F-1 Bearcat was a high-performance development of the Hellcat, and one of the fastest piston-engined fighters ever built, with a spectacular rate of climb. Production F8F-1s (as depicted) differed from the prototypes in having an R-2800-34W Double Wasp engine and a dorsal fin fillet. (US Navy)

Eastern Aircraft Division of General Motors under the designation F3M-1; Bearcat production by the Canadian Car and Foundry Co. was also considered under the designation F4W-1, but no orders were placed.

Production got under way at a quite fantastic speed. The first F8F-1 was delivered on 1 December 1944 and the first operational squadron, VF-19, started to equip with Bearcats on 21 May 1945. The aircraft was almost combat-ready when the war ended. Production F8F-1s had the R-2800-34W Double Wasp, which gave 2,400hp with water-injection for take-off and an emergency combat rating of 2,800hp, and they also had a slightly greater fuel capacity and a dorsal fillet to the fin. The Bearcat's performance was so good that Grumman eventually built 770 F8F-1s in spite of the large-scale cut-backs following VJ-Day, as a result of which no fewer than 5,253 F8F-1s and all the F3M-1s were cancelled.

The F8F-1s were followed by 126 F8F-1Bs, in which four 20mm M-2 cannon replaced the wing-mounted machine guns, but 30 of these were completed as F8F-1N night fighters with APS-6 radar in a pod on the starboard wing leading edge in a manner similar to the F6F-3N and -5N Hellcats; two F8F-1s had first been fitted with this radar in a Trial Installation. A few F8F-1s were later modified into F8F-1D drone-director ships, as were some F8F-2s, which became F8F-2Ds. The F8F-2, which appeared in 1948 after two XF8F-2 prototypes, featured a taller fin and rudder very similar in outline to the F7F-3 Tigercat's, as well as a revised engine cowling, the -1B's cannon armament and some additional armour protection. Grumman built 293 of this variant, plus twelve more F8F-2N night fighters with the same APS-6 pod-mounted radar as the F8F-1N and 60 more F8F-2Ps for photo-reconnaissance with a camera installed in the rear fuselage and only two 20mm wing cannon. Bearcat production ended in May 1949 after 1,264 of all variants had been built – a remarkable total in view of the advent of jet fighters. By this time twelve Navy squadrons had F8F-1s, whilst the same number were equipped with F8F-2s.

One civil Bearcat (the Grumman G-58A), registered N7247C, was built for Major 'Al' J. Williams, well known as a display and aerobatic pilot who had previously used the G-22 *Gulfhawk II* and the G-32 *Gulfhawk III*, registered NC1051 and a variant of the F3F-2 fighter. Named *Gulfhawk IV*, the G-58A Bearcat, very similar to an F8F-1, was written off after a landing at Major Williams' private airstrip at New Bern, North Carolina, some time in 1948 or 1949. Williams claimed that the starboard undercarriage leg did not lock down, although Grumman counter-claimed that he ground-looped the G-58A, the under-fuselage drop tank scraping the runway and the ensuing fire destroying the aircraft. Later, an F8F-2 was restored to the US register and painted in the same colour scheme as *Gulfhawk IV*. Not long after the war an F8F-1 was 'civilianized' with the registration NL3025, the letter 'L' denoting a 'Limited' status applied to certain military aircraft. Another civil G-58A Bearcat was N700A owned by Grumman, which was assembled from spares and was very similar to an F8F-2, though with all its armament and military equipment deleted. Painted red overall and resplendent with black fuselage flash and cowling leading edge, N700A had a 'tuning fork' type aerial for its Bendix MS-192C VHF radio on top of the fin, as well as a knife-like dorsal aerial, while the ventral drop tank was modified for use as a luggage compartment.

The Bearcat's great speed and manoeuvrability made it attractive to foreign air forces, of which two, those of France and Thailand, eventually operated it. More than 250 refurbished aircraft, mostly F8F-1s with a revised fuel system, served with *l'Armée de l'Air* in the Indo-China war. After some costly French reverses in northern Indo-China in the autumn of 1950, General de Lattre de Tassigny was appointed area C-in-C in December that year, and under his direction *l'Armée de l'Air* began to play a much more significant role in the war against the Viet Minh. The Bearcats, Douglas B-26 Invaders and other US-built aircraft forced the enemy to move by night and hampered their deployment, especially when napalm bombs began to be used against them. This renewed effectiveness of airpower, and the use of napalm, enabled the French to inflict a number of reverses on the Viet Minh during 1951. For the next two years the war was largely a conflict of movement, with both sides tending to avoid major confrontations, but the more highly mechanized French, because of their dependence on roads, found themselves at a disadvantage against an enemy who used their superior mobility to gain freedom of movement throughout the countryside.

In November 1953 the village of Dien Bien Phu was taken by paratroop assault from Douglas C-47s as part of a plan to stop Communist divisions moving down from Tongkin into northern Laos. Two airstips were built here to link this new base with French forces around Hanoi, and the French strategy was to draw the Viet Minh into a set battle in which their firepower would be able to inflict a decisive defeat. Six napalm-armed Bearcats were deployed at the larger airstrip on alert but, to French dismay and surprise, the Viet Minh succeeded in manhandling their artillery into position, shelled the airstrips on 10 March 1954 and overran the outer defensive positions, setting up anti-aircraft guns in the hills around the

Left: The French Air Force acquired more than 250 Bearcats from 1951, mostly F8F-1s with a revised fuel system, for use in Indo-China against the Viet Minh. They equipped eight squadrons, including a reconnaissance unit that had cameras mounted in its aircraft's drop tanks. This French F8F-1B, serialled 5172 and fitted with outsize drop tanks, is seen on a pierced steel planking (PSP) runway in Indo-China. (ECPA)

valley in which Dien Bien Phu was situated. This meant that neither Fairchild C-119 Packets nor Douglas C-47s could fly low enough to parachute in supplies or reinforcements accurately. The French ran short of artillery ammunition and their garrison was finally overrun on 7 May after bitter fighting and heavy French losses. This severe defeat led to the partitioning of Vietnam into North and South, separated by a Demilitarized Zone, and some of the surviving French Bearcats were later taken over by both the North and South Vietnamese Air Forces.

The Royal Thai Air Force received 29 F8F-1Bs and 100 F8F-1s under the MDAP programme after it was reorganized by a US Military Air Advisory Group in the early 1950s. Six of the Thai Bearcats, plus a Douglas C-47, paid a goodwill visit to RAF stations and squadrons in Singapore and Malaya late in 1953. The surviving Thai Bearcats still equipped one of the Air Force's two close-support wings as late as 1963, but the type was withdrawn from Thai service not long afterwards.

The Racing Bearcats
By 1964 there were 22 F8F Bearcats on the US civil register, of which eight were active, and among the owners was the Confederate Air Force based at Har-

lingen, Texas. The Bearcat made its racing début in the US National Air Races held at Sky Ranch, north of Reno, Nevada, in September that year, when three F8F-2s qualified for heats in the Unlimited Class races. Two of these were standard airframes, but the third, N1111L owned by Lockheed test pilot Darryl Greenamyer, had a very small, cut-down cockpit canopy and sealed landing flaps. After qualifying second at 359.51mph, Greenamyer found the view from the small canopy too restricted and this, plus the critical weight-balance of the F8F-2, made it too tricky to land on the narrow Sky Ranch runway. He chose to alight instead on the wider runways of Reno Municipal Airport after coming fourth in the finals, but was disqualified for failing to land at the race site as the rules demanded. The two other F8F-2s in the race, Mira Slovak's N9885C, (painted white overall and bearing the name of its sponsor, Smirnoff, but actually owned by Bill Stead) and Commander Walter Ohlrich's N7827C, were both standard, and the former won the race on points. The same three Bearcats competed against three P-51D Mustangs at the 1965 US Nationals on 12 September at the same Reno venue, and this time Greenamyer's N1111L had its wings cut down to 28ft 6in span and fitted with downturned

Hoerner tips, and had a Douglas Sky-raider airscrew with spinner and an even smaller teardrop canopy. He won at an average speed of 375.1mph with his engine well throttled back, the prize money being a mere $2,000. A fortnight later, at the Las Vegas International Air Races held at Boulder City Airport, the same aircraft qualified at a record 423.4mph over the ten-lap, 93½-mile course. In the main race itself for the Paul Mantz Trophy, Greenamyer had to pull out because of problems with his modi-fied 3,300hp engine in the ninth lap after an exciting duel with Chuck Lyford's

P-51D Mustang N2869D, which went on to win.

For the 1966 Los Angeles National Air Races, held on 27–30 May at Fox Field, near Lancaster, California, Greenamyer had modified his Bearcat yet again, giving it a midget racer-sized 'bubble' canopy, and lightening it by 700lb by removing the complete electrical system and all but a few feet of the hydraulic circuity, this now being fitted with a nitrogen bottle for a once-only undercarriage retraction. The Double Wasp was made up of parts of four different engines to give about 3,300hp; it had a two-speed supercharger

Above: G-58A N700A was owned by Grumman and was one of several Bearcats to be 'civilianized'; it was assembled from spares and combined an F8F-1 engine with an F8F-2 airframe. (Grumman)

Left: F8F-2 N1111L, formerly BuNo 121646, was flown by Lockheed test pilot Darryl Greenamyer in the US Nationals from 1964. It was subjected to a whole series of modifications, including very small bubble canopies, cropped wings with Hoerner wing tips, an airscrew spinner and an oversized propeller, and had a stripped and lightened airframe. It is seen here as *Conquest I*; as such, it broke the world's piston-engined speed record at 482.462mph. (P. Kirkup)

from an R-2800-CB17, and water-injection was provided from a 75 gallon tank. To absorb the extra power a 13ft 6in diameter, four-blade propeller like that on the Douglas AD Skyraider was fitted, with a spinner, and its larger diameter necessitated three-point take-offs and landings to avoid damaging the tips. The white exterior was highly waxed and polished. In addition to the cropped wing span of the previous year, Greenamyer removed 18in from the top of the fin and rudder, but this made the Bearcat slide sideways and start to roll at 450mph, and after flying a few laps the pilot discovered that his rudder control was inadequate for high-speed racing turns. This problem also prevented a planned attempt on the world 3km piston-engined speed record at Lancaster.

The expression 'hot ship' really meant something with this Bearcat for, because of its extra power and stripped-down interior, Greenamyer had to wear Alaskan mukluks (fur boots) to keep his feet from blistering, and the throttle had to be heavily taped to dissipate some of the heat. For the 1966 US Nationals, held at Stead Airport near Reno on 21–25 September, the Bearcat, now showing the name of its Smirnoff sponsor instead of Mira Slovak's F8F-2 since the latter had quit racing, had its fin and rudder restored

to their normal height. This time Greenamyer was luckier, beating five P-51D Mustangs to take the race at an average of 396.221mph over the ten-lap, 80.04-mile course. He also won the 1967 Nationals at the same place at an average speed 4mph slower. Another Bearcat contender that year was John Church in N148F, a black F8F-2 with a gold registration and trimmings.

On 16 August 1969 Greenamyer, his Bearcat now named *Conquest I*, broke the world piston-engined speed record by averaging 482.462mph in four flights over a 3km straight-line course at Edwards Air Force base in the Mojave Desert. He flew at 300ft in a temperature of 100°F, and was watched by about 300 spectators. He thus broke the 30-year-old world absolute air speed record of 469.22mph set by *Flugkapitän* Fritz Wendel on 26 April 1939 in the Messerschmitt Me 209V1 (which, for propaganda purposes, the Germans had presented to the world as the 'Me 109R'). A world record attempt the previous summer by Greenamyer at Edwards was unsuccessful because a master-rod bearing in his engine had failed. On 21 September that year he once again won the Unlimited Championship race, sponsored by Harrah's casino of Reno, at Stead Airport. The race consisted of twelve laps of an

Below: F8F-2 N7827C, formerly BuNo 121752, was raced by Commander Walter Ohlrich in the US Nationals from 1964 to 1971. It later had a modified R-2800-9W engine with water methanol injection, and was named *Tom Cat* and later *Miss Priss*. The white colour scheme seen here is set off with a red cowling and spinner with white stripes, a blue fuselage flash and registration, red wing and tailplane tips, and a red racing number. (P. Kirkup)

½-mile course, and *Conquest I* worked up the record speed, for a closed course, of 412.631mph. Two years later, at the 1971 Nationals, he again broke the same closed-course speed record, at 413.987mph.

There were two other Bearcats in the 1969 field of six, a standard F8F-1 owned and flown by Gunther Balz, registered N9G and with a very attractive white and red colour scheme with gold trim. This unfortunately came last, but F8F-2 N777L, *The Able Cat*, flown by TWA co-pilot Lyle Shelton, managed fifth. Shelton had rebuilt this Bearcat almost from scratch from BuNo 16629, which he had found at Valparaiso, Indiana, earlier that year. The aircraft had been badly damaged in a take-off or landing accident, and it was further damaged when it was removed from the runway, the net result being a wrecked port wing, tail and canopy and a missing engine. Shelton obtained a 2,700hp Wright R-3350-26WA Cyclone engine from a Douglas AD Skyraider driving a DC-7 four-blade propeller and spinner, and designed a new engine mounting. He gradually managed to buy or borrow enough missing parts to make up a complete airframe, and one of the most ambitious rebuilds ever of a Second World War fighter was completed in a mere seven months.

Walter Ohlrich's F8F-2, previously named *Tom Cat* and now *Miss Priss*, did not qualify for the finals but it won the Consolidation race. It now had a modified R-2800-9W engine with a water-methanol system of 75–80 gallons capacity used for power-boosting during the race. This system was used to carry fuel for the 1,667-mile Harold's Club Transcontinental Trophy race from Milwaukee, Wisconsin, to Reno on 14 September, in which Ohlrich came eighth. He had designed his own plastic fuel tanks for this race, for which *Miss Priss* was also fitted with two big underwing drop tanks from a Douglas AD Skyraider. In 1972 *Miss Priss* was sold to John Herlihy, who raced it under the name *Sweet P*; it later became N800H *Bearcat Bill*.

For the 1970 Nationals Greenamyer's Bearcat was fitted with a cine camera at the top of the fin in order to photograph the races in which he flew, but the camera did not function properly. A new Bearcat contender that year was Ron Reynolds with F8F-2 N5005. In June 1971 Lyle Shelton won the first Unlimited race on the East Coast, at Cape May, New Jersey, at 360.15mph in his F8F-2.

For the 1973 season, starting with the Great Miami Air Race on 16–21 January, another new Bearcat was John Sliker's F8F-2 N7701C *Escape II*, which he fitted

Below: Lyle Shelton's F8F-2 N777L, at first named *The Able Cat*, was notable in being rebuilt from a crashed airframe and fitted with a Wright R-3350-25WA engine from a Douglas AD Skyraider driving a DC-7 four-blade propeller. Flying this machine in 1973, Shelton became the first man ever to win three Unlimited races in a year. The colour scheme is white and purple. (P. Kirkup)

with a 2,400hp R-2800-CB17 Double Wasp taken, complete with cowling, from a Martin 2-0-2 airliner. This had the disadvantage of a big carburettor air scoop on top of the cowling, which added drag and restricted the pilot's view forward, yet in spite of this encumbrance *Escape II* qualified for the Unlimited Class race at Reno/Stead that September at 407.390mph. For the 1975 Nationals the intake scoop was removed and the intake relocated inside the cowling, but the aircraft crashed on 15 September. Michael Smith had also fitted his F8F-2, N9885C, formerly flown by Mira Slovak, with an R-2800-CB17 without such a scoop in 1973, but after this was put out of action when an oil line came loose a similar engine from a Douglas DC-6B was fitted, and with this he was able to qualify. Lyle Shelton won the Unlimited Class race in his R-3350-engined F8F-2, now with a cut-down cockpit canopy and renamed *Phast Phantom*, at an average speed of 428.155mph fopr the ten laps of the 9.815-mile course, thus breaking the closed-course speed record that Darryl Greenamyer had twice before set. Shelton broke this record again at Reno on 10 September 1974 at 432.252mph, and Greenamyer took the record from him a year later at 435.556mph. Shelton had

also won the twelve-lap Roscoe Turner Speed Classic at the 1973 Great Miami Air Races at 373mph, and won again at the California Air Classic held at Mojave on 18–21 October at 396mph, becoming in 1973 the first man ever to win three Unlimited races in a year. He won the Unlimited race again at the Reno Nationals on 11 September 1975, averaging 429.916mph around eight laps of the 9.815-mile course. However, at the California Air Classic at Mojave in June 1976, Shelton's Bearcat was badly damaged in a wheels-up landing in one of the qualifying heats, after an oil leak had resulted in an engine stoppage.

In the last few years the P-51D Mustang has regained its old pre-eminence in Unlimited Class racing, and at Reno in 1983 twenty of the 32 contenders were P-51Ds and one a P-51H. Only two Bearcats, an F8F-1 and an F8F-2, took part. The radial-engine challenge has been taken up anew by Britain's Hawker Sea Fury, now equipped with the big 36-cylinder, four-row Pratt & Whitney R-4360 Wasp Major. With prize money increasing, and winning speeds topping the 425mph mark, it may well be that more of these Wasp Major-powered Sea Furies will displace the Bearcats as the P-51D's chief contenders.

Above: F8F-1 NL9G first appeared in the US Nationals in 1969 as N9G, owned and flown by Gunther Balz; as shown here, it was later painted in the markings of the Royal Thai Air Force, which operated 129 Bearcats. The roundel is red/white/blue/white/red, as is the national flag on the black and white fin and rudder 'checkerboard'. Just visible beneath the cockpit canopy is the red tiger's head emblem of the Thai Air Force's 1st Fighter-Bomber Wing. (Air-Britain)

Feline Jet Fighters

In January 1945, as the first Bearcats were coming off the production line, Grumman began work on a jet night fighter as one of four finalists in the Navy's first design competition for such an aircraft, which was eventually won by the Douglas F3D Skyknight. After seven weeks the Grumman project took shape as the G-75 or XF9F-1, with four 1,500lb s.t., Navy-sponsored Westinghouse J30 (or 19XB-2B) turbojets in the wing roots and a crew of two in tandem; four engines were necessary to give the required performance since, at that time, a more powerful turbojet was unavailable in the United States. A contract was signed for the XF9F-1 on 11 April 1946. The aircraft would be equipped with nose radar and a crew of two, but there were doubts about how best to install the wing-mounted engines and also about the desirability of using four turbojets of such low power. The Navy agreed to change the XF9F-1 contract to cover a single-seat day fighter, and Grumman proposed several G-79 layouts, most of them with a single large turbojet in the fuselage. In May 1947, following successful tests by the US Navy of two imported Rolls-Royce Nene turbojets at the Naval Air Material Center, Philadelphia, the previous December, Pratt & Whitney took out a licence to build the British engine in an Americanized version to be known as the J42. The Navy had been attracted by the Nene's excellent power-to-weight ratio – it gave 5,000lb s.t. for a weight of 1,700lb – and the Nene came to be known as 'The Needle Engine' for its part in stimulating competition and development among US turbojet manufacturers.

The F9F Panther

Grumman had decided to use a single, 5,000lb s.t. Nene in the fuselage for the XF9F-1, with air intakes in thickened wing roots and the jet exhausting at the rear of the fuselage under the tail; in this form the aircraft was designated G-79D. The original XF9F-1 contract was amended in August 1946 to cover three XF9F-2 prototypes – BuNos 122475 and 122477, plus a static test airframe – and in translating the G-79D into the XF9F-2 the cockpit was moved back and the fin and rudder were changed from a shape resembling the Bearcat's to one of a lower aspect ratio, triangular form. The XF9F-2

contract also covered design information for a swept wing version of the project, and this eventually led to the F9F-6, but Leroy Grumman and vice-president Bill Schwendler declined to submit the original sweptback project under the August 1946 contract, partly because of the limited data for this type of layout then available.

The first XF9F-2 prototype, powered by an imported Nene, took off on its maiden flight on 24 November 1947 in the hands of Corwin 'Corky' Meyer, who landed it on one of the long runways at New York's Idlewild Airport. The first prototype later had wing-tip tanks and four 20mm M-2 cannon fitted. The second prototype, BuNo 122477, made its first flight in March 1949; the third prototype, 122476, was the first XF9F-3, and flew on 16 August 1948 powered by a 4,600lb s.t. Allison J33-A-8 (or Model 400) turbojet, this engine having been delivered to Grumman only that month. The Allison J33 was regarded as an insurance against the failure of the Nene and J42.

The F9F Panther was a rugged aeroplane, fully in keeping with the tradition that had given its makers the nickname 'Grumman Ironworks'. The first twelve production aircraft did not have wing-tip tanks, and fuel was carried only within the fuselage, but subsequent aircraft (except, at first, the XF9F-2 and XF9F-3 prototypes) did have these tanks, which were made permanent to ensure a cleaner fit and to overcome the difficulty of jettisoning them both simultaneously. The wings folded upwards hydraulically and could take two 500 or 1,000lb bombs on racks or six 5in HVAR (High-Velocity Aircraft Rocket) projectiles on zero-length launchers. Split, slotted flaps were installed, and the wing leading edges had variable camber. Four 20mm M-2 cannon were arranged in the nose, and air brakes were fitted beneath the forward fuselage. An interesting point is that the F9F was equipped with a Martin-Baker ejection seat, before such seats had entered service with the RAF. Both the Panther's nose and the complete rear fuselage could be removed on dollies to give access to the engine and armament, and on at least one occasion the rear fuselage parted company

with the rest of the airframe when the arrester hook engaged the wires during a landing.

Both the J42 and J33 powerplants proved difficult to install, and getting this right necessitated a number of modifications to the airframe. The Navy placed an initial order for 47 F9F-2s with the 5,750lb s.t. J42-P-8 turbojet and 54 F9F-3s with the J33-A-8 engine, both these variants, which first flew in November 1948, being produced simultaneously and named Panther. The F9F-2 proved to be the superior version, and so the F9F-3s were re-engined from 1950 to become -2s. The first operational Panther unit was VF-51, which received its first F9F-3s in May 1949; these were followed by the first F9F-2s delivered to the Navy's *Blue Angels* aerobatic team. Service entry was trouble-free, and the aircraft proved to have an excellent performance and manoeuvrability, although a wing fence was later added to the F9F-2 and -3 just outboard of each main intake. A total of 567 F9F-2s were built, in addition to the converted aircraft.

On 3 June 1950 F9F-2 Panthers from the carrier *Valley Forge* became the Navy's first jet fighters to see combat when they went into action over Korea, and on 9 November that year an F9F-2 flown by the CO of VF-111 became the first Navy aircraft to shoot down a jet when it destroyed a MiG-15. F9F-2s flew nearly half the Navy's combat missions in Korea, mainly in ground-attack sorties both from Navy carriers and Marine airstrips ashore, using 5in HVARs or 1,000lb bombs. For the fighter role, two 150 US gallon drop tanks were sometimes carried on wing racks. Some F9F-2s with six underwing stores pylons were temporarily designated F9F-2B, and some were converted into F9F-2D director ships (later designated DF-9B) for controlling target drones or RPVs (remote-controlled pilotless vehicles). Further machines were converted into F9F-2KDs for use as drone directors or as target drone aircraft themselves, and the -2D and -2KD variants were used in support of such missile programmes as the Chance Vought Regulus 1 and 2, the Douglas/Sperry Sparrow 1, the McDonnell Triton and Grumman's own Rigel long-range surface-to-surface

Above: The F9F-5 was powered by a Pratt & Whitney J48, a licence-built version of the Rolls-Royce Tay. Compared to the F9F-2, the -5 also had a 2ft longer rear fuselage and a taller fin and rudder. (Grumman)

missile for the Navy. Twenty surplus F9F-2 Panthers were later supplied to Argentina's *Aviación Naval*, together with two TF-9J Cougar swept-wing two-seat trainers. These equipped Attack Squadron 1, a component of Escuadra Aéronavale 3 (EA 3) at the Punta de Indio base across the River Plate estuary from Montevideo, and were finally replaced by sixteen Douglas A-4Q Skyhawks delivered in 1972.

One F9F-2, BuNo 123084, was re-engined with an Allison J33-A-16 turbo-jet of 5,850lb s.t. dry (6,450lb with water-injection) to become the XF9F-4; 109 F9F-4s were ordered with this engine, but in the event were completed as F9F-5s. The F9F-5 featured a 24½in-longer rear fuselage and a taller fin and rudder, and was powered by a 6,250lb s.t. Pratt & Whitney J48-P-2, J48-P-4 or J48-P-6A turbojet, or a 7,250lb s.t. J48-P-8. The J48 was a licence-built version of the Rolls-Royce Tay, a more powerful development of the Nene, but it had not gone into production for any British aircraft. The XF9F-5 prototype – which was F9F-2 BuNo 123085 re-

engined with a J48-P-2 – first flew on 21 December 1949, but F9F-5 deliveries did not begin until the last F9F-2s were completed in August 1951. Altogether 595 F9F-5s were built, plus the 109 ordered as F9F-4s and another 36 F9F-5Ps with K-17 and trimetrogen cameras for vertical and oblique photo coverage in an extended nose, the -5P also having a General Electric G-3 autopilot and some equipment changes.

Some F9F-5s were equipped with special electronics, and a few featured a nose-mounted in-flight refuelling probe manufactured by the US subsidiary of the well-known British company Flight Refuelling Ltd. One F9F-5 was modified in 1954 to have blown flaps, invented by John D. Attinello of the Naval Air Test Center at Patuxent River, Maryland, and of the same basic type as were later fitted to such aircraft as the F-104 Starfighter and Supermarine Scimitar. Some F9F-5s and -5Ps were converted into drone-director ships or target drones as F9F-5KDs; this variant was similar to the F9F-2KD and was redesignated DF-9E in 1962. Many F9F Panthers were used as advanced trainers from 1953 onwards, as they were replaced in service by the F9F-6 Cougar and subsequent aircraft. In 1952 F9F-5s were retrofitted with a radar-ranging gun sight in a small bulge under the nose, and this was also fitted to F9F-6 Cougars whilst they were on the production line.

The Swept-Wing Cougar

The fitting of a swept wing to the basic Panther enabled its production life to be extended by another seven years. The original swept-wing XF9F-2 design study called for under the August 1946 XF9F-2 contract was not taken to the stage of a formal proposal, and the first official approaches for a swept-wing Panther development were not made until early 1950, almost a year after the type had first

entered service. These were the subject of a Navy contract of 2 March 1951, which called for three prototypes of the XF9F-6, or Grumman G-93. A completely new wing with 35 degrees of sweepback and over 40 per cent greater area was designed, together with a swept tailplane of narrower chord and fittd with a powered elevator. These were married to the same fuselage and vertical tail surfaces as the Panther, although by the time design work was completed little of the F9F-6 was common to the F9F-5 apart from the nose. The powerplant was the same 7,250lb s.t. P&W J48-P-8 as that fitted to some F9F-5s.

The new wing had a different aerofoil section from that of the -5, larger trailing-edge flaps, much larger split flaps on the centre section, automatic leading-edge

Left: Some F9F-5s were converted into F9F-5KD target drones; BuNo 126277, of VU-1, is seen here. This variant was later redesignated DF-9E. (R. L. Trimble)

Left: The first swept-wing version of the F9F series was the F9F-6 Cougar (later redesignated F-9F), which had a new wing with 35 degrees of sweepback, larger flaps, leading-edge slats, wing fences and spoilers for lateral control, as well as a swept tailplane. (Grumman)

Above: The F9F-7 (F–9H) was very similar to the F9F-6 but was powered by a 6,350lb s.t. Allison J33-A-16A turbojet instead of a P&W J48-P-8. This variant was the first of the F9F series to retain the Allison engine throughout its service life. (D. O. Olson, via J. M. G. Gradidge)

slats and, for lateral control, hydraulically operated, spanwise spoilers on the wing upper surfaces at 75 per cent of the chord line in place of conventional ailerons. Very prominent root fillets faired the wing into the fuselage, and the engine intakes were extended forward of the leading edge to a point almost level with the windscreen. The definitive F9F-6 wing had inboard fences, the leading-edge outer slatted section was slightly drooped and the spoilers extended from the wing tips to the inboard fences. The wing-tip tanks of earlier versions were deleted, and two 150 US gallon drop tanks or 1,000lb bombs could be carried on underwing racks, or alternatively six 5in HVAR projectiles on zero-length launchers; the fixed armament, four 20mm M-2 cannon, remained unchanged. The prototype XF9F-6 first flew on 20 September 1951, and the swept-wing versions were named Cougar. F9F-6 production totalled 646, and the first unit to receive the aircraft was VF-32, which was issued with its new equipment from November 1952. The aircraft was relabelled F-9F in the 1962 tri-service designations.

The F9F-6P, of which 60 were built, was an unarmed photo-reconnaissance variant with K-17 and trimetrogen cameras (for vertical and oblique coverage) in an extended nose; it later became the RF-9F. Like the Panther, the Cougar had a quickly detachable nose and rear fuselage to give easy access to the armament, electronics, powerplant and other equipment. The hydraulically adjustable tailplane was linked to the flap control to provide constant longitudinal trim during flap extension. The F9F-6D (later DF-9F) and F9F-6PD were drone-director ship conversions of some F9F-6s and two F9F-6Ps; some -6s were converted into target drones as the F9F-6K (later QF-9F), with wing-tip radomes and new electronic equipment in the nose, and with revised and updated special equipment this variant became the F9F-6K2 (later QF-9G).

The 168 production F9F-7 (later F-9H) Cougars were very similar to the F9F-6 but had the Allison J33-A-16A turbojet of 6,350lb s.t. (7,000lb s.t. with water-injection). This was the first of the Panther/Cougar line to retain the Allison engine throughout its service life. The F9F-8 (later F-9J) first flew on 18 December 1953; there was no XF9F-8. The first -8, BuNo 131063, had test instrumentation installed and a nose probe for performance measurement. The F9F-8 reverted to the Pratt & Whitney J48-P-8A of 7,250lb s.t. (8,500lb s.t. with water-injection) and was a development of the F9F-6 with greater speed and range; in January 1954 one of these aircraft exceeded Mach 1 in a shallow dive. The -8 differed from the F9F-6 in having the leading-edge slats replaced by fixed, cambered, leading-edge extensions outboard of the wing fences. The wing trailing edges were also extended and span was reduced, whilst the wing chord was increased by no less than 22 per cent. Deleting the hydraulic system for the leading-edge slats gave space for an additional 30 US gallons of fuel in each wing, and the centre fuselage was made 8in longer to take an extra 80 US gallons of fuel; the shape of the cockpit hood was also revised, to improve the pilot's view to the rear. Altogether 662 F9F-8s were built, several later being converted to QF-9J target drones and some to the F9F-8B (later AF-9J) attack variant with four Philco/Martin AAM-N-7 Sidewinder infra-red homing air-to-air missiles (AAM) on underwing pylons, or the early Martin ASM-N-7 Bullpup air-to-surface missiles (ASM). The YF9F-8B prototype later became the YAF-9J, and many

Left: The F9F-8B (later redesignated AF-9J) was an attack variant of the -8 which could carry four Philco/Martin AAM-N-7 Sidewinder infra-red air-to-air missiles on underwing pylons, or Martin ASM-N-7 Bullpup air-to-surface missiles. F9F-8Bs like BuNo 131071 seen here were converted from -8s and had a revised nose. (Grumman)

Left: This TF-9J Cougar, BuNo 146405, was photographed at NAS Miramar, California; assigned to VT-10, it is painted white overall, with a red nose and tail and black lettering. (R. Bulinski)

Left: One of the two TF-9J Cougars supplied to Argentina's *Aviación Naval* to convert pilots to the F9F-2 Panthers of Attack Squadron 1, 3-A-151 shown here is overall black, with white lettering and leading edges, and carries the national flag on the nose. (A. Reinhard)

AF-9Js were later used for missile-training as TAF-9Js. The F9F-8P for photo-reconnaissance, which first flew on 21 August 1955, had two pairs of downward-looking trimetrogen cameras and a single forward oblique camera in an extended nose that was longer and more drooped than the F9F-5P's. A total of 110 F9F-8Ps, which later became RF-9Js, were built.

The last of the Panther/Cougar line was the F9F-8T (later TF-9J) two-seat trainer, the YF9F-8T prototype of which, BuNo 141667, first flew on 4 April 1956. This version, which was later designated YTF-9J, had the forward fuselage lengthened by 34in in order to accommodate a second cockpit, both the pupil and instructor (in the rear cockpit, well above the pupil) having Martin-Baker ejection seats and standard F9F-8 controls and instrumentation. The canopy was hinged at the rear to open clamshell-fashion, and the aircraft could be flown as a single-seater from the front cockpit. Only two 20mm M-2 cannon were fitted, but the same external weapons loads as the F9F-8's could be carried, and the -8T could also be used as an operational fighter. Altogether 400 F9F-8Ts were built, bringing total Cougar production to 2,046 for the Navy and Marine Corps. The last -8T was delivered to the Navy on 2 February 1960.

F9F-8Ts replaced Panthers in many squadrons and were used for the third phase of Navy pilot training after the Beech T-34B Mentor and the Rockwell T-2B Buckeye. The Cougar was the first swept-wing type to be used by the US Navy's *Blue Angels* aerobatic team, which flew them from 1955 to 1958. Some of the F-9J Cougar variants remained in second-line use with various Reserve units until the early 1970s, the TF-9J even being used on combat missions in Vietnam, and the type was not finally withdrawn until February 1974, when the last users of the TF-9J, VT-4, retired their aircraft. Altogether total Panther/Cougar production numbered 3,410 aircraft, and the first of the various drone conversions was made in 1955. Two TF-9Js used for test flying were designated NTF-9J.

Below: The last of the Panther/Cougar line, the TF-9J (formerly designated F9F-8T) two-seat trainer had the forward fuselage lengthened by 34in to take a second pilot. Only two 20mm M-2 cannon were fitted, but the aircraft could carry the same external stores as the F9F-8. (Grumman)

The F11F Tiger

Preliminary design work started in 1951 on a final, advanced development of the F9F Panther/Cougar series known as the Grumman G-98, and the Navy ordered three prototypes on 27 April 1952 (one a static test airframe) as the XF9F-8, which later took the designation XF9F-9 when the F9F-8 Cougar appeared. However, the G-98 very soon materialized, with the Bureau of Aeronautics' agreement, as a completely new design to meet the need for higher performance, as shown to be desirable by the experience of the Korean War and, in particular, the MiG-15's combat capabilities: the G-98's design, like that of the F-104 Starfighter, gave priority to performance at the expense of other variables. Ultimately the G-98 had only its Martin-Baker ejection seat in common with the Cougar, and it lacked the more 'muscular' appearance of the Panther/Cougar series. It had a thinner wing than the F9F-6 Cougar, of only 6½ per cent thickness/chord ratio, fuselage-side intakes for the 7,500lb s.t. Wright J65-W-7 turbojet (a US-built version of the British Armstrong Siddeley Sapphire), a low-set slab tailplane, twin steerable nosewheels, and mainwheels retracting into the lower fuselage. The new NACA-developed 'Area Rule', with the fuselage 'waisted' to compensate for the volume of the wing (in order to achieve minimum transonic and supersonic drag),

was followed, the Tiger, as the G-98 was named, being the first type designed from this basis.

The very thin wing had full-span leading-edge slats, blown flaps over the whole fixed portion of the trailing edge extending in one piece to the wing-tip hinge line, and spoilers for lateral control rather than ailerons. The wing tips folded upwards manually for carrier stowage. One feature unusual for the time was that the upper and lower skins of the main wing box were each milled from a single slab of light alloy machined to shape. The leading-edge slats, wing spoilers, rudder and all-flying tailplane were powered. Fuel was carried in the entire wing box, as well as in cells in the fuselage and also in the fin, and 'finger' type ventral air brakes were fitted to the fuselage in line with the wing trailing edge. An in-flight refuelling probe could be accommodated in the nose, and a ram air turbine provided emergency hydraulic power. The Tiger's armament comprised four 20mm cannon, and four AIM-9 Sidewinder 1A or 1C AAMs could be carried on underwing pylons, or two Sidewinders and two 150 US gallon drop tanks.

Powered by a Wright J65-W-7 without reheat, the prototype XF9F-9 first flew on 30 July 1954, piloted by Corwin 'Corky' Meyer. The second prototype flew in October that year, and in January 1955 the same aircraft was flown with an after-

Below: The F11F-1 Tiger was a development of the F9F series to meet the need for a fighter of higher performance. It was the first aircraft to have a fuselage designed from the start to incorporate the 'Area Rule', and had spoilers instead of ailerons for lateral control. (US Navy)

burning J65-W-8, which gave 10,000lb s.t. with reheat (later replaced by a J65-W-18), and some other changes were made. The first six production F9F-9s were regarded as YF9F-9 service test aircraft, and many of the first dozen Tigers had the non-afterburning J65-W-7 rather than the more usual 7,450lb s.t. J65-W-18, which gave 10,500lb s.t. with afterburning. In April 1955 the type was redesignated F11F-1, and became the F-11A under the 1962 tri-service designation system.

Unfortunately, problems with the J65 were soon experienced, and Grumman became sufficiently concerned to build two Tigers, BuNos 138646 and 138647, fitted with a 14,800lb s.t. (with reheat) General Electric J79-GE-3A turbojet as an alternative powerplant. In this form the aircraft were designated F11F-1F, and had enlarged air intakes and a larger rear fuselage, as well as forward sweep on the inboard portions of the wing leading edges. The Tiger had been easily supersonic with the J65 – indeed it was the first supersonic jet in Navy service – but the J79 engine gave the two 'Super Tigers' a Mach 2 performance; however, despite achieving a speed of 1,220mph and a record altitude of 76,940ft the F11F-1F did not go into production.

Forty-two F11F-1s were built on the first Navy contract (ending with BuNo 138645), and these were followed by a

further 157 which had a longer nose with provision for all-weather radar (although in practice this was never fitted), the in-flight refuelling probe being relocated to starboard. The first deliveries of the Tiger to an operational squadron were made in March 1957 to VA-156 (which, despite its 'Attack' designation, was actually a day fighter unit), and the last of the second bath of 157 was accepted by the Navy in December 1958. Five other squadrons were equipped with Tigers, two in AIRLANT (Naval Air Force, Atlantic Fleet) and three in AIRPAC (Naval Air Force, Pacific Fleet). Tigers also replaced Cougars in the Navy's *Blue Angels* aerobatic team, but from 1959 the F11F began to be withdrawn from service, moving to Advanced Training Command units in 1962 after being replaced by F-8

Top: F11F-1s of the US Navy *Blue Angels* aerobatic team speed past the Statue of Liberty during one of their displays. (Grumman)
Above: One of the two F11F-1F Tigers built with 14,800lb s.t., reheated General Electric J79-GE-3A turbojets as an alternative to the Wright J65; the 'waisted' fuselage is clearly in evidence. The F11F-1F had enlarged air intakes and a larger rear fuselage, and the J79 gave it a Mach 2 performance. (Grumman)

Crusaders in carrier-based squadrons. An unusual incident took place on 21 September 1956 when an F11F-1 actually shot itself down, colliding from behind with some 20mm cannon shells it had fired about a minute previously.

A photo-reconnaissance version of the Tiger had originally been ordered as the F9F-9P, but an order for 85 F11F-1Ps was later cancelled, as were a further 231 F11F-1s. The F11F-1T was a proposed two-seat operational trainer variant with the fuselage lengthened by 12in so as to accommodate the second cockpit and the all-up weight reduced by 500lb. The Tiger never really achieved its full sales or development potential because, although a good aeroplane, it was soon succeeded by even better designs such as the F-4 Phantom and F-8 Crusader.

The Swing-Wing Jaguar

Not long after the first flight of the XF9F-2 Panther prototype, Grumman started work on a programme for a variable-sweep aircraft. It was funded by the US Navy, which was then concerned about the problems of operating high-speed jets on board its carriers. To accomplish flight-deck landings a straight wing with leading-edge slats and flaps was the best arrangement, but for maximum speed a highly swept wing was necessary, and variable wing sweep was seen as a possible way of reconciling these requirements. Grumman first discussed the XF10F-1 single-seat, variable-sweep

fighter with the Navy in January 1948, and at first it featured a variable-incidence wing, which could lower deck landing speeds and afford a better view for the pilot, but this was soon realized to be only a partial solution. On 7 July 1949 Grumman made a formal proposal for a transonic fighter using some early data from the USAAF's Bell X-5 variable-sweep research aircraft. The X-5 had been based on the German Messerschmitt P.1101 variable-sweep jet fighter and research aircraft which, nearly complete but not flown by the end of the war, had been investigated in May 1945 by an Allied intelligence team headed by Robert J. Woods, Bell's chief designer and co-founder. He arranged for the P.1101 to be taken to Wright Field in the United States, together with most of the German design team who had worked on it, and here it was redesigned into the Bell X-5, which first flew on 20 June 1951, nine years after the German project first appeared on the Messerschmitt drawing boards.

Grumman's July 1949 proposal envisaged a high-mounted wing in which the earlier wing sweep of 42.5 degrees would be decreased to 13.5 degrees for take-off, cruise and landing, the wing roots being 'translated' forward on rails mounted in the fuselage as the wing was swept back for high-speed flight. The wings moved in this way because in the Grumman proposal they were attached to a linkage driven by a hydraulic actuator mounted

on the centreline, so that the wing root slid axially as the actuator rotated. This wing movement was also necessary to keep the wing's centre of pressure roughly in line with the aircraft's centre of gravity. While the wing was being redesigned from the original variable-incidence configuration, the tailplane was repositioned from the fuselage to the top of the fin, a relocation that would cause pitch-up problems which were not then fully understood. The XF10F-1 first flew with a unique, delta-shaped, 'floating' slab tailplane, actuated by a small, manually operated delta surface at the front of a long 'acorn' fairing at the tailplane/fin junction. The wing had a fully swept back area of 450ft^2, full-span leading-edge slats, and slotted Fowler flaps along 80 per cent of the span, whilst an unusual feature was the provision of swivelling pylons for bombs (up to 4,000lb) or drop tanks that could be turned into the line of flight as wing sweep varied. Design gross weight was 27,350lb, of which only 5.5 per cent was estimated to be due to the weight penalty of variable sweep. Large sweep angles effectively ruled out the use of conventional ailerons, hence lateral control was effected by means of inboard spoilers acting above and below the wing, with small outboard ailerons to provide feel. The outer wings folded for carrier stowage, to give a span of 24ft 9in, and the armament would consist of four 20mm cannon.

Following the outbreak of war in Korea, new impetus was given to the programme, and in late 1950 a contract was placed for two XF10F-1s (BuNos 124435–36) and 123 production F10F-1s, to be named Jaguar. Later, twelve more XF10F-1s (128311–22) were ordered, as well as 30 more F10F-1s, and it is astonishing, considering that variable sweep was a very advanced and largely untried concept, that the F10F-1s were ordered 'off the drawing board'. Power was to be provided by a Westinghouse XJ40-WE-8 turbojet, which was limited to a thrust of 7,200lb s.t. throughout the test programme as the development of its afterburner had yet to be completed; with reheat it would have given 11,600lb s.t. At first, however, a J40-WE-6 of 7,600lb s.t. was fitted. The engine was fed by two 'cheek' type intakes in the nose, and the jet pipe exhausted under the tail in a manner similar to the F9F-2 Panther's. Only one XF10F-1, BuNo 128311 (the third prototype to be ordered) left the ground, making its first flight at Edwards Air Force Base, California, in great secrecy on 16 April 1952, piloted by Corwin 'Corky' Meyer. It went on to make over 200 flights in twelve months of testing.

The XF10F-1 was successful in some important respects. Varying the wing sweep produced little trim change after a tailplane of higher aspect ratio was fitted, and the redesigned stabilizers were eventually fully swept, with an irreversible linkage. The stalling speed at landing weight was down to 90mph, but the lateral spoilers produced such large, erratic control forces and flutter when activated that they had finally to be removed, leaving only the ailerons for lateral control. It was also found that the demands on the tail surfaces varied widely according to sweep angle and speed, the rudder being too large for high speeds but much too small for approach and landing, while a much larger tailplane would have been necessary for production F10F-1s. Another considerable problem was that dihedral effect, or the rolling moment due to sideslip, became much worse as the sweep angle increased, with an associated loss of directional stability. The difficulty was alleviated to some extent by fitting small anhedralled delta surfaces known as 'horsals' (horizontal dorsals) on the rear fuselage sides to improve fin effectiveness.

The control problems, particularly with the lateral spoilers and tailplane, finally proved too much, however, and these, together with the snags afflicting the Westinghouse J40 turbojet (which was grounded in March 1953) led to the whole Jaguar programme being terminated. The J40 engine went into only limited production for the McDonnell F3H-1 Demon, and both this and the same company's J46 turbojet, which powered only the Chance Vought F7U-3 Cutlass Navy fighter, were eventually abandoned because of their fundamental and detail defects. As well as the 153 F10F-1s, a further eight F10F-1Ps with a camera nose were also cancelled.

Far left: The XF10F-1 Jaguar variable-sweep combat aircraft was only partially successful because of control problems with the lateral spoilers and tail surfaces, and also on account of problems with its engine. The first prototype XF10F-1, BuNo 124435 (shown), was eventually destroyed in crash barrier tests at Johnsville Naval Air Station near Philadelphia. (Grumman)

The Jaguar was a notable pioneering effort, and the variable-sweep design experience gained from it helped to pave the way for the F-111, for which Grumman was an associate contractor with General Dynamics, designing and manufacturing the undercarriage, rear fuselage and horizontal stabilizers, and arrester gear.

The F-14 Tomcat

In April 1968 the United States Congress called a halt to further development of the General Dynamics F-111B, which had failed to meet the Navy's requirements for an advanced, carrier-based, air superiority fighter. The -B version of this most controversial of warplanes, which was assembled by Grumman and had first flown on 18 May 1965, had a greater wing span and area than the USAF's F-111A; it was also to have had six Hughes AIM-54 Phoenix air-to-air missiles. Nine development F-111Bs were built, of which the last four had the definitive Pratt & Whitney TF30-P-12 turbofans of the 28 production aircraft on order. The cancellation of the F-111B left a big gap in the Navy's planned inventory, and to set in motion the task of filling this it sent requests for proposals on 21 June 1968 to five companies for what was to be known as the VFX carrier-based fighter. By December that year the Grumman G-303 and the McDonnell Douglas design were selected as finalists, the G-303 being already well advanced when further development of the F-111B was halted. The project encompassed a variable-sweep, twin-engined, two-seat aircraft with a crew comprising pilot and Naval Flight Officer/observer in tandem. The G-303 was named winner of the contest on 15 January 1969, and was henceforth known as the F-14 Tomcat.

Grumman had to produce a detailed mock-up by May of that year, and twelve pre-production YF-14A-GRs were ordered for development trials; there was no XF-14. The Navy initially planned to order 469 F-14 Tomcats, this total later rising to 722 and being cut back to 313 – subsequently being revised to 334 and increased to 403 in 1975, before being 'finalized' at 497 F-14A-GRs, including the development aircraft. (This total is now to be much increased, extending production into the 1990s.) Time was of the essence, and so the same TF30 turbofans as used in the F-111 were chosen to power the new aircraft, an existing electronics system was installed, and the undercarriage was evolved from that of the Grumman A-6 Intruder. The F-14 also benefited from the variable-sweep experience gained with the XF10F-1 Jaguar as well as that from the cancelled F-111B.

All this helped to make possible a maiden flight of the first YF-14A-GR, BuNo 157980, at Bethpage on 21 December 1970, more than a month ahead of schedule and a mere eighteen months after the Navy's first request for proposals – a remarkable achievement for so advanced an aircraft. Despite the loss of the first YF-14A to a hydraulic failure only nine days later during its second flight (the crew ejected safely), the second YF-14A flew on 24 May 1971, and seven more YF-14As were in the air by the end of that year.

Variable sweep was chosen for the F-14 to meet the conflicting needs of carrier compatibility, dogfighting in defence of a carrier task force, and tactical ground attack. Leading-edge wing sweep varies from 20 degrees in the fully forward position to 68 degrees fully swept, with an oversweep angle of 75 degrees for carrier stowage. Optimum sweep is controlled automatically by a Mach Sweep Programmer, which relates sweep to Mach number and altitude, but has provision for manual override. As a result, so the makers claim, the F-14 can out-manoeuvre all previous combat aircraft, and makes a very stable missile launch platform. Small canard foreplanes, known as glove vanes, extend automatically from the fixed portion of the wing leading edge as wing sweep is increased at supersonic speeds; these control the centre of pressure shift which is always a problem with variable-geometry aircraft. Lateral control is achieved via spoilers on the wing upper surfaces. Leading edge slats are fitted, as are trailing-edge flaps occupying virtually the full span. This wing has enabled F-14s to make field take-offs in less than 1,000ft and landings in under 1,500ft at normal, 20-degree sweep angles. Twin, outward-

Right: The second pre-production YF-14A Tomcat shows its planform with the wings fully forward; optimum sweep is controlled automatically by a Mach Sweep Programmer. The F-14's armament includes an M61A-1 multi-barrel 20mm cannon in the fuselage, plus Sparrow, Sidewinder or Phoenix air-to-air missiles. (Grumman)

Right: An F-14A of VF-1, wearing the US Navy's latest 'low-visibility' paint scheme. (Grumman)

canted fins and rudders are mounted one above each tail pipe, and there is an outward-canted ventral fin beneath.

The all-flying tailplanes are novel in having skins of boron epoxy composite material, and there are speed brakes above and below the rear fuselage, between the bases of the fins. The engines comprise two 20,900lb s.t. Pratt & Whitney TF30-P-412A turbofans with reheat. The crew of two are seated on Martin-Baker GRU-7A rocket-assisted zero-zero ejection seats. A fixed armament, consisting of one General Electric M61A-1 Vulcan multi-barrel 20mm cannon, is located in the port side of the forward fuselage. Four AIM-7E Sparrow medium-range air-to-air missiles can be housed, partially recessed, in the fuselage underside, and two wing pylons, one under each fixed portion of the wing, can accommodate four AIM-9 Sidewinder missiles or two additional Sparrow AAMs or Hughes AIM-54 Phoenix missiles with two more Sidewinders. Up to six Phoenix AAMs – a weapon carried by no other combat aircraft – can be accommodated, four of them on underfuselage pallets. The Phoenix can, in combination with the powerful Hughes AWG-9 nose radar, pick out and destroy a single aircraft from a formation at a range of over 100 miles. For close-in dogfighting the multi-barrel Vulcan cannon is used, with Sidewinder AAMs if required. The maximum external weapon load is 14,500lb, and a drop tank can be fitted beneath each air intake trunk.

The first F-14A deliveries took place in October 1972 to VF-124, the training squadron at NAS Miramar, San Diego, California, for working up with both air and ground crews, and the first two operational Tomcat squadrons, VF-1 and VF-2, worked up at Miramar before embarking on the carrier *Enterprise* in 1974, being followed by VF-14 and VF-32 on board *John F. Kennedy* in 1975. Entry into service was smooth.

Eighty F-14A Tomcats were ordered for the Imperial Iranian Air Force, the first three arriving at Khatami Air Force Base, Isfahan, in January 1976. The aircraft were equipped with the Phoenix missile system but had a slightly different ECM fit from that installed in US Navy machines. All the aircraft had been delivered by August 1978, but after the overthrow of the Shah's regime early in 1979 they were unable to fly owing to a lack of maintenance and, following worsening relations between the new regime and the United States, a repeat order for 70 machines was cancelled. Purges by the Ayatollah Khomeini's revolutionary squads affected all walks of Iranian life, including the military, and by 1981 only seven F-14As of the original 80 were reported to be flying, a shortage of spares, and also probably a lack of trained personnel effectively grounding the remainder. Those that are still flying are probably restricted to patrolling their bases of Shiraz and Khatami against attacks from Iraqi aircraft; otherwise the F-14As have taken little part in the bitter war between the two countries.

By 1 March 1985 507 F-14As, including the twelve YF-14As, had been delivered to the US Navy, and by the end of that year the Tomcat was to equip 24 squadrons (two of which were training units), operating from twelve different carriers and also shore bases at Miramar in California and Oceana in Virginia. A number of improvements to the avionics and other systems of the F-14A have been made or are currently under development. From late 1979 a Northrop TCS (television camera set) has been mounted beneath the nose of some F-14As to search for, acquire and lock on to distant targets, and then display them on monitor screens for the crew, who are thus provided with an unusual way of evaluating a target and the best method of attacking it. A total of 341 of these sets had been ordered by March 1985. In 1979 the 1,760lb TARPS (Tactical Air Reconnaissance Pod System) camera pod was evaluated for carriage on the F-14A, and 49 aircraft were fitted for it in 1980–81. This equipment is mounted under the fuselage, just off the centreline in the tunnel between the engine nacelles. The F-14/TARPS, as this variant is known, fills an important tactical reconnaissance role pending the development of a new PR aircraft.

The F-14B was very similar to the -A but was powered by two 28,100lb s.t. Pratt & Whitney F401-P-400 turbofans. However, difficulties with this variant led

to it being abandoned on the grounds of cost. Two F-14As, BuNos 157986 (the seventh development aircraft) and 158630, were modified into YF-14B-GR prototypes, but only the first of these was flown, making its maiden flight on 12 September 1973. The proposed F-14C development of the -B with new electronics and weapons was likewise a victim of rising costs and remained a 'paper project' only. The seventh development F-14A was later fitted with two General Electric F101DFE (Developed Fighter Engine) turbofans, and undertook a short test programme of 34 flights with these powerplants during July–September 1981. These engines, which form the basis of the General Electric F110-GE-400 turbofans that will power the new F-14D, gave a dramatic improvement in performance.

Grumman was awarded an $863.8 million fixed-price contract in July 1984, with General Electric and Hughes as subcontractors, for an F-14 updating programme to produce the F-14A Plus, which has the F110-GE-400 engines of the -D variant but is otherwise unchanged, and also for the F-14D with these engines, digital avionics and a new radar provisionally designated APG-XX. The F110-GE-400 has a 30 per cent increase in both non-reheat and afterburning thrust over the improved TF30-P-414A engines that power those F-14As delivered at the rate of 24 a year from FY (Fiscal Year) 1983 to FY 1986. Production was due to change from the F-14A to the F-14A Plus variant with the last FY 1986 aircraft, and a further 29 F-14A Plus aircraft will be delivered before the first of some 300 F-14Ds reaches the US Navy in March 1990. The first aircraft, the former F-14B, flew in October 1986. Production is planned to slow to eighteen Tomcats a year in 1987 and 1988, and to twelve in 1989; the last Plus to be manufactured will be the first of the -Ds, after which production will increase again.

The F110-GE-400 powering the F-

Below: An Imperial Iranian Air Force F-14A Tomcat, 3-863, fires a Hughes AIM-54 Phoenix air-to-air missile on a predelivery test flight. (Air-Britain)

14D and the F-14A Plus has an 82 per cent commonality of parts with the F110-GE-100 engines of the USAF's McDonnell Douglas F-15 Eagles and some future General Dynamics F-16 Fighting Falcons. A 4ft 2in 'plug' will be inserted in the GE-400's afterburner section to match the engine to the F-14's airframe contours and inlet positions. With the -400 engines the F-14's deck-launched intercept radius and combat air patrol (CAP) time on station will be increased, it is expected, by 60 per cent and 35 per cent respectively as a result of both a lower fuel consumption (after-burning specific fuel consumption will be 30 per cent lower than that of the TF30-P-414A engine of the last F-14As) and the fact that the F110-engined version will be capable of being launched without the use of reheat.

The F-14D will have new digital avionics for weapons management, navigation, display and control functions, and it will also feature the ALR-67 threat-warning recognition system, the ALQ-165 airborne self-protection jammer (ASPJ), the JTIDS (Joint Tactical Information Distribution System) data-link, an infra-red search and track sensor (IRST), a programmable radar signal processor and a Northrop TCS system in the nose. The APG-XX radar under development for the F-14D is based on the Hughes AN/AWG-9 radar of the F-14A, and will be able to counter sophisticated ECM techniques. The -D variant will also have AIM-120 AMRAAM (Advanced Medium Range Air-to-Air Missiles), whilst other new missile variants to be added to the existing Tomcat inventory are the AIM-9M Sidewinder, the AIM-

7M Sparrow and the AIM-54C 'digital' Phoenix. The F-14D will also have Martin-Baker NACES ejection seats.

A full scale F-14D development pro-gramme is planned. This will involve five aircraft, including the YF-14B prototype previously fitted with General Electric F101DFE engines, which flew with definitive F110-GE-400s in September 1986 as part of the F-14A Plus pro-gramme. Three more aircraft will be used for radar and avionics development work, in conjunction with a Douglas TA-3B Sky-warrior twin-jet attack bomber used for observation. One aircraft will be com-pleted to full F-14D standard and will join the -D variant's test programme after serving in F-14A Plus development. The first flight of the F-14D is scheduled for the second quarter of 1988.

F-14A deliveries were halted on 29 April 1985 after the discovery of cracks in a bulkhead in some aircraft, and those Tomcats in service with the fleet were grounded while Grumman and US Navy teams began work to install a reinforce-ment in the 248 F-14As affected. The Navy and Grumman agreed to resume deliveries in October, the cost to Grum-man of the retrofit programme being $30 million. Future production aircraft will have a redesigned bulkhead with a longer service life, and all the aircraft affected by the cracks will have a reinforcement in-stalled by mid-1986. This was not the first time that this outstanding combat aircraft had been troubled by costs rising above predicted levels: at one time Grumman actually refused to continue the Tomcat programme, claiming that it would lose $105 million on its existing contracts if it did so.

Above: The YF-14B, formerly the seventh pre-production YF-14A, was later fitted with two General Electric F101DFE (Derivative Fighter Engine) turbofans, with which it made 34 test flights during July–September 1981. These engines, which gave a dramatic increase in performance, form the basis of the GE F110-GE-400 selected to power the new F-14D. (Grumman)

Sub-Hunters and Early Warners

The TBM-3W/TBM-3S Avenger and AF-2W/AF-2S Guardian anti-submarine hunter/killer aircraft of the early postwar years played a very useful stop-gap role, but as the 1950s dawned it became clear that they would be outdated by the new missile-armed, nuclear-powered submarines then being planned. It was therefore a logical step to combine in one design the hunter and killer roles previously performed by two separate aircraft, which would, like them, be able to operate from aircraft carrier decks, carry enough fuel for long search missions at low altitudes plus a substantial load of detection equipment and offensive weapons, and be capable of accommodating new search devices and strike weapons as these became available. On 30 June 1950 the US Navy, having initiated a programme for just such an aircraft, awarded a prototype contract to Grumman for their G-89 design as the XS2F-1. The first of two XS2F-1 prototypes, BuNos 129137 and 129138, completed its maiden flight on 14 December 1952.

The S2F Tracker

At first sight this rather small aeroplane, with two medium-sized piston engines – 1,450hp Wright R-1820-76W Cyclones – seemed a little out of place amongst faster turboprop types like the Fairey Gannet and larger land-based anti-submarine aircraft such as the Lockheed P2V Neptune. But the Tracker, as the production S2F-1 was named, can best be regarded as a larger, twin-engined development of the Avenger able to undertake both the hunter and killer roles of the TBM-3W and TBM-3S. It has a capacious fuselage with an internal weapons bay, APS-38 search radar in a retractable, ventral, 'dustbin' type radome just aft of the bay, an ASQ-10 MAD (magnetic anomaly detection) boom that can be retracted into the rear fuselage beneath the tail, provision for carrying eight sonobuoys in the rear of each engine nacelle and, for night identification, a 70 million candlepower searchlight mounted under the starboard wing leading edge.

The crew of the S2F-1 normally com-

Below: The XS2F-1 Tracker, the first prototype of which (129137) is seen here, was essentially a larger, twin-engined successor to the Avenger, able to undertake both the submarine hunter and killer roles of the TBM-3W and TBM-3S. Three 5in HVAR rocket projectiles are carried under each wing, but the underwing searchlight is not yet installed. (Grumman)

prises the pilot, co-pilot/navigator and two radar operators, and the weapons bay can carry two Mk. 101 depth bombs, or electric, acoustic-homing torpedoes, or four 385lb depth charges, while there are three attachment points under each wing for 5in HVAR projectiles, 250lb bombs, depth charges or torpedoes. Two torpedoes can be carried under each wing as a ferry load. The low-speed manoeuvrability so important to ASW aicraft was ensured by almost full-span flaps, fixed leading-edge slats and long-span spoilers on the wing upper surfaces for lateral control, augmenting the small ailerons. The use of such basically similar flaps, slats and spoilers was also a feature of the F9F-6 and -7 Cougar, the XF10F-1 Jaguar, the F11F-1 Tiger and the F-14A Tomcat. The Tracker's wings fold upwards and inwards hydraulically from outboard of the engine nacelles for carrier stowage, reducing the span to 27ft 4in, and internal tankage for 1,598 Imperial gallons of fuel was sufficient for an S2F-1 to spend some five hours patrolling on station at a range of 230 miles. The first fifteen production Trackers were YS2F-1s used for development work, and these became YS-2As, and later S-2As, under the new 1962 tri-service designations. The S2F-1 (later S-2A) differed from the prototypes in having 1,525hp Wright R-1820-82WA Cyclones and various equipment changes, and it first entered service with Anti-Submarine Squadron VS-26 in February 1954; within ten years S-2As and the later S-2Ds were equipping eight more first-line squadrons, the replacement training units VS-30 and VS-41, and most US Navy Air Reserve Training Units.

Altogether 740 S-2As were built, of which 108 were diverted from US Navy orders to foreign countries under MAP programmes. The Italian Air Force acquired 48 S-2As, which were operated by its 86°, 87° and 88° Gruppi (Squadrons), while 60 were supplied to the Japanese Maritime Self-Defence Force where they equipped Nos. 11, 12, 13 and 14 Squadrons and No. 204 Air Training Squadron. Six S-2As were supplied to Argentina's *Aviación Naval* in 1964 for operation by Patrol Squadron I from the fleet carrier *Veinticinco de Mayo*. To these were added another six of the later S-2E Trackers in 1978–79. Several Argentine Trackers operated from Port Stanley during the Falkland Islands campaign of April–June 1982, both the S-2As and S-2Es by then normally being stationed at the Comandante Espora base. Some of the Japanese S-2As were later converted to target-tugs under the Japanese designation S2F-U, instead of S2F-1U as the US Navy knew this variant. Over 50 of the latter, which later became US-2As, were converted from S2F-1s and replaced the Navy's Douglas UB-26J Invaders in the target-towing role. The S2F-1T (later TS-2A) was an ASW training variant, 207 of which were converted from S2F-1s. It could carry up to 25 Mk. 15 Mod. 8 practice depth charges in the weapons bay. The S2F-1S (later S-2B) was the -1 modified to have the AQA-3 'Jezebel' passive long-range acoustic search equipment and its associated 'Julie' active (explosive) echo-ranging equipment, which worked with 60 underwater sounding charges dropped through a fuselage dispenser. With updated 'Julie/Jezebel'

Above: An S2F-1 about to be catapulted off a carrier deck. The production S2F-1 (later designated S-2A) differed only slightly from the XS2F-1s and the fifteen pre-production YS2F-1s, and first entered squadron service with VS-26 in February 1954. (Grumman)

equipment the -1S became the S2F-1S1 (later S-2F), whilst some utility-type conversions very similar to the S2F-1U but incorporating some S-2B/S-2F features became US-2Bs; 66 S-2As were also converted to US-2B standard, and one S-2F to a US2F.

In March 1954 De Havilland Aircraft of Canada was awarded a prime contract to build the S2F-1 Tracker under licence for the Royal Canadian Navy, and the first of 43 Canadian-built aircraft was formally delivered on 12 October 1956, these being designated CS2F-1. A further 57 CS2F-2s followed, very similar to the CS2F-1s but fitted with improved search and operational equipment, although not the enlarged weapons bay and larger fin and rudder of the Grumman-built S2F-2. Both Canadian versions had 1,525hp Wright R-1820-82WA Cyclones and Hamilton Standard propellers built by Canadian Pratt & Whitney, and a number of these aircraft later became CS2F-3s when fitted with updated search and operational equipment. The CS2F variants were later given the Canadian Armed Forces designation CP-121, and they served with VS 880 aboard the carrier HMCS *Bonaventure* and with the shore-based utility squadrons VU 32 (which had ten CS2F-2s and eight CS2F-1s in 1963) and VU 33 (which had CS2F-1s amongst other types). VU 32's Trackers were used for target-towing as well as training. The eighteen surviving CP-121s still fly ASW sorties from the CAF base at Shearwater.

Some CS2F-1s were also supplied to the Brazilian Air Force's 1° Grupo de Aviacão Embarcada, which operated thirteen S-2A and CS2F-1 Trackers from the country's only aircraft carrier *Minas Gerais*. The Air Force is responsible for providing fixed-wing aircraft and crews for this ship, although there is a small naval air arm equipped with helicopters. Seventeen ex-RCN CS2F-1s (later designated CS-2As), were also supplied to the Royal Netherlands Naval Air Service for operation by No. 1 Squadron from the Doctor Plesman Airport at Curaçao in the Dutch West Indies. This service also operated a further 28 Grumman-built S-2As with Nos. 2 and 4 Squadrons aboard the carrier *Karel Doorman*, replacing

TBM-3W and TBM-3S Avengers, and some S-2As were also among the types used by No. 5 Training Squadron at Valkenburg. Fairey Aviation of Canada modified eighteen Dutch S-2As to S-2N standard, and four of them later became US-2N utility variants. Uruguay's *Aviación Naval* used three S-2As for air–sea rescue as well as ASW work, and these were supplemented by six ex-US Navy S-2Gs during 1983. Nine S-2As and 30 S-2Es equipped the Taiwanese (Chinese Nationalist) Air Force's single maritime reconnaissance squadron, whilst ten S-2F Trackers supplied in 1966 form the main part of the Thai Navy's only MR squadron, based at Bangkok.

The S2F-2 (later S-2C), of which 77 were built for the US Navy, featured an extension of the weapons bay on the port side only to enable the aircraft to accommodate larger homing torpedoes of a new type, and to compensate for the higher operating weights the tail surfaces were slightly enlarged. Forty-eight S-2Cs were later converted into US-2C (formerly S2F-2U) utility variants for use by Utility Squadrons VU-2 and VU-7, while some S-2Cs with a camera installation became RS-2Cs (formerly S2F-2Ps). The S-2C was really an interim variant, but the G-121 or S2F-3 (later S-2D), which first flew on 20 May 1959, introduced a number of important design changes. The forward fuselage, 18in longer and 3¼in wider, gave slightly roomier accommodation for the pilots and radar operators, the wing span was increased by 2ft 11in and the tail surfaces were further enlarged, the internal fuel capacity being increased to 3,762 Imp. gallons. The rear of each

Below: De Havilland Aircraft of Canada built 100 S2F-1 Trackers under licence, of which 43 were CS2F-1s (like the aircraft seen here) and 57 CS2F-2s; a number of these were later modified to CS2F-3 standard. These three variants, which were later designated CP-121, differed chiefly in the standards of search and operational equipment fitted. (De Havilland Canada)

engine nacelle was modified to take sixteen instead of eight sonobuoys, ECM (electronic countermeasures) antennae now appeared at the wing tips, a more powerful searchlight of 85 million candlepower was fitted on the starboard wing, and the retractable MAD boom was lengthened. A 'Sniffer' passive submarine exhaust trail detector was now carried, and there was also a Ground Track Plotter that provided the pilot with an instantaneous picture of any given tactical situation, so eliminating the computing and plotting duties that previously had to be done by the crew.

The S-2D entered operational service in May 1961 and within a couple of years was equipping fifteen Navy ASW squadrons, many of which also had S-2As. Altogether 119 S-2Ds were built, and some of these were later converted to ES-2D electronic trainer variants and US-2Ds for utility and target-towing duties. The S2F-3S (later S-2E) was essentially similar to the S-2D but had the same AQA-3 'Jezebel' and 'Julie' search and echo-ranging equipment as fitted to the S-2B (formerly S2F-1S), as well as a tactical navigation system. It also had provision for carrying the 'Betty' nuclear depth charge, guided missiles under the wings, and 7.62mm miniguns. Forty-five S-2Es were built, the last twelve being diverted from US contracts to the Royal Australian Navy, where they equipped VS 816 Squadron aboard the fleet carrier HMAS *Melbourne*. Nine Australian Trackers were lost in a disastrous hangar fire in December 1976, but others were acquired and strength built up to nineteen aircraft, of which sixteen were of S-2G standard with updated electronics. Six Trackers flew from *Melbourne* with VS 816 and three S-2Es were flown from Darwin on surveillance duties, while four more S-2Gs were held in storage in 1981; subsequently, all nineteen were shore-based at Nowra, New South Wales, and employed on coastal reconnaissance pending their withdrawal from service in 1984 following the decision to scrap *Melbourne*. Peru's naval air arm, the *Servicio Aéronavale*, also operates S-2E Trackers, nine being employed on ASW duties from the Jorge Chavez air base, and in 1982 these were modernized at Grumman's St.

Augustine, Florida, plant. Japan's Maritime Self-Defence Force later acquired 21 S-2F Trackers to supplement its S-2As, and these equipped No. 11 Squadron at Kanoya; the surviving fourteen S-2As equipped No. 14 Squadron at Atsugi in 1981, and another S-2A also served with No. 61 at the same base.

The S-2G, which was actually produced by the Martin Marietta Corporation, was an interim ASW variant for use pending the entry into service of the Lockheed S-3A Viking early in 1974. The prototype S-2G was converted in 1972 by Martin Marietta, which then manufactured kits for the Navy to convert 49 S-2Es to S-2G standard. The -G featured updated electronics, some of which were similar to the Lockheed S-3A's, including an ECM pod under each wing and a forward-looking infra-red (FLIR) scanner in a retractable

Top: The S2F-2 (later S-2C) differed from the S-2A in having slightly enlarged tail surfaces and a weapons bay extended (on the port side only) to carry larger homing torpedoes. (Grumman)
Above: The S-2G Tracker was an interim ASW variant intended to fill the gap before the entry into service of the Lockheed S-3A Viking early in 1974. It had updated electronics some of which were similar to those installed in the S-3. (Grumman)

turret under the forward fuselage. Fifty S-2Fs were later modified to have AN/AQA-7 DIFAR (Directional Acoustic Frequency Analysis and Recording) sonobuoy processing equipment.

The Tracker was retired from US Navy service on 28 August 1976, but it had already found a new use in civilian life in fighting forest fires. In 1973, after the TBM-3 Avenger had been withdrawn from this work after a number of crashes, the California Division of Forestry leased a batch of 50 TS-2A Trackers from the US Navy to modify for this role, and these were sub-leased to various operators to replace the Avengers. Part of the S-2A's fuselage keel spar was removed to accommodate a fire retardant chemical tank of 800 US gallons capacity discharging from the bottom of the fuselage, and the cockpit was rearranged for single-pilot operation, all military equipment being deleted and as much other equipment as possible removed to save weight.

By 1978 fire-fighting Trackers were being operated by the Aero Union Corporation of Chico, California (three TS-2As), the Hemet Valley Flying Service of Hemet, California (eight TS-2As), and the Sis-Q Flying Service of Santa Rosa, California (six TS-2As), while a further 35 TS-2As were held in storage by the California Division of Forestry, some of these being allocated to the above-mentioned operators for use as spares; 34 of these were cancelled from the US register in 1985. In Canada several CS2F-1 Trackers were similarly modified for the Ontario Provincial Government – the first operator to use them in this role in Canada – and for use in Saskatchewan. Conair Aviation acquired two ex-Royal Canadian Navy/Canadian Armed Forces CS2F-1s, C-GHQY and C-GHQZ, which started fire-fighting in British Columbia in 1977 and are also equipped to spray the spruce budworm in the forests of New Brunswick and Quebec. Conair acquired a third CS2F-1, C-GHPU, in 1985.

The Trader and Tracer
For the COD (carrier onboard delivery) role the Grumman G-96 or TF-1 (later C-1A) Trader was evolved. A new fuselage with accommodation for up to nine

Above: This Canadian-built CS2F-1 was one of several modified for forest fire bombing and used by the Ontario Provincial Government's Ministry of Natural Resources. (De Havilland Canada)

passengers in quickly removable, rear-facing seats, or 3,500lb of freight, was married to the S-2A's wings and engines and the S-2D's enlarged tail surfaces. The fuselage was slightly deeper and more rounded than the S-2A's, and to secure the cargo in high-deceleration (up to $20g$) arrested carrier landings a 'cage' device was used, consisting of two parallel sets of removable vertical bulkheads secured between upper and lower longitudinal rails. The TF-1 made its first flight in January 1955, and a total of 87 TF-1s were built, for use by Fleet Logistics Support and Transport Squadrons VR-21, VR-24 and VR-40. Four of the TF-1s were completed as TF-1Q (later EC-1A) ECM variants, these having the maker's designation G-125.

The XWF-1, based on the S2F-1, was projected in 1954, to fulfil the carrier-

based airborne early warning (AEW) role. Two prototypes were to have been built, but the XWF-1 was succeeded by the TF-1W project, derived from the TF-1 Trader and subsequently developed into the WF-2. The WF-2 (later E-1B) Tracer, as it was named, carried an APS-82 radar system for detecting ships and high- or low-flying aircraft in a 32ft×20ft, 'teardrop' shaped radome made of fibreglass honeycomb sandwich and mounted on a short pylon above the fuselage. The radome housed a 17½ft antenna rotating six times a minute, and the two radar operators monitored identical 10in screens. TF-1 BuNo 136792 was converted into an aerodynamic prototype of the WF-2 (Grumman G-117) with an aluminium-skinned radome, first flying in this form on 1 March 1957. Twin fins and rudders were now featured, the single vertical tail surfaces being cut down in

height so that the rear of the radome rested on them, and the carrier stowage system was redesigned so that the wings folded back to lie alongside the fuselage instead of upwards. Extensive electronics were carried for all-weather operations, including tacan, IFF and a radar altimeter. The first of 88 production WF-2s to be built first flew in February 1958, initially equipping Airborne Early Warning Squadrons VAW-11 and VAW-12, from which detachments were deployed to the various Carrier Air Wings. The WF-2 was known as the 'Willy Fudd' to its pilots.

The Hawkeye

The success of the WF-2 Tracer, coupled with the Navy-inspired development of airborne radars able to detect targets beyond the line of sight of ships, led to the W2F-1 Hawkeye, the first aircraft to be designed from the start for airborne

Top: The C-1A (formerly TF-1) Trader was a version of the S-2A for the COD (carrier onboard delivery) role with a new fuselage accommodating up to nine passengers or 3,500lb of freight. C-1A 146053 seen here is from the carrier *Constellation*. (US Navy)

Above: The WF-2 (later E-1B) Tracer was an airborne early warning version of the S2F-1 with APS-82 radar in a 'teardrop' shaped radome above the fuselage. This equipment necessitated twin fins and rudders and a revised wing folding system. (Grumman)

early warning surveillance. By 1956 the development of such radars had led to the concept of a Naval Tactical Data System (NTDS), located in fleet headquarters, which would enable a task force commander to view all the information on the disposition of ships and aircraft (both friendly and enemy) needed to control his forces and get an overall tactical picture of any combat situation. The NTDS would process, organize and display information received from ships and aircraft in the combat area, and in particular from an Airborne Tactical Data System (ATDS) mounted in an aircraft such as the W2F-1. The ATDS compartment in the W2F-1's main cabin, with three radar controllers, was the nerve centre of the aircraft's intercept-control system, the ATDS being linked to the NTDS. The W2F-1 was thus equipped to direct friendly carrier-based aircraft in both attacking and defensive missions, and to handle almost any combat situation, for example detecting high-performance enemy aircraft approaching a task force.

The Grumman design that became the W2F-1 was the 5 March 1957 winner of an industry-wide competition for a carrier-borne AEW radar picket, and in its initial version (later designated E-2A) was fitted with APS-96 long-range search radar with the scanner rotating six times per minute inside the 24ft-diameter radome mounted above the fuselage. The radome developed sufficient lift in flight to offset its weight, and it could be lowered almost 2ft for stowage in carrier hangars. The unusual airflow patterns over and around the radome necessitated

a tail unit consisting of four fins and three rudders mounted on a tailplane with 11 degrees of dihedral. The first of three W2F-1 prototypes flew on 21 October 1960, but this aircraft did not have fully operational electronic and AEW systems, which were first taken aloft in a fully equipped aircraft on 19 April 1961. Power was provided by two 4,050eshp Allison T56-A-8 turboprops driving four-blade, 13ft 6in diameter Aeroproducts N41 reversible-pitch airscrews. The single main wheels retracted forwards and rotated to lie flat in the bottom of the very deep nacelles; the twin nosewheels retracted backwards. There was also a retractable tail skid, as well as an 'A' frame arrester hook under the tail. The crew of five, which included two pilots, were provided with a downward-hinging entry door, with built-in steps, in the port side of the centre fuselage. The outer wing panels could be folded hydraulically to lie along the rear fuselage, leading edges down, and rubber de-icing boots were fitted along the wing and tail surface leading edges.

The first delivery of the E-2A Hawkeye was made on 19 January 1964 to VAW-11 at San Diego for use in training air and ground crews, and this unit became operational on the carrier *Kitty Hawk* in 1966, providing E-2A detachments as required to other carriers in the Pacific. In 1965 E-2As were issued to VAW-12, this unit providing similar detachments to the Atlantic Fleet. Altogether 62 E-2As were built, the last being completed early in 1967, and in a retrofit programme completed in December 1971 most were

Above: All E-2As were later modified to E-2B standard, the -B model differing in having a Litton Industries L-304 computer and improved equipment reliability. This E-2B is from VAW-116, operating from *Constellation*. (US Navy)

brought up to E-2B standard. Two aircraft, however, became TE-2A crew trainers and two were converted to YE-2C prototypes, whilst a further pair were modified into YC-2A Greyhound prototypes.

An E-2A fitted with AN/APS-111 radar and an AN/APA-164 radome antenna first flew on 17 August 1966. This radar system gave reduced ground clutter but was not chosen for a production Hawkeye. The E-2B was very similar to the -A but featured a Litton Industries L-304 micro-electronic general-purpose computer and several improvements in equipment reliability. An E-2A was modified into the E-2B prototype and first flew in this form on 20 February 1969; production E-2Bs later equipped RVAW-110, VAW-112, VAW-113, VAW-115, VAW-116 and VAW-117.

The E-2C was a new and greatly improved version, with completely revised avionics, including a Randtron Systems AN/APA-171 antenna system in the radome with General Electric AN/APS-120 search radar and an OL-93/AP radar data processor. The new radar can spot distant airborne targets despite heavy sea or land background 'clutter', as well as surface targets. The three crew members in the ATDS compartment are the combat information centre officer, air traffic control officer and radar operator, who have three identical display stations, each with a 10in main and a 5in auxiliary display, the former showing target track information. For accurate navigation back to the carrier after hours on patrol, a Litton Industries LN-150 CAINS (Carrier Aircraft Inertial Navigational System) is fitted, and, as on the E-2B, a Litton L-304 computer links and processes the radar, communications, navigation and passive detection data and can also automatically transmit intercept solutions to friendly fighters or to ground control. The OL-93/AP radar data processor was later replaced, from the 34th E-2C, by the AN/APS-125 Advanced Radar Processing System (ARPS), and earlier E-2Cs were later retrofitted with this equipment. The E-2C also has uprated Allison T56-A-425 turboprops of 4,910eshp driving Hamilton Standard four-blade, reversible-pitch propellers.

The first of two YE-2C prototypes took to the air on 20 January 1971, followed by the second prototype a year later. The first production E-2C made its maiden flight on 23 September 1972, and the aircraft entered service with VAW-123 at Norfolk, Virginia, in November that year, first going to sea on board the USS *Saratoga* late in 1974. It subsequently equipped RVAW-120 (a training unit), VAW-121, VAW-122, VAW-124, VAW-125 and VAW-126, and by the end of 1984 over 90 E-2Cs had been delivered, with production continuing to a planned total of 113 for the US Navy. E-2Cs now equip fifteen squadrons. From 1983 new E-2Cs were fitted with the General Electric AN/APS-138 search radar, which is also being retrofitted to E-2Cs delivered earlier. This has a new antenna, an enhanced Litton AN/ALR-73 passive detection system with triangulation and the ability to recognize exotic emissions from such sources as ships or submarines, and an expanded computer memory capacity. The AN/APS-138 radar can detect airborne targets anywhere in a surveillance 'envelope' measuring three million cubic miles, while at the same time watching marine traffic. More than 600 targets can be tracked automatically and simultaneously, and more than 40 airborne intercepts controlled. The two TE-2Cs are crew trainer variants of the E-2C.

Four E-2C Hawkeyes from US Navy orders were supplied to the Israeli Defence Forces/Air Force for use in a shore-based airborne early warning role; these were delivered in July and August 1978, and an option was taken on two more. The aircraft proved their worth especially during the 1982 war against Syrian and Palestine Liberation Organization (PLO) forces in the Lebanon (Operation 'Peace for Galilee'). The Syrian fighters in this conflict were only two minutes from their bases, whereas the Israeli pilots, some of whom had to fly from the Negev region in the south of Israel, were between 10 and 40 minutes from their bases. Most of the 80-plus Syrian Air Force aircraft shot down by the Israelis in the 1982 fighting went down over the Beka'a Valley region of the Lebanon, less than a minute from the Syrian border and the location for Syrian batteries of Russian-made surface-to-air missiles. The Syrian pilots could, moreover, slip back over their border without being pursued, as Israeli aircraft were not allowed to cross into Syria, but because the E-2Cs could detect the enemy fighters actually taking off, they gave vital early warning and enabled the Israeli strike aircraft attacking the Syrian missile sites to take up tactically advantageous positions before being intercepted. The result was that the Syrians lost all their SAMs in the Lebanon, and the Israelis lost only some ten aircraft.

The next export customer for the E-2C was Japan's Air Self-Defence Force, which placed an initial order for four in 1979, followed by four more later. It was not until February 1983 that the first two were delivered to Misawa Air Base, headquarters of the Northern Air Defence Force, thereby establishing the JASDF's Surveillance Group. Another four E-2Cs are required to complete the early warning coverage of Japan, making twelve in all, but funds to order these have not so far been made available. The first of four E-2Cs acquired by Egypt for the sum of $1,100 million was delivered to the Arab Republic of Egypt Air Force early in 1985, these aircraft being of course shore-based like the Israeli Hawkeyes. The latest

export customer is Singapore, which in 1984 ordered two E-2Cs, plus two more on option. All Hawkeye exports so far have been of the E-2C, but the E-2X is a projected export variant with some of the sophisticated avionics deleted and a simplified standard of equipment, for sale to those countries not cleared for security reasons to operate the standard E-2C.

In 1982 NASA's Ames Research Center, as part of its studies concerning the military applications of upper-surface blowing as first applied to the Boeing YC-14 STOL military transport, revealed a design study of an E-2C Hawkeye variant powered by four General Electric TF34 turbofans mounted so as to exhaust over the wing and provide USB. NASA estimated that this variant would be 125kts faster than the standard E-2C – giving it a longer time on station despite a slightly shorter endurance – and that the approach speed would have been only 65kts. With TF34 turbofans and USB, the E-2C could maintain a height of 43,600ft, or 14,600ft more than the standard E-2C, thus giving a proportionate increase in the area scanned by its radar. Although some redesign of the tail would have been necessary to keep it out of the jet efflux, it was claimed that the

Below: The first of four E-2Cs for Egypt was delivered to the Arab Republic of Egypt Air Force early in 1985. (Grumman)

TF34-powered E-2C could, if built, have provided unrivalled AEW coverage for a fleet.

US Navy E-2Cs have more recently entered the war against the drug smugglers, helping to catch those flying cocaine and marijuana shipments from Colombia to Florida. The emphasis has now shifted to 'coke', which has a much higher street value than marijuana and which, because in its white powder form it is so easy to conceal and smuggle in commercially viable quantities, has led to the large-scale use of light aircraft for smuggling. In their first 90 days in the 'drug war' role, during October–December 1981, the E-2Cs assisted in the seizure of 45 aircraft and over $300 million worth of drugs.

The Greyhound
To replace the TF-1 Trader in the COD (carrier onboard delivery) role, Grumman proposed a transport version of the E-2A soon after the Hawkeye programme started, and three prototype YC-2As were ordered, one of which would be for static test. The first of the two airworthy machines, BuNo 148147, made its maiden flight on 18 November 1964; both were converted from E-2As. The C-2A Greyhound, as it was known, featured a wider and deeper fuselage married to the same wings, engines and tail unit as the E-2A's and a similar undercarriage, but with a stronger nose gear, adapted from the A-6A Intruder's, to cater for higher all-up weights. Unlike the E-2A the aircraft had no tailplane dihedral. The fuselage can seat up to 39 troops in three longitudinal rows of seats, or 28–32 passengers, or, in the casevac role, twelve

litters with four medical attendants. Cargo, loaded through a door with an integral ramp which folds up into the underside of the rear fuselage, can be carried instead. There is provision for a remotely controlled cargo handling winch in the cargo compartment, and the C-2A can be launched by catapult, using nose-tow gear, and make arrested landings. The first seventeen C-2As could be fitted with two 350 or 450 US gallon external fuel tanks on the sides of the fuselage and, for long range ferrying, six 243 US gallon tanks can be accommodated in the main cabin in place of seats. There is also provision for an in-flight refuelling probe above the front fuselage, although this item of equipment was not specified for US Navy C-2As.

The first production Greyhounds were built during 1966–67, one dozen being designated C-2A-05-GR and the remaining five C-2A-10-GR. The first C-2A deliveries were made to VRC-50, a Fleet Tactical Support unit, from December 1966; of this first production batch, twelve were still in service in 1984. The C-2A was put back into production with a Navy order for 39 more, for which Grumman announced an advanced procurement contract on 8 February 1982 and initial deliveries of which were scheduled for May 1985. These new aircraft will have the E-2C's uprated Allison T56-A-425 turboprops and avionics, improved anti-corrosion protection, better passenger comfort and a new auxiliary power unit (APU) for self-sufficient operation at remote locations independent of ground services. Deliveries of this second batch will be completed in 1989.

Above: The C-2A Greyhound was a replacement for the C-1A Trader in the COD role and had the E-2A's wings, engines and tail unit married to a new, deeper fuselage seating up to 39 passengers or troops, or twelve litters with four medical attendants. This C-2A, from VR-24, is seen landing on board the carrier *Independence* with the Sixth Fleet in the Mediterranean Sea. (US Navy)

Mohawk and Intruder

During 1956 military requirements were formulated which led to two of Grumman's most distinctive looking aeroplanes, the OV-1 Mohawk battlefield surveillance aircraft for the US Army and the A2F-1 Intruder attack bomber for the Navy. Neither would have won any prizes for elegance or good looks, but each reflected in its appearance the specialized and demanding specifications it had to meet. The Grumman G-134, as the Mohawk was designated, was the company's first design for the US Army – and the latter's first turboprop aeroplane – and was conceived to meet joint Army and Marine Corps requirements. These called for exceptional STOL performance with good low-speed control characteristics, and the ability to operate from rough forward airstrips, whilst carrying a wide range of electronic surveillance equipment for a variety of tactical observation roles.

The OV-1 Mohawk

The result was an unusual aeroplane with a performance approximately midway between that of light AOP types such as the Piper L-18 Super Cub and Cessna L-19 Bird Dog and that of jet fighters. The Mohawk's crew of pilot and observer were seated side by side on Martin-Baker J5 ejection seats in a cockpit giving a very good all-round view. Triple fins and rudders and full-span leading edge slats gave good low-speed control, and, unlike the S2F Tracker and the later jet fighters, the Mohawk had conventional-size ailerons and flaps instead of spoilers for lateral control. There were forward-opening air brakes on each side of the fuselage aft of the wing.

Power was at first provided by two 1,008eshp Lycoming T53-L-3 turboprops driving Hamilton Standard three-blade, reversible-pitch propellers. Turboprops were chosen not only because this type of engine had a higher power-to-weight ratio than a piston engine and was cheaper, more reliable and simpler to maintain – very important for an aircraft operating from forward airstrips – but also because the high-octane aviation fuel required for piston engines, especially in forward battle areas, constituted a greater fire risk. Moreover, the Lycoming T53 was in widespread use in the US Army's many hundreds of Bell UH-1 Huey heli-

Below: The OV-1 Mohawk battlefield surveillance aircraft for the US Army has side-by-side seating for the crew of two, triple fins and rudders for good low speed control and Lycoming T53 turboprops, and carries cameras and surveillance equipment. This is the first production OV-1A. (Grumman)

copters. From 1962 Mohawks of all versions were equipped, both on the production line and by retrofit, with 1,150eshp Lycoming T53-L-7 or T53-L-15 engines. A fuel tank in the fuselage over the wing had a capacity of 297 US gallons, and a 150 US gallon Aero 1C drop tank could be carried under each wing.

For better downward visibility, the sides of the Mohawk's cockpit canopy were bulged. Dual controls were fitted, except when electronic surveillance equipment was carried, while removable flak curtains could be installed on the forward and after cockpit bulkheads. The main wheels retracted outwards from the wing roots into the engine nacelles, instead of inwards from the nacelles, and the nose-wheel retracted backwards into the fuselage. An alternative wheel-ski landing gear was also designed for the Mohawk.

Nine YAO-1A-GR Mohawks were ordered for service tests in 1957, these being redesignated YOV-1A-GR under the 1962 tri-service arrangements. The first, 57-6463, made its maiden flight on 14 April 1959, all nine test aircraft being completed by the end of that year. The US Navy acted as the Mohawk programme manager for the Army and Marine Corps, but the Marines withdrew from the project before the first test aircraft flew and their projected OF-1 version, which would have had additional fuel tankage and provision for underwing armament, and for which four YOF-1s had been ordered, was abandoned. The nine service test aircraft each had two underwing pylons for drop tanks or up to 2,700lb of external stores, and were

equipped with a KA-30 high-resolution camera system in the fuselage, together with extensive radio equipment, IFF and VOR/tacan. The production AO-1A-GR (later OV-1A-GR), of which 64 were built, was the basic visual photographic variant, with the same KA-30 or (later) KS-61 camera system in the fuselage for horizon-to-horizon coverage, and provision for a nose camera; two additional underwing pylons could be fitted. The first 18 OV-1As had a Collins FD-105 integrated flight system and some changes in radio and navaids over the YOV-1As, with provision for fitting a radar altimeter, ILS system, autopilot, doppler and other radio equipment and navaids that were installed in the nineteenth and later OV-1As. All versions of the Mohawk can carry 52 flares for night photography in each of two removable, upward-firing pods mounted above the wing roots. Two OV-1As were later modified to OV-1B standard, one of these going to the US Navy.

The OV-1A entered operational service in 1961 with units of the US Seventh Army in Germany, and started operations in Vietnam with the 23rd Special Warfare Aviation Detachment in July 1962. Two years later President Johnson's signing of the Gulf of Tonkin Resolution marked the beginning of a growing and irrevocable US commitment to the Vietnam War, and in 1964 some armed Mohawks, designated JOV-1A-GR, were operated by the 11th Air Assault Division in South-East Asia, being handed over to the 73rd Aerial Surveillance Company in 1965. Mohawks were usually unarmed, but these few JOV-1As were modified to

Above: The OV-1B was equipped with APS-94 SLAR (side-looking airborne radar) in a long, torpedo-like radome under the starboard side of the forward fuselage which could produce a permanent radar photographic map of the terrain below. The wing span was increased by 6ft on this model. (Grumman)

have four additional underwing pylons (making six in all) for carrying light bombs, 12.7mm machine gun pods or 2.75in rocket projectiles. OV-1As, -Bs and -Cs in Vietnam were also fitted with grenade launchers, Minigun pods or small guided missiles under the wings. Yet the Mohawk played only a limited part in the Vietnam conflict, partly because its basic concept was overshadowed by the development of helicopter gunships such as the Bell UH-1 Huey family, and also because of the widespread use of ADSIDs (Air-Delivered Seismic Intruder Devices) dropped in planned patterns by F-4 Phantoms along the Ho Chi Minh Trail. These transmitted seismic information by remote control to listening aircraft for onward relaying on Viet Cong movements of men and supplies down this Trail. RPVs (remotely piloted vehicles, or small pilotless aircraft) were also used in Vietnam for battlefield surveillance.

The OV-1B-GR Mohawk, of which 100 were built, was distinguished by having APS-94 SLAR (side-looking airborne radar) in a long, torpedo-like container under the forward fuselage on the starboard side. Wing span was increased by 6ft, the fuselage air brakes were deleted, and there was no provision for dual controls. The APS-94 SLAR could produce a permanent radar photographic map of the terrain on either side of the aircraft's flight path, on either 4in×5in cut film or 70mm film strip, and an in-flight film processor enabled the observer to see a developed photographic image within seconds of the film being exposed. The -B's other radio equipment, electronics and navaids were very similar to those of the later production OV-1As. At least two OV-1Bs were transferred to the US Navy.

The OV-1C-GR, of which 129 were built, was also very similar to the later production OV-1A, but had UAS-4 infra-red surveillance sensor equipment in the underside of the rear fuselage, and single instead of dual controls; a forward-looking panoramic camera was also fitted. A number of OV-1Cs were fitted with updated electronics during 1966–67, and at the same time the wing leading-edge slats were deactivated.

Four OV-1C airframes were assigned to completion in 1967 as YOV-1D-GR service test aircraft. The OV-1D-GR, of which 37 were built, incorporated three photographic systems, a KA-60C 180-degree vertical panoramic camera, a similar KA-60C forward-looking panoramic camera and a KA-76 vertical camera. The OV-1D could also be converted from an infra-red to a SLAR surveillance capability (or *vice versa*) in an hour, by fitting the AN/AAS-24 infra-red surveillance system or the AN/APS-94D SLAR. The OV-1D thus combined in one airframe the operational capabilities of the OV-1A, -B and -C, but it also had more extensive radio equipment and navaids than earlier versions, and could carry ECM pods, flare or chaff dispensers or an LS-59A photoflash unit on the underwing pylons; furthermore, it had a strengthened landing gear, was fitted with underwing hardpoints for 'stores', and was equipped with an inertial navigation system (INS). Finally, more powerful Lycoming T53-L-701 turboprops of 1,400shp were fitted to the OV-1D, the last of which was completed in December 1970. Many OV-1Bs and OV-1Cs were converted to OV-1D standard at Grumman's Stuart plant near Miami from 1981, and a total of 110 such conversions were planned, 80 being completed during

Below: This OV-1C, 61-2706, was one of several Mohawks that carried armament on six underwing pylons; the JOV-1A was a very similar armed variant, whilst some OV-1As, -Bs and -Cs in Vietnam also carried underwing ordnance. (Grumman)

1981–82. A dozen OV-1Bs were also modified to become RV-1D-GR tactical reconnaissance variants for 'elint' (electronic intelligence gathering).

The OV-1E-GR was a projected version of the OV-1A Mohawk with a modified forward fuselage to accommodate a large cabin aft of, and integral with, the cockpit, for advanced electronic surveillance duties, crew proficiency training or cargo transport; SLAR radar or infrared surveillance equipment could have been fitted, but the OV-1E was not built. Sixteen OV-1Bs were in fact converted for 'elint' duties as EV-1E-GRs, with AN/ALQ-133 'Quick Look II' surveillance radar, a ventral radome and wing-tip radar pods, plus various equipment changes. Early in 1976 two EV-1Es were supplied to the Israeli Defence Force/Air Force for the 'elint' and battlefield surveillance roles, equipped with SLAR pods.

The A-6 Intruder

In 1956 the Navy issued a requirement for a low level, long-range, carrier-based attack aircraft able to deliver nuclear or conventional weapons on to small targets completely obscured by weather or darkness. This requirement reflected Korean War experience and called for a high subsonic performance, at tree-top height so as to fly under the enemy's radar, and a heavy weapons load. The design contest, which lasted from May to December 1957, involved eleven submissions from eight companies, and on 31 December that year Grumman's G-128 proposal, to be known as the A2F-1 Intruder, was judged the best. It became the subject of the Navy's first 'cost plus incentive fee' contract in March 1959 when four of eight YA2F-1 (later YA-6A and A-6A) development aircraft were ordered. The first of these made its maiden flight on 19 April 1960, quickly followed into flight status by the remaining seven YA2F-1s.

The high/mid-wing Intruder was designed around two 8,500lb s.t. Pratt & Whitney J52-P-6 'straight' turbojets mounted side by side in the fuselage, the jetpipes of which were arranged to be swivelled downwards hydraulically through 23 degrees on the first four YA2F-1s, to shorten the take-off run by deflected jet thrust. The other four YA2F-1s had the jetpipes fixed and angled downwards, although there was provision for swivelling them, and production Intruders had them permanently angled downwards at 7 degrees. The fuselage was area-ruled, although the aircraft was designed to be subsonic, and an unusual feature in a machine of this category was that there was no internal weapons bay. Nevertheless, up to 15,000lb of external stores could be carried under five weapons attachment points, four under the wings and one under the fuselage, each of these points having a load capacity of 3,600lb. Up to thirty 500lb bombs could be carried in clusters of three, or four Martin AGM-12B Bullpup air-to-surface missiles, or two Bullpups and three 2,000lb bombs.

The absence of a weapons bay made possible a slim, tapering fuselage and a very compact airframe. The Intruder's wing span is actually 1ft less than the Avenger's but the maximum take-off weight of the A-6E – 60,400lb – is much more than twice its own empty weight and nearly four times the maximum weight of the TBF-1 Avenger. Unlike the Royal Navy's similarly sized Blackburn Buccaneer, the Intruder does not use supercirculation or flap-blowing techniques to make possible a smaller wing. The crew of two, pilot and bombardier/navigator, are seated side by side on Martin-Baker GRU5 ejection seats under a rearward-sliding canopy. The seats can be reclined to reduce fatigue during low-level operations, and the bombardier/navigator (B/N) is seated to starboard slightly behind and below the pilot. He controls the very comprehensive navigation, radar and attack systems which are integrated into the DIANE (Digital Integrated Attack Navigation Equipment) system, and an integrated display enables the pilot to 'see' the target and geographical features at night or in bad weather by means of two viewing screens in the cockpit.

The wings are swept back 25 degrees at the quarter-chord line, and feature almost full-span leading-edge slats and trailing-edge flaps to give excellent slow-flying qualities. Instead of ailerons for lateral control there are inset spoilers (or

Above: Production A2F-1 (A-6A) Intruders, like this one in VA-176 markings, differed little from the YA2F-1s. Note the perforations in the fuselage air brakes, and also the flight refuelling probe and leading edge slats. (J. M. G. Gradidge)

flaperons') forward of, and of the same span as, the trailing-edge flaps. An unusual feature is that the trailing edge of each wing tip outboard of the flaps splits to form speed brakes above and below the wing when extended. There are two short fences above each wing, the outer panels of which fold upwards and inwards. On early-model Intruders a door-type air brake was fitted on each side of the rear fuselage.

The bottom of the fuselage between the engines is recessed to carry a semi-exposed store. A distinctive, low aspect ratio fin and rudder are featured, with an antenna in the rear part of the fin immediately above the rudder. The all-moving tailplane has no separate elevators. The twin-wheel nose gear retracts backwards, the single wheel main units retract forwards and inwards into the air intake fairings, and there is an A-frame arrester hook under the rear fuselage. Up to four 300 US gallon drop tanks can be carried under the wings, and a detachable flight refuelling probe is fitted just ahead of the windscreen.

Two initial orders for 69 production A2F-1s (later A-6As) were placed in 1962 and 1963, and these differed only slightly from the development aircraft in having 9,300lb s.t. J52-P-8A or J52-P-8B turbojets with jet pipes at a fixed, downward angle, as well as a larger rudder; the A-6A also introduced the wing-tip speed brakes. Altogether 482 A-6As were built, the last being delivered in December 1969, and

the first A-6A to enter Navy service was accepted officially on 1 February 1963 by VA-42 at NAS Oceana. The first Marine Corps unit with A-6As was VMA(AW)-242, which equipped with the type at NAS Cherry Point in October 1964. Later, 119 A-6As were converted to A-6E standard with the -E model's new Norden navigation and attack radar; most later versions of the Intruder were modified from A-6As, and by 1984 the A-6A, A-6B and A-6C variants were no longer operational. Three YA-6As and three A-6As later used for miscellaneous testing were designated NA-6A, and one NEA-6A was similarly employed. A projected three-seat operational trainer variant of the A-6A was the TA-6A, seating an instructor and two pilots, but this was not built.

During 1965 A-6As began operating in Vietnam, flying initially from the carrier *Independence*. Navy and Marine Corps A-6 units flew many air strikes in the war, proving their ability to make pinpoint bombing attacks on targets that almost no other aircraft could hit accurately until the General Dynamics F-111 was deployed in combat. After the Paul Doumer road and rail bridge over the Red River at Hanoi had been put out of action by USAF bombing and repaired several times in 1966, the North Vietnamese started to ferry railway freight cars across the river, and in October 1967 a lone A-6A from the carrier *Constellation* armed with eighteen 500lb bombs and piloted by Lt. Cdr. Charles Hunter, made a low-level night attack on the ferry's loading slip not far from the bridge. Only eighteen miles from the target, the first of sixteen surface-to-air missiles, which could be distinguished by its trail of burning propellant, was launched to meet the A-6A. One SAM missed the Intruder by only 200ft, but the attack was pressed home successfully at roof-top height, and the loading slip was destroyed. In another night attack, on 18 April 1966, two A-6As from the carrier *Kitty Hawk* put the Uongbi power station near Haiphong out of action by dropping all 26 of their 1,000lb bombs on it, thus knocking out one-third of North Vietnam's electricity supply. The A-6A's heavy weapons load and its DIANE system enabled it to achieve results in attacks like these that would have necessitated a whole squadron of Second World War bombers.

The EA-6A (formerly A2F-1Q), which first flew as a prototype in 1965, was a special electronic countermeasures (ECM) version for Marine Corps A-6A strike units, retaining partial A-6A strike capability but equipped for electronic jamming and intelligence-gathering within a combat area. Some parts of the DIANE system were deleted, and the EA-6A could be distinguished externally by a radome at the top of its fin and (for most operations) ECM pods under the wings. It carried over 30 different antennae to detect, classify, record and jam enemy radiations and transmissions. A-6A BuNo 149935 was converted into the YEA-6A

(formerly YA2F-1Q) prototype, and three more YA-6As and three A-6As were likewise converted to EA-6As, to be followed by 21 EA-6As built as such. This variant led to the four-seater EA-6B Prowler described later. The A-6B, of which nineteen were converted from A-6As for use by one Navy squadron, was equipped to test and launch the General Dynamics AGM-78 Standard ARM (Anti-Radiation Missile) intended to destroy ground-based SAM and anti-aircraft gun sites by homing in on the radiation waves emitted by ground radars. The A-6B differed from the -A chiefly in its electronics, and it had three different configurations ranging from limited to full strike capability. A-6A BuNo 149486 was also used to test the General Dynamics BGM-109 Tomahawk SLCM (Sea-Launched Cruise Missile), making the first air launch of an anti-ship Tomahawk from under its wing at the Pacific Missile Test Center on 29 March 1976.

The A-6C Intruder, twelve of which were produced (by modifying A-6A airframes), featured a turret-like fairing under the fuselage housing FLIR (forward-looking infra-red) sensors and an LLTV (low-light-level television) camera to provide an enhanced night attack capability, by permitting detailed identification and acquisition of targets not discernible by the A-6A's radar. One A-6C was later modified to A-6E standard with the -E's Norden navigation and attack radar.

One A-6A was modified into a proto-type inflight-refuelling tanker aircraft, with a hose and reel unit in the rear fuselage, first flying in this form on 23 May 1966. The KA-6D was the production tanker variant, and was fitted with tacan as well as with underwing fuel tanks. It can transfer more than 21,000lb of fuel immediately after take-off, or 15,000lb at a distance of 288 miles from the parent carrier. It can also be used as a day bomber or as a control aircraft for air–sea rescue operations. A total of 78 A-6As and seven A-6Es were modified to KA-6Ds; by 1984 all the older A-6s in service were being converted to A-6E/TRAM or KA-6D standard, the later KA-6Ds having no weapons capability.

The A-6E, which first flew on 10 November 1970, is similar to the A-6A but has, in place of the original DIANE system of the -A model, a Norden AN/APQ-148 multi-mode navigation/attack radar coupled to an IBM AN/ASQ-133 solid-state digital computer similar to the type first tested on the EA-6B. The first A-6Es had been deployed to a squadron in September 1972, and 129 examples of this variant were ordered, while many A-6As were converted to A-6E standard by fitting the new avionics. Planned procurement of the -E model totalled 348 aircraft in 1985, and current conversions of earlier A-6s are to A-6E/TRAM standard, to which all A-6Es already built are being modified. The -E also has some detail changes from the A-6A, the latter's

fuselage air brakes being deleted, while the powerplants are 9,300lb s.t. J52-P-8B turbojets.

The A-6E/TRAM (Target Recognition and Attack Multisensor) variant of the A-6E first flew on 22 March 1974 without sensors, and on 22 October that year with them fitted. This variant has a Hughes electro-optical sensor package, containing both FLIR and laser tracker-designator equipment, housed in a small turret under the nose. There are other

Below: The KA-6D tanker for in-flight refuelling has a hose and reel unit in the rear fuselage and usually carries four 300 US gallon drop tanks. Seventy-eight KA-6Ds were converted from A-6As and seven from A-6Es; later KA-6D conversions now have the weapon system capability deleted and provision for carrying five 400 US gallon drop tanks. (US Navy)

Left: The A-6E/TRAM (Target Recognition and Attack Multisensor) variant has a turreted electro-optical sensor package housed under the nose and can fire laser-guided weapons. All existing A-6Es are being modified to A-6E/TRAM standard, and 50 of the latter are being fitted to carry four McDonnell Douglas AGM-84A Harpoon anti-ship missiles. (Grumman)

improvements to the avionics, and laser-guided as well as conventional weapons can be fired by the TRAM variant. Under plans made early in 1981, fifty A-6E/TRAMs are equipped to carry four McDonnell Douglas AGM-84A Harpoon anti-ship missiles, and all new production A-6Es and converted aircraft will be able to carry Harpoons. The A-6E/TRAM variant was first deployed at sea in May 1980.

More than 600 A-6 Intruders have been built, and about 250 were in US Navy service early in 1982. They currently equip eighteen Navy and Marine Corps squadrons and three readiness training squadrons. A major updating programme of the Intruder under a July 1984 contract will result in the A-6F with new avionics and radar, and with a non-afterburning General Electric F404-GE-400D turbofan in place of the Pratt & Whitney J52. Air-to-air or stand-off, air-to-surface missiles will be carried, and the A-6F will have a new cockpit based on CRT (cathode-ray tube) technology and with digital avionics. Survivability will also be enhanced. The A-6F is scheduled for completion in 1989, with first deliveries to the US Navy in 1990.

The EA-6B Prowler

Whereas the Grumman EA-6A counter-measures aircraft retained a partial strike capability, the EA-6B Prowler was drastically redesigned so that its entire warload consisted of the most advanced and comprehensive ECM equipment ever fitted to a tactical attack aircraft. Two extra crew members (ECM officers) were seated side by side in a rear cockpit to operate the ALQ-99 ECM equipment, the forward

fuselage being lengthened by 4ft 6in to take the extra accommodation. Work on the EA-6B started in 1966, Grumman being awarded a prototype design and development contract in the autumn of that year, and the first of two A-6As converted into EA-6B prototypes, BuNo 149479, made its first flight on 25 May 1968; these two later became NEA-6Bs, and a third EA-6B for static testing was converted from a YA-6A. The first four EA-6Bs were pre-production aircraft, and procurement of the EA-6B is planned to total over 90 aircraft. Production in 1984 was eight aircraft, with six built in 1985 and twelve in 1986, and six will be built annually until 1991. The first Prowler deliveries were made in January 1971, and by mid-1977 ten EA-6B squadrons were in Navy service, designated VAQ-129 to VAQ-138 inclusive. The first Marine Corps Prowler squadron, VMAQ-2, began training in September 1977.

The EA-6B has a fin-tip radome similar to, but larger than, that of the EA-6A. It contains sensitive surveillance receivers for long-range detection of enemy radars, and information from their emissions is fed into a central digital computer for display and recording. Ten high-powered electronic jamming transmitters are carried in five ECM pods, two under each wing and one under the fuselage. Electric power for each pod is generated by a ram air turbine driven by a small windmilling propeller on the nose of the pod. These ECM containers initially provided jamming coverage of the four radar wavebands then in use in South-East Asia; three EA-6B squadrons served in Vietnam, where they played an important role. The 24th and later EA-6Bs were of

the so-called EXCAP variety, with an enhanced jamming capability to cover a further three frequency bands, each pod covering one such band. The first 23 aircraft were later modified to fit them for an improved on-board system after tests with a prototype began in 1975.

Apart from the extra crew space, the EA-6B has strengthened wings to cater for a higher gross weight and greater fatigue life. The underfuselage structure is 'beefed up' in the regions of the landing gear attachments and arrester hook, the undercarriage and hook also being strengthened for the higher gross weight. More powerful J52-P-408 turbojets of 11,200lb s.t. are fitted, which provide 20 per cent more sea level thrust than the A-6E's powerplants, whilst fuel capacity is also greater than that of the A-6E. Martin-Baker GRUEA7 ejection seats are provided for the flight crew.

The first 21 EA-6Bs were later modified by Grumman to ICAP (Increased Capability) standard with a new defensive ECM system, the ECM equipment in wing and fuselage pods having improved jamming capability and substantially

increased jamming efficiency (the EXCAP variant could cope only with individual emitters but the ICAP variant could jam several emitters forming a weapon system). The ICAP model also featured the ACLS (Automatic Carrier Landing System) for carrier recovery in zero-zero weather conditions.

The ICAP-2 variant, now succeeding the original ICAP model, first flew on 24 June 1980 and features further improved jamming capability, with improved emitter identification and correlation, software and display improvements, better reliability and easier maintenance. ICAP-2 can now cope with groups of weapons systems such as an air defence complex, and earlier EA-6Bs are being modified to this standard. The latest update programme is ADVCAP (Advanced Capability), work on which began in 1983. This involves a new Litton Industries receiver/processor group for still further improved tactical jamming capability. The first six of these systems was scheduled for delivery in 1987, with production envisaged for 1991, and in due course EA-6Bs will be modified to ADVCAP standard.

Above: Developed from the EA-6A, the EA-6B Prowler has very advanced and comprehensive ECM equipment, and two extra crew members (ECM officers) side by side in a rear cockpit to operate it. This EA-6B of VAQ-129 carries five ECM pods under the fuselage and wings containing high-powered jamming transmitters. (Grumman)

Left: The ICAP-2 variant of the EA-6B features a further improved jamming capability over the earlier ICAP (Improved Capability) model; the ICAP-2 Prowler can now cope with groups of weapons systems such as an air defence complex, and each of its ECM pods can generate signals in any one of seven frequency bands instead of the single band of the original pods. (Grumman)

Ag-Cats and Gulfstreams

As the Second World War drew to a close, there seemed to be the promise of a large market in the immediate future for privately owned aircraft, and several companies outside the well-established lightplane manufacturers such as Piper and Taylorcraft built designs for this market. Grumman entered the field with two three-seater lightplane prototypes, the G-63 Kitten, built in 1944 and having a tailwheel undercarriage, and the G-72 Kitten, built in 1946 and similar to the G-63 but with a fixed, unspatted nosewheel undercarriage. Both aircraft were powered by the 125hp Continental C125 six-cylinder, horizontally opposed engine, which gave the G-72 a cruising speed of 130mph. However, the Kitten did not go into production, partly because the hoped-for postwar light aircraft boom did not materialize to the extent anticipated, and partly because of Grumman's more pressing commitments with the F9F Panther and other US Navy projects. The two Kittens were used for a time as executive 'hacks' by Grumman officials, and the G-72 was later flown as a single-seater with various items of test equipment in place of the two other seats. Both Kittens were still flying as late as 1949. Apart from the commercial amphibians, of which the Widgeon ceased production at the end of 1948, the two Kittens remained for a decade Grumman's sole venture into civil aviation.

The Ag-Cat

In 1956 Grumman, after flight testing the French-designed Fouga CM 170 Magister jet trainer, took an option to build the type under licence in both its CM 170R and navalized CM 175 Zéphyr forms. In the event, this option was not exercised, but if it had been Grumman-built Magisters might have been sold in due course to civilian flying schools in the United States as well as to the military.

The company's first really successful attempt to diversify outside the naval and military field was the G-164 Ag-Cat single-seat agricultural biplane for crop-dusting and spraying, the prototype of which first flew on 27 May 1957. The type was certificated in the Restricted (Agricultural) category on 20 January 1959, being fitted initially with an uncowled 220–225hp Continental W670 nine-cylinder, air-cooled radial engine, and it received FAA approval for patrolling and surveying on 9 April 1962.

Ag-Cat production was subcontracted to the Schweizer Aircraft Corporation of Elmira, New York, one of America's leading sailplane manufacturers, and the first Ag-Cat deliveries were made to Uruguay and Puerto Rico in 1959. By 1979 Schweizer had built 2,455 Ag-Cats – 1,730 G-164As, 659 G-164Bs, 44 G-164Cs and 22 G-164D Turbo Ag-Cats – and the aircraft was in service in some

Below: The G-63 Kitten prototype NX41808 seen here was built in 1944 to meet the large postwar market foreseen for private owner aircraft. It was a three-seater with a 125hp Continental C125 'flat six' engine, but it did not go into production. (Grumman)

Bottom: The G-72 Kitten was also built with a view to the postwar market. A three-seater with the same engine, it originally had a fixed, unspatted nosewheel undercarriage, and a single fin and rudder very like that of the G-63, but the aircraft was later modified to have a retractable nosewheel gear and twin fins and rudders, as shown. (Grumman)

34 countries. In January 1981 Schweizer purchased all rights to the Ag-Cat design and resumed production in October that year with an improved variant of the G-164B known as the Ag-Cat Super-B. This was offered in two versions, the Ag-Cat Super-B/600, with a 600hp Pratt & Whitney R-1340 Wasp nine-cylinder radial, and the very similar Ag-Cat Super-B/450, which differed chiefly in having a 450hp R-985 Wasp Junior radial. These are now the two main production versions, and have superseded earlier variants. In addition to the original Continental W670-6N (or R-670-4), W670-16 (R-670-11) or W670-6A (R-670-5) radial, the Ag-Cat was also available with other types of engine, such as the 240hp Gulf Coast W670-240, the 245hp Jacobs L-4M or L-4MB and 275–300hp Jacobs R-755A2M1 seven-cylinder radials, the 450hp Pratt & Whitney R-985 Wasp Junior, and the 600hp R-1340 Wasp engine. The Wasp-powered versions were known as G-164A Super Ag-Cats, and their extra power made possible a greater payload of dry or liquid agricultural chemicals.

The Ag-Cat has a welded steel tube fuselage structure covered with duralumin sheet to withstand the rough usage of crop dusting operations and incorporating removable side panels. The constant-chord, single-bay, staggered wings are two-spar aluminium structures with aluminium covering on the top surfaces, around the leading edges and back to the front spar on the undersurfaces, the remainder of the lower wing surfaces being fabric-covered. There are no flaps, but light alloy ailerons are fitted to all four wings for making tighter turns, and the upper and lower wings are interchangeable on each side. The wing tips are of fibreglass. The wire-braced tail surfaces consist of fabric-covered, steel tube frameworks, and a wire for deflecting cables runs from the tip of the fin to the top of the cockpit canopy. The pilot sits in a raised position in the cockpit (which was open on earlier versions) for a better forward view, with a reinforced fairing aft of the cockpit to protect him in the event of an accident involving a turn-over. An enclosed cockpit was optional on earlier aircraft, but it is now standard on the Super Ag-Cat, with air-conditioning an 'optional extra'.

Forward of the cockpit, over the aircraft's centre of gravity, is a fibreglass hopper for dry or liquid agricultural chemicals. This was of 35ft^3 capacity on early versions, and could take up to 2,000lb or 260 US gallons of chemicals.

Below: The G-164 Ag-Cat single-seat agricultural biplane was first certificated with a 225hp uncowled Continental W670 nine-cylinder radial, as fitted to N74055, one of the prototypes, seen here. (Grumman)

The Super Ag-Cat B features a larger hopper of 40ft³ capacity that can take 300 US gallons of chemicals, whilst the Super Ag-Cat C introduced a 66.7ft³ capacity hopper that could take 500 US gallons. The chemicals are discharged through a distributor beneath the fuselage, and the Super Ag-Cat can be fitted with a low-volume, ULV or high-volume spray system with leading- or trailing-edge booms, depending on the type of crops to be treated. A spray or dust distribution system is available, and the Super Ag-Cat can also be used for water-bombing forest fires.

Fuel is carried in an upper wing centre-section tank that held 32.7 US gallons in early Ag-Cat versions and 46 US gallons in the Super Ag-Cat. Optional wing tanks in one or both sides of the centre section bring the Super Ag-Cat B's fuel capacity to 64 or 80 US gallons; the Super Ag-Cat C has a standard tankage of 80 US gallons. The main wheels on the cantilever spring steel undercarriage legs have Cleveland heavy-duty, air-cooled disc brakes, and the tailwheel is steerable. A 12V or 24V electrical system for navigation lights and engine starter is another optional extra, as is a radio installation.

Ag-Cat Developments

The first version of the Super Ag-Cat was the Super Ag-Cat A, which was certificated in the Restricted (Agricultural) category on 4 March 1966. This came in two variants, the Super Ag-Cat A/450 (the basic aircraft), fitted with a 450hp Wasp Junior R-985 radial driving a Hamilton Standard constant-speed propeller with twin AG-100-2 metal blades, and the Super Ag-Cat A/600 powered by a 600hp Wasp R-1340 radial driving a very similar airscrew; the earlier G-164 Ag-Cat variants were fitted with a Grumman (Sensenich) ground-adjustable, two-blade metal propeller. Production of the Super Ag-Cat A ended in December 1977. The Super Ag-Cat B, which was certificated in the Restricted (Agricultural) category on 18 November 1975, was similar to the A/450, with the same Wasp Junior engine (with which it was known as the Super Ag-Cat B/450), but featured an increase in wing span of 6ft 4in, to 42ft 3in, to allow longer booms to be fitted, for a broader swath of spray or dust. The fuselage was lengthened, a larger hopper was fitted, and the fin and rudder were heightened, with the fin chord increased. In 1977 the basic B/450 variant was supplemented by the Super Ag-Cat B/525, equipped with a 525hp Continental/Page R-975 nine-cylinder, air-cooled radial driving a Hamilton Standard constant-speed propeller with twin AG-100 metal blades.

The Super Ag-Cat C/600, the prototype of which first flew on 27 February 1976, is similar to the B/450 but has a 600hp Wasp R-1340 radial. The C model has the fuselage lengthened by about 4ft 2in to take the larger, 500 US gallon hopper, and deepened, giving a standard fuel capacity greater than that of the B. The C/600 was certificated in the Restricted (Agricultural) category on 23 November 1977. The 1977 model Super Ag-Cats featured several minor but important improvements, such as a simplified hopper door, provision for an air intake filter of larger volume, and a new, specially contoured pilot's seat. When Schweizer took over the Ag-Cat design rights in 1981 and put its improved G-164B Ag-Cat Super B/600 and Super B/450 into production, the company made several changes over the earlier B model, chief amongst which was the raising of the upper wings by 8in to improve the pilot's view and to increase the load-carrying capability, operating speed and rate of climb. A hopper of greater capacity (53.5ft³, or 400 US gallons) than the earlier B model's is now featured, and a 3ft 2in wide stainless steel gatebox and bottom loader valve are now standard equipment. Numerous other airframe and equipment improvements have been made. The same R-1340 Wasp and R-985 Wasp Junior engines as before are fitted, driving a Pacific Propeller 12D40/AG100 two-blade, constant-speed metal airscrew.

In the spring of 1984 Schweizer was flight-testing an Ag-Cat Super B fitted with a 700hp Thunder TE495-TC700 water-cooled, turbocharged V-8 piston engine as an alternative to the R-1340 Wasp, and a variant with this powerplant may go into production. If it does, it could conceivably revive the First World War tradition of water-cooled aero

Left: A 1977 model G-164A Super Ag-Cat A showing the external stiffeners on the fuselage sides introduced with the Wasp-powered Super Ag-Cats. The A model came in two variants, the Super Ag-Cat A/450 with a 450hp Wasp Junior R-985 radial, the basic variant, and the Super Ag-Cat A/600 with a 600hp Wasp R-1340. (Schweizer Aircraft)

Left: A 1977 model Super Ag-Cat B/525 with a nine-cylinder, 525hp, Continental/Page R-975 radial. The aircraft was otherwise the same as the B/450. (Schweizer Aircraft)

Left: Schweizer's improved variants, the G-164B Ag-Cat Super B/600 with a 600hp Wasp R-1340 and the Ag-Cat Super B/450 with a 450hp Wasp Junior R-985, showed several changes over the earlier G-164B, chief amongst which was that the upper wings were raised by 8in to improve the pilot's view. The hopper capacity is now 400 US gallons, although this B/450 has a 325-gallon hopper. (Schweizer Aircraft)

engines such as the Hispano-Suiza V-8 and the Austro-Daimler. In another attempt to find an alternative to the R-1340 Wasp, Serv-Aero Engineering of Salinas, California, had earlier re-engined Super Ag-Cat N947X with a 560hp Alvis Leonides radial driving a Dowty-Rotol R289 three-blade propeller. Although slightly less powerful than the R-1340 Wasp, the Leonides reduced drag and increased propeller efficiency, to give an improved overall performance. Another 'one-off' variant was the Super Ag-Cat trainer N6904Q shown at the 1979 Paris Salon. This had the hopper removed and in its place featured an open cockpit for the pilot under instruction, the existing enclosed cockpit being retained unchanged.

Partly to overcome the shortage of spares and components for the now elderly R-1340 Wasp engine, which had been out of production for some years,

Frakes Aviation of Cleburne, Texas, who had produced the Turbo Mallard conversion, re-engined a Super Ag-Cat in 1977 with a 750shp Pratt & Whitney PT6A-34 turboprop driving a Hartzell three-blade metal propeller. This variant was known as the Turbo-Cat. The PT6A turboprop, in a slender two-piece fibreglass cowling, gave much less drag than the uncowled radial engines of previous versions, as well as offering economies in maintenance costs and fuel consumption, greater reliability and increased time between overhauls. The first Turbo-Cat was evaluated by Air Rice of Katy, Texas, and it was followed by a second Frakes Turbo-Cat conversion, which, with a 750shp PT6A-34AG derated to 540shp, made its first flight in June 1978.

Gulfstream American, the successor to Grumman, began work on a prototype PT6-powered G-164D Turbo Ag-Cat D, very similar to the Turbo-Cat, in February

1978. The aircraft first flew on 19 July 1978, and that September construction of the first pre-production Turbo Ag-Cat D began. This variant, generally similar to the Super Ag-Cat C/600, was offered in three versions, the Turbo Ag-Cat D/T, with a 680shp PT6A-15AG turboprop and a 500 US gallon hopper; the Turbo Ag-Cat D/ST, as the D/T but with a 750shp PT6A-34; and the Turbo Ag-Cat D/SST, also as the D/T but with an 850shp PT6A-41. The PT6 drives a Hartzell HC-B3, TN-3D/T10282A+4 constant-speed, fully feathering and reversible-pitch, three-blade metal propeller. The basic fuel capacity is 80 US gallons in three wing tanks, and an electrical system is now a standard feature of the D model; the PT6 increases the length to 34ft 4in. Frakes Aviation also offers PT6 conversions of the various Super Ag-Cat A, B and C variants, which are also fitted with Frakes vortex-control wing tips as well as the new engine; Frakes claims that a 30ft streamer will fly steady in the airflow behind these wing tips. The 1983 prices for such versions varied from $150,000 for a Super Ag-Cat A with PT6A-15 to $250,000 for a Super Ag-Cat C with a PT6A-34.

The Turbo Ag-Cat D variants, which were marketed in Europe by Dornier, have now been succeeded in production by Schweizer's own turbine version, the PT6A-powered G-164B Ag-Cat Turbine, which is very similar to the Super-B. This is available with three optional power-plants, the 500shp PT6A-11AG, the 680shp PT6A-15AG, or the 750shp PT6A-34AG. With the latter engine, the 1983 price of an Ag-Cat Turbine was $285,000, compared with $230,000 for PT6A-11AG-powered version; that year's price for the piston-engined Ag-Cat Super-B/450 was $125,000, and for the Super-B/600 variant $133,000. Although one of the most expensive agricultural aircraft available, the Ag-Cat was the most popular in this category in the USA in 1983: 250 were operating in the state of Arkansas alone, where soya beans, cotton and other crops are grown.

So far all turboprop Ag-Cat variants had been PT6-powered, but in 1980 a version of the Super Ag-Cat C with the Garrett TPE331, known as the Marsh G-164 C-T Turbo Cat, was certificated. This was developed by Marsh Aviation of Mesa, Arizona, and featured a 778shp Garrett TPE331-1-101 turboprop de-rated to 600shp. Other improvements included automatic start sequencing, automatic fuel nozzle purging, and engine inlet and fuel filter anti-icing, whilst the

Left: A Marsh G-164 Turbo Cat conversion of a Super Ag-Cat A, showing the slightly deeper cowling of the Garrett TPE331-1-101 turboprop compared to that of PT6-powered versions. (Marsh Aviation)

Garrett engine gave improved reliability and performance and an increased payload. Optional extras on the Turbo Cat are an air-conditioning system for the pilot, single-point refuelling, and a hydraulic spray system. By 1981 six Turbo Cat conversions had been completed (one of a G-164A, four of G-164Bs and one of a G-164C), but no more have since been produced, although the model is still available to prospective customers.

At the US National Agricultural Aviation Association meeting at Las Vegas, Nevada, at the end of 1982, three new Ag-Cat variants were revealed – a twin-engined modification known as the Twin Cat, a version with a 1,200hp Wright R-1820-202A Cyclone radial engine known as the King Cat, and an Ag-Cat B with a larger hopper of 450 US gallons capacity in a lengthened fuselage, known as the Maxi Cat. The last variant was created by Aero Mod General of Spokane, Washington, who claimed that 40 per cent greater production for each hour of operations was possible with the Maxi Cat conversion, but no more was heard of the Maxi Cat after the 1982 NAA meeting.

The Maxi Cat was succeeded by a new Aero Mod conversion known as the Super Ag Max, which could be made to A- and B-series Ag-Cats and consisted of lengthening the fuselage by 2ft 9in (a 2ft section ahead of the cockpit and a 9in 'plug' to the rear of it) to accommodate a fibreglass hopper of 430 US gallons capacity. Wing span is increased by 2ft 9in over the Super Ag-Cat B to 45ft, and the wing spars are replaced by new members with heavier flanges. These modifications are claimed to give a speed increase of about 15mph and a 27 per cent increase in fuel efficiency. By late 1984 some fifteen Super Ag-Cat Bs and five Super Ag-Cat As converted to Super Ag Max standard had been delivered to various customers, including three to South Africa, where a few King Cats are also in service.

The Twin Cat version was produced by removing the Wasp engine and replacing it by a streamlined nose fairing on which two 350hp Lycoming TIO-540-A2C turbocharged 'flat six' engines were mounted, one held on each side of the nose fairing by a tubular framework. These powerplants drove three-blade

propellers and conferred the advantages of twin-engined safety on the Ag-Cat, which already had one of the best safety records of any agricultural aircraft. The twin Lycomings, which have a 1,500-hour Time Between Overhauls period, give an extremely uniform spray distribution, and it is claimed that the Twin Cat can take off, be ferried, land and taxi with either engine shut down, whilst stalling speed is said to be 10kts below that of the standard Ag-Cat's. Three of these twin-engined conversions were produced by a company named Twin Cat, of Ormond Beach, Florida, and these had completed 2,000 hours in service in the states of Colorado, Idaho, Nebraska, Oregon and Washington by the time Twin Cat N8459K was shown at the 1982 NAAA meeting. Interest in the Twin Cat was shown by operators in South Africa, Australia and Canada.

The King Cat is the most powerful Ag-Cat variant so far, and the first such conversion, of a G-164C Super Ag-Cat C/600, had the engineering work carried out by Serv-Aero Engineering (who also produced the Leonides Ag-Cat) for the Mid-Continent Aircraft Corporation of Hayti, Missouri, who have undertaken all subsequent King Cat conversions – of which eighteen had been completed by early 1984. The 1,200hp R-1820-202A Cyclone drives a three-blade, metal propeller, and the hopper capacity is 500 US gallons, or 4,000lb of dry chemicals. A Super Ag-Cat C/600 can be converted into a King Cat by Mid-Continent, or a kit is available for installation of the Cyclone by the customer or his maintenance organization. Optional extras available for the King Cat include Serv-O ailerons, an increased fuel capacity of 114 US gallons, Collins cockpit air-conditioning, and a 500 US gallon water-bombing system for forest fires.

The Gulfstream I
In the mid-1950s it became clear that there would soon be a need for an executive transport to replace the several hundred Douglas DC-3s, Lockheed Lodestars, Martin 2-0-2s and 4-0-4s and other piston-engined airliners used in the United States in this role. The great majority of these aircraft were unpressur-

ized and, with the introduction of Vickers Viscounts by Capital Airlines in 1954, the US air-travelling public has begun to get a taste for the superior smoothness of turbine-powered travel. This advantage would surely be expected as a matter of course by business aircraft users, and so it was entirely logical that Grumman's first executive transport, the G-159 Gulfstream I, which conducted its maiden flight on 14 August 1958, should be powered by two 2,190shp Rolls-Royce RDa.7/2 Dart 529 or 529-8E turboprops, the same basic engine that powered the Viscount and also Fairchild's licence-built version of the Fokker Friendship airliner, the F-27.

With a crew of two, the Gulfstream I seated 10–14 passengers in a pressurized cabin 1ft less in diameter and shorter than that of its chief competitor for executive sales, the Fairchild F-27, and had hydraulically operated, self-contained air-stairs at the entrance forward of the cabin. There was a pressurized baggage compartment in addition to luggage space in the forward cabin, and a toilet compartment with hot and cold water. The interior furnishings and equipment were left to the customer's choice, and were installed by specialist firms to whom Gulfstream Is were delivered 'green' (i.e. without such cabin furnishings or customer avionics). A variant seating 24

passengers in a high-density interior was also projected for possible sale to the US local service airlines, then largely equipped with DC-3s, but this was not built. Two decades later, however, the stretched 32–38 passenger Gulfstream I-C was devised for a very similar market, the US commuter airlines.

The Gulfstream I received FAA Type Approval on 21 May 1959, and was the first US twin-engined executive type certificated to cruise at 30,000ft. Its range with maximum fuel and allowances for 45 minutes' holding and 200 miles' diversion was 2,540 miles, which meant that it could cross the United States from coast to coast with only one refuelling stop; in terms of both range and cruising altitude, it was a great improvement on types like the DC-3 and Lodestar. These were strong selling points and, when production ceased in February 1969, a total of 200 Gulfstream Is had been built, including the military VC-4A and TC-4C. The US Coast Guard took delivery of Gulfstream I BuNo 1380 (later renumbered 02 and formerly N791G) in 1963 as a staff transport under the designation VC-4A, but an order for a second was later cancelled. The VC-4A replaced the Coast Guard's two Martin RM-1s (later VC-3As), which were staff transport versions of the 4-0-4 airliner. The Navy had planned to procure a navigational trainer

Below: The Gulfstream I was designed to provide pressurized and turbine-powered travel for executives who had previously relied on unpressurized, piston-engined types such as the Lockheed Lodestar, DC-3 and Martin 2-0-2. It had two 2,190shp Rolls-Royce Dart 529 turboprops of the same type that powered the Viscount and Friendship. (Grumman)

and transport version of the Gulfstream I in 1962, and the designation T-41A was at first allocated, later changed to TC-4B when the Air Force's version of the Cessna 172F came into service.

An order for ten TC-4Bs was deleted from the 1964 defence budget, but in 1966 the Navy ordered nine TC-4Cs as bombardier/navigator trainers for the A-6A Intruder, with the A-6A's radar in an enlarged nose and stations for up to six B/Ns in the main cabin, with equipment to teach them to operate the A-6A's DIANE system. The TC-4C, equipped with 2,185shp Dart 529-8X turboprops, first flew on 14 June 1967 and was named Academe. Two TC-4Cs were updated to A-6E/TRAM configuration in mid-1978, two others then being of A-6E standard and four more of the original A-6A standard; all eight were upgraded to A-6E/TRAM configuration by 1980. TC-4Cs are attached to A-6 Intruder squadrons, such as VA-42 and VMAT-202.

The Gulfstream I is of conventional, all-metal construction with single-slotted flaps, and the main undercarriage units retract forward of the main wing box spars to avoid cut-outs in the primary wing structure; the main gear units can also be lowered for use as speed brakes, and the nose undercarriage unit retracts forwards. Integral fuel tanks in the wings have a capacity of 1,550 US gallons, and the Darts drive Rotol four-blade, constant-speed propellers. There is an auxiliary power unit (APU) for ground operation of cabin air-conditioning, radio and other services, and Bendix X- and C-band weather radar is fitted.

Gulfstream I N36G was used to flight-test the new General Electric CT7 turbo-prop based on the T700 military helicopter engine and chosen to power the new Saab-Fairchild SF.340 commuter airliner. The Gulfstream first flew with the 1,600shp CT7 in September 1982, the engine replacing the port Dart turboprop and being installed in an SF.340 nacelle; it drove a Dowty propeller with four composite blades. General Electric found that, when throttled back to give the same power as the CT7, the Dart – a much older design, of course – had a fuel consumption about 40 per cent higher.

During the first half of 1979 Gulfstream American (the former Grumman American) conducted engineering studies and market surveys for a new, 'stretched', 32–38 passenger commuter airline version of the Gulfstream I known as the GAC 159-C Gulfstream I-C. Gulfstream American had acquired the jigs, tooling and fixtures for the Gulfstream I when it took over Grumman American in September 1978, and existing airframes were converted to Gulfstream I-C standard by means of a 9ft 6in increase in fuselage length to bring the overall length to 74ft 3in. This fuselage 'plug' enabled the I-C variant to seat up to 38 passengers at 29in pitch three abreast, or 32 passengers at 34in pitch. There was a toilet and carry-on baggage compartment at the front of the cabin, plus a 144ft^3 capacity baggage compartment at the rear. The former

Above: Nine TC-4C Academes were ordered as bombardier/navigator trainers for the A-6A Intruder; they were fitted with the A-6A's radar in the enlarged nose and with stations for up to six B/Ns in the main cabin learning to operate the A-6A's DIANE system. TC-4Cs were later updated to A-6E/TRAM equivalent configuration. (Grumman)

Above: From 1975 the Gulfstream II could be fitted with wing tip fuel tanks, as shown here on HZ-AFI of the Saudi Arabian airline Saudia. Engine 'hush kits' could also be fitted. (J. M. G. Gradidge)

circular cabin windows were replaced by rectangular ones, the nose was reshaped, and a 'wraparound' windscreen of the type used on the Gulfstream III was fitted. The maximum payload was now 7,600lb, or up to 8,500lb for the all-cargo variant, which had a large freight door 6ft 10in wide and 5ft 4in high in the port side of the rear fuselage. Maximum take-off weight in the passenger role was 36,000lb, and basic operating weight 23,550lb. The Dart turboprops were retained, although the General Electric CT64 and Avco Lycoming T55 turbo-props were considered as other possible power-plants for the Gulfstream I-C.

During the summer of 1979 Gulfstream I N5400C was converted into the I-C prototype by inserting the fuselage 'plug', first flying in this form on 25 October 1979. The first I-C to be delivered to a commuter airline went to Air North of Burlington, Vermont, on 11 November 1980, a second I-C following later. Other commuter airlines to order I-Cs were Chapparal Airlines of Abilene, Texas, who bought two and later leased a third; Air US of Denver, Colorado, two; Consolidated Airways of Indiana, six; Excellair of Colorado, two; and Royale Airways of Shreveport, Louisiana, which has a fleet of ten. Orion Air of Raleigh, North Carolina, a contract cargo-carrier flying express delivery services of small packages, also operated a fleet of ten. The latest airline operator of the Gulfstream I on scheduled services is the Leeds/Bradford-based regional carrier Brown

Air, which planned to inaugurate Leeds/Bradford–Frankfurt services in December 1985 with a 24-passenger Mk. I. By 1984 Gulfstream I-C conversions were no longer being produced, but the basic concept of stretching a low-time, well-maintained executive turboprop into a 32–38 passenger airliner for around two-thirds the cost of a brand-new aircraft had proven itself.

The Gulfstream II and III

With the growing acceptance of jet travel in the 1960s, a jet-powered development of the Gulfstream I was a logical step, and Grumman announced its decision to start production of the twin-turbofan G-1159 Gulfstream II on 17 May 1965. The first production Gulfstream II – no prototype was built – flew on 2 October 1966 and, after completion of the flight-test programme, was delivered to the National Distillers & Chemical Corporation on 6 December 1967, the type having received FAA certification on 19 October that year. Production of the Gulfstream II ended in 1979, and altogether 256 GIIs (as they are often called) had been delivered by 1 January 1981, including one for the US Coast Guard designated VC-11A. Cabin interiors and customer avionics, except for the Sperry SP-50G automatic flight control system fitted as standard, are installed by distributors for the type or by specialist companies in 'green' airframes

The Gulfstream II differs from the turboprop Mk. I in having two 11,400lb s.t. Rolls-Royce RB.163 Spey 511-8 turbofans mounted in nacelles on the rear fuselage. Rohr target-type thrust reversers are fitted, forming the aft portions of the nacelles when in the 'stowed' position. From aircraft No. 166, delivered in July 1975, a 'hush kit' for each engine was incorporated, and these kits could be fitted to earlier Gulfstream IIs retrospectively if required. Up to 23,300lb of fuel could be carried in integral tanks in the wings, and in 1975 a Gulfstream II was flight-tested with wing-tip tanks, which increased the fuel capacity to 26,800lb and enabled the maximum take-off weight to rise to 65,500lb from the 57,500lb of earlier aircraft. These tanks gave a range improvement of up to 12 per cent with maximum fuel, for a slight cruise performance penalty, and made possible a range of 3,662 miles with allowances for 45 minutes' holding and 230 miles' diversion, thus enabling a Gulfstream II to fly across the United States, coast to coast and non-stop.

Up to nineteen passengers are accommodated in a pressurized and air-conditioned cabin just 1ft longer than that of the Gulfstream I, with a large baggage compartment at the rear. The crew numbers two or three. The cabin entrance door forward on the port side has integral airstairs, and there is an auxiliary power unit in the tail compartment. A new and larger wing with a moderate sweepback of 25 degrees at the quarter-chord line replaces the Gulfstream I's unswept wing. It is fitted with one-piece, single-slotted, Fowler-type flaps, and spoilers are mounted forward of the flaps to assist the ailerons in lateral control and also act as air brakes. The main undercarriage units retract inwards into the wings and the nose gear, which, like the main gear, has twin wheels, retracts forwards. The T-tail surfaces are all swept back.

The Coast Guard acquired Gulfstream II N862GA as a VIP and staff transport, designated VC-11A. It was to have had Bureau Number 1451, but was renumbered 01 in a new Coast Guard series for VIP aircraft, 02 being the VC-4A variant of the Gulfstream I. Two Gulfstream IIs were specially modified for use by NASA as flying simulators to help train astronauts for Space Shuttle Orbiter

landings. The first of these flew at Bethpage on 29 September 1975, and both were delivered in mid-1976. Based at NASA's Johnson's Space Center, Houston, Texas, they are known as Shuttle Training aircraft. They have been fitted with special equipment, and have modified aerodynamic and engine controls added to the conventional controls: two aerofoil-shaped fairings, for example, are fitted under the wing roots. By using these special controls and cockpit displays an astronaut flying the Gulfstream II can simulate the Shuttle Orbiter in various control modes during approach and landing.

A retrofit programme is now offered to customers in which their GII can be fitted with the Gulfstream III wing with winglets, thus becoming the Gulfstream II-B. The new wing gives some 900nm extra range over the original GII, and provides a significant improvement in fuel efficiency. The work involves some structural modifications to permit increases in take-off weight, operating speeds and cruising heights. The prototype II-B conversion was made on GII N711SC of the Southland Corporation of Dallas, Texas, and this first flew as a II-B on 17 March 1981, completing FAA certification trials on 17 September that year. Since then orders for over 40 II-B conversions from GIIs have been placed.

The Gulfstream III, first announced on 10 November 1976 as a development of the Gulfstream II, was in its original form intended to have a NASA/Grumman supercritical wing (i.e. a wing designed to cruise above the critical Mach number) fitted with winglets at the tips; these would give a further improvement in cruising fuel consumption by increasing the wing's efficiency in cruise, through a reduction in the tip vortices. A larger cockpit with an improved field of view was also to have been a feature, together with an enlarged cabin, a quieter flight deck environment and a more streamlined nose for improved aerodynamics. Work on the Gulfstream III was, however, temporarily suspended in the spring of 1977, but the programme was resumed a year later as a less ambitious design showing a wing of conventional instead of supercritical aerofoil section, with extended leading edges incorporating additional fuel tankage in place of the earlier wing tip tanks, and NASA (Whitcomb) winglets at the tips. Wing sweepback was slightly increased to 27° 40′ at the quarter-chord line, the fuselage was lengthened by inserting a 2ft section aft of the flight deck, and the nose radome was made longer and more streamlined. The flight deck has improved crew accommodation and a new 'wrap-around' windscreen. The cabin still seats up to nineteen passengers, but there is now more space per passenger than in the Gulfstream II. The Collins EFIS-85 electronic flight instrument system was approved for the Gulfstream III (often referred to as the GIII) in March 1983, and the Sperry EDZ-600 and EDZ-800 EFIS are optional alternative systems. A new electrical system was fitted in GIIIs from 1983.

A prototype Gulfstream III converted from a GII, N901G, made its first flight on 2 December 1979, followed by a second prototype on 24 December the same year, GIII FAA certification being received on 22 September 1980. In April 1980 the third production Gulfstream III, N300GA, for delivery to the Ivory Coast Air Force, set two World Class Clk records when it flew non-stop from Savannah, Georgia, to Hanover in West Germany, a distance of 4,569.91 miles, in 8 hours 58 minutes at an average speed of 511.12mph. The aircraft was then displayed at Hanover's 1980 International Air Show. This was the first of several such Class Clk records (for jets of

25,000–35,000kg all-up weight) to be set by GIIIs, and it was broken on 15–16 February 1981 when another Gulfstream III flew from Kona Airport, Hawaii, to Washington, DC, non-stop (a distance of 4,778 miles) in 8 hours 50 minutes. Later a new Class Clk record for distance in a straight line was set by a GIII flown by R. K. Smyth and H. E. Rohr for 5,005.40 miles non-stop from Kuchiro in Japan to Los Angeles; Smyth and W. J. Hodde had already set a Class Clk altitude record of 52,000ft on 3 May 1980 in a Gulfstream III.

During 8–10 January 1982 the first production GIII, N100P (*The Spirit of America*), owned by the National Distillers & Chemical Corporation, captained by Harold Curtis and with four other crew members and five passengers aboard, smashed another Class Clk record by flying round the world in 47 hours 39 minutes at an average speed of 489.3mph over a distance of 23,490 miles, and this

Above: An artist's impression of a Gulfstream II modified to flight test a new propfan/engine combination by Lockheed-Georgia under the supervision of NASA's Lewis Research Center in Cleveland, Ohio. Flight testing under the Propfan Test Assessment Program was expected to begin early in 1987, the fan and engine being mounted on the port wing only. (Gulfstream)

Below: The Gulfstream III has winglets at the tips to improve the wing's efficiency in cruise, a 2ft fuselage extension and an improved flight deck; the wing's leading edges are also extended and incorporate extra fuel capacity. The Gulfstream II can be retrofitted with the GIII's wing, to produce the Gulfstream II-B. (J. M. G. Gradidge)

flight set up fifteen records over recognized point-to-point courses en route. Leaving from Teterboro, New Jersey, the GIII made refuelling stops at Geneva, Bahrain, Singapore, Guam, Hawaii and Chicago, and cruised at between 37,000ft and 45,000ft; the flight broke the previous Class Clk record, set up six years earlier by a Lear Jet 36, by over nine hours. The flight also marked the 100th anniversary of the Old Grand-Dad Distillery Company, owned by National Distillers, the GIII's registration, N100P, appropriately denoting 100 per cent proof. National Distillers had also owned both the first production Gulfstream I and the first GII. Another notable Class Clk round-the-world record, this time over the North and South Poles, was set by Brooke Knapp in a GIII during 15–18 November 1983, averaging 334.81mph.

These record flights helped to convince prospective GIII customers of the superior performance made possible by the new wing, and by 1 April 1982 123 Gulfstream IIIs had been delivered, with nine more on order. These included three for the Royal Danish Air Force specially equipped for maritime surveillance, fishery patrol and protection and air–sea rescue duties. The aircraft serve with No. 721 Squadron at Vaerløse, near Copenhagen, and each is allocated a one-month period of duty in rotation based at Sondestrom, Greenland. The GIIIs replace the eight Douglas C-47s formerly in service. The Royal Danish Air Force's fishery patrols cover 212,155 square miles around Greenland and 112,708 square miles around the Faroe Islands, a region so great that in bad weather a flight of over 900 miles to the nearest airfield might be necessary. The GIII's exceptional range is therefore very useful. For fishery patrols the Danish GIIIs carry a crew of seven, consisting of two pilots, a flight engineer, a navigator, an observer, a photographer and a radio operator. The aircraft are also equipped to carry out air drops and casualty evacuation (up to fifteen litters), as well as search and rescue (SAR) missions.

The radio operator's station is on the port side of the cabin immediately aft of the door, with a purpose-built observer's station directly opposite to starboard. Aft of the radio operator's position is the navigator's station, which has a master console for the Texas Instruments AN/APS-127 sea-surveillance radar, with antennae in the nose radome. There is also a Litton 72R INS and a VHF navigation system, with provision for the later installation of a VHF/Omega nav system if desired. There is an upward-opening cargo door, measuring 5ft 3in by 6ft 11in, in the starboard side of the fuselage forward of the wings, and a cargo roller conveyor system in the after cabin floor. There is also an overhead cable system for attaching drop-load parachute lanyards, and a flare-launching system in the after fuselage, to port, just behind the wing. The existing baggage door in the port side can be used to air-drop emergency supplies and survival equipment. With a reduced fuel load, 4,551lb of cargo can be accommodated, or 1,870lb with a maximum fuel load. With three crewmen aboard, a payload of 1,600lb and NBAA (National Business Aircraft Association) VFR reserves, the Danish GIIIs have a range of 4,721 miles cruising at Mach 0.77.

The next military variant of the Gulfstream III was the C-SAM (for the Special Air Missions role) or C-20A, to give it its US Air Force designation. This aircraft was modified for USAF airlift requirements, with a crew of four and seating for fourteen passengers. A contract to lease three C-20As from the manufacturers was announced on 7 June 1983, and these will replace Lockheed C-140B/JetStar VIP transports. An option was also taken on eight additional C-20As for purchase in FY (Fiscal Years) 1983 and 1984, and the first C-20A was delivered on 16 September 1983 to the 89th Military Air Wing at Andrews Air Force Base, Texas.

The Gulfstream SRA-1 is a special multi-mission version of the GIII first publicly displayed at the 1984 Farnborough SBAC show, the prototype, N47449, having first flown on 14 August that year. The SRA-1 is equipped with fully integrated systems for electronic surveillance, reconnaissance, maritime patrol and sea surface surveillance, and anti-submarine warfare. Its interior can rapidly be rearranged for carrying VIPs, as an 18-passenger personnel transport with flight attendant, for the casevac role with fifteen litter patients and medical staff, or as a freighter carrying up to 6,000lb of priority cargo. The prototype SRA-1 has six underwing hardpoints for external stores, each capable of carrying up to 2,000lb. McDonnell Douglas Harpoon anti-ship missiles, Hughes AGM-65 Maverick TV-guided air-to-surface missiles, Sting Ray torpedoes or Paveway laser-guided bombs can be carried under the wings. A 19ft long side-looking radar pod (Motorola SLAMMR) is fitted under the fuselage, and the same cargo door as on the Danish GIIIs is installed; this door can, again, be used to drop flares, survival gear and rescue equipment. There is also an optically flat window for a panoramic camera or one taking infra-red images. The cabin is fitted out with five sensor consoles for use with such maritime patrol systems as the Texas Instruments AN/APS-134(V)2 surveillance radar; infra-red detection systems, MAD equipment and acoustic processors are also installed. The SRA-1 can fly surveillance missions of over nine hours at altitudes of about 45,000ft, covering a total area of 1.5 million square miles.

The Gulfstream IV

With American Jet Industries buying out Grumman's 80 per cent holding in the Grumman American Aviation Corporation in September 1978, the company was renamed the Gulfstream American Corporation and, from 15 November 1982,

the Gulfstream Aerospace Corporation. Production of the Gulfstream II was continued at Savannah, Georgia, and Grumman continued to develop the GIII under contract to Gulfstream after the takeover by American Jet Industries, and to provide after-sales service and support for both the GII and GIII, receiving a royalty on all GII and GIII sales made after 31 December 1979. Development of the GIII led to the G-1159C Gulfstream IV, or GIV, on which design work was begun in April 1982. The GIV prototype, N404GA, was rolled out at Savannah on 11 September 1985 and made its first flight eight days later. It was first displayed in public at the National Business Aircraft Association (NBAA) Convention at New Orleans, on 24–26 September, being flown into the city's Lakefront Airport by Gulfstream's president, Allen Paulson. N404GA had logged only eight hours' flying when the Convention began, but the GIV already had a sizeable backlog of orders, 83 having been sold.

The GIV is almost a new aeroplane, differing from the GIII in having a structurally redesigned wing up to 900lb lighter, with the same degree of sweepback as the GIII's and an advanced sonic 'rooftop' (i.e. very similar to superitical) wing section, a fuselage lengthened by 4ft 6in with a sixth window on each side of the cabin, new landing gear with new brake and steering systems, a carbonfibre rudder, and a flight deck incorporating six advanced Sperry CRT (cathode-ray tube)

Below: The C-20A is the USAF's VIP/staff transport version of the Gulfstream III for the C-SAM (Special Air Missions) role, seating fourteen passengers. This C-20A, the first of three to be ordered, is in service with the 89th Military Air Wing at Andrews Air Force Base, Texas. The USAF ordered eight more GIIIs, seven of which are to be C-20Bs with airframe and avionics improvements. (Gulfstream)

displays and digital avionics. The GIII's Speys are replaced by two 12,420lb s.t. Rolls-Royce RB.183-03 Tay 610-8 turbofans, the Tay being a straightforward development of the Spey 555 with a new front fan to increase the bypass ratio from less than 1:1 to 3:1; this engine also incorporates high-efficiency components developed in Rolls-Royce's advanced engineering and RB.211 programmes, including wide-chord fan blades. The Tay turbofan was made possible by an agreement between Rolls-Royce and Gulfstream announced in March 1983 for a large order for the more fuel-efficient Tay to power the GIV. It is worth recalling that the original Rolls-Royce Tay, a slightly larger and more powerful development of the Nene, which first flew in the second prototype Vickers Viscount in March 1950, was built under licence by Pratt & Whitney as the J48 and as such powered the F9F Panther and Cougar. The GIV's Tays, which have target-type thrust-reversers, combine with the new wing section to give a design range of 5,100 miles at 530–577mph.

The cabin still has standard seating for nineteen passengers, the same as the GIII, and a crew of two or three. The GIV has a maximum ramp weight of 70,200lb, can take off in 5,100ft, and can land in 3,200ft. Steeper approaches and shorter landing runs are made possible by three spoilers on each wing uppersurface at the 12 per cent chord line, just forward of the flaps; these spoilers operate together as air brakes or differentially to assist roll control. A proposed commuter/regional airliner version of the GIV known as the Gulfstream IV-B was announced by the manufacturers in March 1985, the design of this variant having been prompted by enquiries from two US airlines. The IV-B would seat 24 first-class passengers and four crew in a fuselage 18ft 6in longer than that of the GIV, with fuselage 'plugs' forward and aft of the wing centre-section. The GIV's wings, engines, tail unit and systems would remain unchanged. The IV-B would have an empty weight of 36,300lb, a maximum take-off weight of 78,300lb and a maximum range, with IFR reserves, of 4,376 miles.

A corporate airliner variant of the GIV and an all-cargo version known as the Gulfstream Cargoliner have also been proposed. The latter would have 2,230ft^3 of cargo space and a 15,000lb payload capacity. Maximum range would be 3,454 miles, and the Cargoliner would be very useful for small, high-speed consignments or emergency cargoes where urgent delivery were essential.

Below: The roll-out of the Gulfstream IV prototype at Savannah, 11 September 1985. FAA certification of the GIV was expected in September 1986, with deliveries to begin later that year. (Gulfstream)

The AA-1 and AA-5 Lightplanes

Both the Ag-Cat and Gulfstream ranges had proven to be highly successful moves away from Grumman's past dependence on US Navy orders, but further diversification into the cheaper lightplane end of the civil market was sought, and in the autumn of 1972 a merger was planned with the American Aviation Corporation of Cleveland, Ohio. This became effective on 2 January 1973 when the Grumman American Aviation Corporation was revealed as a new subsidiary of the Grumman Corporation, the new company continuing to build, at Cleveland, the two-seat AA-1 Trainer, the very similar Tr-2, and the larger four-seat AA-5 and Traveler, of which over 1,100 examples had already been built by American Aviation. These types were now marketed alongside the Gulfstream II and Super Ag-Cat by Grumman American Aviation.

The AA-1 and Tr-2

The AA-1A Trainer, the design of which had begun in October 1969, was a specialized trainer version of the AA-1 American Yankee, formerly known as the Bede BD-1 and designed by Jim Bede, later to produce the unconventional rear-engined BD-5 which was marketed in piston-engined, jet-powered and sailplane forms. The American Yankee was designed as a low-cost, two-seat, sporting and utility aircraft with aluminium honeycomb construction in the fuselage and metal-to-metal bonding throughout the airframe. The prototype first flew on 11 July 1963, and American Aviation was formed in 1964 to develop and produce it. The company completed its 500th aircraft on 12 March 1971, a total made up of 456 AA-1 American Yankees and 44 AA-1A Trainers, the first production Yankee having first flown on 30 May 1968.

The prototype AA-1A Trainer took off for its maiden flight on 25 March 1970, followed by the first production aircraft on 6 November that year; FAA Certification in the Normal and Utility categories was granted on 14 January 1971. The Trainer differed from the Yankee chiefly in having a modified wing section with revised leading and trailing edges, as well as dual controls as standard, some changes in equipment, and main wheels with lower tyre pressures. A different propeller was available optionally for improved cruising performance. Among the earlier customers for the AA-1A Trainer was Philippine Air Lines, for whom an order for ten for use as primary trainers was announced in January 1972. The 1974 model, designated AA-1B, featured new, bucket-type seats for the two pilots, repositioned flight instruments and other accessories and a quieter cabin. The AA-1B was offered in Standard Trainer, Basic Trainer and Advanced Trainer variants with differing instrumentation and other equipment. The 1977 model, designated AA-1C, featured a more powerful Lycoming 0-235-L2C 'flat four' engine of 115hp driving a Sensenich two-blade, fixed-pitch, metal propeller, and suitable for operation on 100-octane, low-lead-level fuel, instead of the 108hp Lycoming 0-235-C2C and McCauley two-blade propeller of earlier versions. The AA-1C also featured a larger tailplane and elevators, as well as improved sound-proofing and dual shock absorbers on the nosewheel unit, while wheel spats were now standard. The AA-1C was also offered in a variant known as the T-Cat, which had some additional instrumentation and equipment.

All the AA-1 variants have side-by-side seating for two people under a large, transparent, sliding canopy, with an optional seat for a child and space for 100lb of baggage aft of the seats. The fixed nosewheel undercarriage has cantilever, leaf-spring type mainwheel legs of fibreglass and a tubular steel nose gear with a large, free-swivelling fork holding the nosewheel; wheel spats are optional on the AA-1A and AA-1B. The Alclad wing skin and ribs are attached to the tube-type, circular-section main spar by adhesive bonding, and the main spars serve as integral fuel tanks, giving a total capacity of 24 US gallons. There are refuelling points at the wing tips. The ailerons are of bonded construction, with honeycomb ribs and Alclad skin, and the plain flaps, rudder and elevators are of very similar design. The fuselage has an aluminium honeycomb cabin section, the use of honeycomb eliminating false floors and making possible a greater usable cabin space relative to the cross-sectional area. The fin and two tailplanes are interchangeable, and are also of adhesive-bonded aluminium.

The Tr-2 variant, introduced in October 1971, was very similar to the AA-1A Trainer, but was intended to meet the dual roles of advanced trainer and sports lightplane with de luxe equipment; it had virtually all the optional extras of equipment of the AA-1A as standard features. When marketed in parallel with the AA-1C it was renamed Lynx, equipped to a very similar standard as the T-Cat variant of the AA-1C, with certain additional items.

The AA-5 and Traveler

The AA-5 and its de luxe variant the Traveler are enlarged versions of the AA-1 series seating a pilot and three passengers in a more commodious cabin. The wing span is increased by 7ft, and the chord is greater, while the fuselage is slightly longer and the tail surfaces are enlarged, with a dorsal and ventral fin added and anti-spin fillets at the tailplane leading edge roots. A 150hp Lycoming 0-320-E2G 'flat four' engine is fitted, driving a McCauley two-blade, fixed-pitch, metal propeller; the total fuel capacity is now 38 US gallons in two integral wing tanks, there being refuelling points in the wing upper surfaces. Design of the AA-5 began in June 1970 and was quickly completed, the prototype making its maiden flight on 21 August that year; FAA certification was granted on 12 November 1971. The

Traveler de luxe variant of the AA-5 incorporates as standard various instruments and extra items of equipment that were optional on the AA-5.

The 1974 model AA-5, to which the name Traveler now applied (the previous variant of this name now becoming the AA-5 Traveler Deluxe) introduced the same improvements featured on the AA-1B Trainer, such as new, bucket-type seats for the pilots; in addition, the rearmost cabin window on each side was extended by 1ft, the baggage compartment was enlarged, with an external door to it on the port side, and the dorsal fin was restyled. The Traveler Deluxe now featured a single-axis autopilot, and the 1976 model of this variant was renamed Cheetah when marketed alongside that year's AA-5A, having dual controls as standard, as well as various extra instruments that were previously optional. The AA-5A also featured a redesigned engine cowling, and the ventral fin was now deleted from both the AA-5A and Cheetah. In place of the 38 US gallons standard tankage, these models could now be fitted optionally with two integral fuel tanks in the wings with a total capacity of

52.6 US gallons. The AA-5B, introduced late in 1974, differed from the AA-5A in having the more powerful Lycoming 0-360-A4K 'flat four' engine of 180hp driving a McCauley two-blade, fixed-pitch, metal propeller, and the optional 52.6 US gallons fuel tankage of the AA-5A was made standard. The Tiger was the de luxe variant of the AA-5B, having the same additional instruments and equipment as the Cheetah. Production of the basically equipped AA-5 Traveler ceased in 1977, although that of the de luxe Cheetah and Tiger models continued, the 1,000th Tiger being delivered on 21 November 1978.

The GA-7 and Cougar

Grumman American's first original design was the GA-7 four-seat light twin, the first flight of which was announced on 20 December 1974. This aircraft, known as the Cougar in its de luxe version, was designed mainly for business use and for private pilots who already have IFR experience in high-powered, single-engined lightplanes. The production prototype GA-7, registered N877X, first flew on 14 January 1977, and first production deliveries began in February 1978. The powerplants offered are two 160hp Lycoming 0-320-D1D 'flat four' engines driving Hartzell two-blade, constant-speed, fully feathering, metal propellers. The possibilities of a turboprop version of the GA-7 were considered, although this was never built. The Cougar has, as standard, radio aids that are optional on the GA-7, and certain additional instruments and equipment, as well as dual controls. There is provision for lightweight radio antennae in the nose cone.

The all-metal structure is basically similar to the AA-1 and AA-5 series, with a two-spar, light alloy wing with skins attached to the ribs and spars by metal-to-metal bonding; the single-slotted, Fowler-type flaps are electrically operated. The fuselage cabin section, like that of the AA-1, is of aluminium honeycomb construction, with a semi-monocoque rear fuselage using metal-to-metal bonding. Baggage can be carried aft of the rear seats, and there is another 12ft^3 of baggage space in the nose. The nosewheel retracts forwards and the main gear units

retract outwards into the wings. The two integral wing tanks have a total capacity of 118 US gallons.

The Grumman Corporation's 80 per cent holding in Grumman American Aviation was, it was announced, bought out on 1 September 1978 by American Jet Industries Inc. of Van Nuys, California, which made a cash offer to the holders of the remaining 20 per cent of stock. This was accepted and, as a result, Grumman American ceased to be a Grumman subsidiary and took the name Gulfstream American Corporation, which was changed to Gulfstream Aerospace Corporation on 15 November 1982. At the time of AJI's take-over it had built over 4,000 aircraft, and the head office and works continued at Savannah, Georgia, whither the company had moved from the former American Aviation works at Cleveland, Ohio. AJI specialized in the modification and repair of all types of executive aircraft and airliners, including all-cargo and passenger-cargo conversions of the Convair 580, the Fairchild Hiller FH-227 and Lockheed Electra turbo-props, the Electra being fitted by AJI with a big cargo door, a strengthened floor and

Above: The AA-5A and its de luxe variant the Cheetah (formerly called the Traveler De Luxe) featured a redesigned engine cowling, the ventral fin of the AA-5 and Traveler being deleted. This is a Cheetah. (Author)

Below: The AA-5B and its de luxe variant the Tiger (the latter is depicted) differed from the AA-5A in having the more powerful Lycoming 0-360-A4K engine and a greater fuel capacity. (Author)

a palletized cargo loading system. AJI had also devised turboprop conversions of the Cessna 402 and 414 light twins, which became the Turbo Star 402 and Turbo Star Pressurized 414 when fitted with Allison 250 turboprops.

AJI also designed the unorthodox Hustler Model 400 six-passenger executive transport, which in its original form had an 850shp PT6A-41 turboprop in the nose and a 718lb s.t. Williams WR19-3-1 turbofan in the rear fuselage as a standby engine. The Hustler Model 400 prototype, N400AJ, first flew on 11 January 1978 powered only by the PT6A-41, and it was later decided that the Williams standby turbofan would be replaced by a Pratt & Whitney JT15D-1 to produce the Hustler Model 500. This involved some design changes, including an increase in fuselage length, and later still the PT6A-41 was replaced by a Garrett TPE 331-10 turboprop. These powerplant changes and other development work on the Hustler were carried out by Gulfstream American, who also devised the Peregrine 600 two-seat jet trainer based on the Hustler 500 and designed as a replacement for the USAF's Cessna T-37s. This had the Hustler's forward engine replaced by a new front fuselage seating two side by side, and no wing-tip tanks. The powerplant was a 3,000lb s.t. JT15D-3 turbofan, and a version with two 1,200lb s.t. Williams WR44 turbofans, fed by two

dorsal NACA intakes and tandem seating was also studied, as well as a six-seater executive version with the same engines. The Peregrine first flew on 22 May 1981, but in the end neither it nor the Hustler went into production.

Gulfstream American continued to build the AA-1C and T-Cat/Lynx, the AA-5, Cheetah and Tiger variants, the GA-7 and the Cougar for a time after the AJI take-over, but production of the AA-1 and AA-5 range was ended after AJI's acquisition of what was now Gulfstream American had been completed, and some time later GA-7 and Cougar production also ceased. Marketing of the Super Ag-Cat and Turbo Ag-Cat variants continued until responsibility for these aircraft was taken over by Schweizer in 1981, as related in the previous chapter. In 1985 Gulfstream Aerospace was bought out by the Chrysler Corporation, which wanted to diversify away from car manufacture and needed to benefit from aerospace and avionics technology. Gulfstream retains its identity and continues with the GIII and GIV executive jets, but its Turbo Commander range of light turboprop twins, acquired in 1981 from Rockwell International's General Aviation Division, is now up for sale. With the disposal of its light aircraft and executive jet range, Grumman has thus reverted to its former role as a manufacturer of combat aircraft mainly for the US Navy.

Above: The GA-7 four-seater light twin and its de luxe variant the Cougar (seen here) was the last type produced by Grumman American before it assumed the name Gulfstream American. (Author)

Ravens and Forward-Swept Wings

As related in Chapter 6, Grumman's experience with the pioneer variable-sweep XF10F-1 Jaguar led to its collaboration with General Dynamics as an associate contractor on the F-111, Grumman designing and manufacturing the undercarriage, rear fuselage, tailplane and arrester gear for the USAF's F-111A and the Navy's F-111B versions. The latter was intended as a carrier-based fleet defence fighter with up to six Hughes AIM-54 Phoenix air-to-air missiles, and had a wing span 7ft greater than that of the F-111A. The first F-111B, assembled by Grumman, had its maiden flight on 18 May 1965. Seven development F-111Bs were built, the first five with Pratt & Whitney TF30-P-1 turbofans and the last two with the more potent TF30-P-12 engines intended to power the two dozen production F-111Bs on order; the seventh and last development -B was used as a test-bed for the Phoenix missile. But the F-111B failed to meet the Navy's requirements, and in April 1968 Congress called a halt to its further development, a decision which led directly to the procurement of the F-14 Tomcat.

The EF-111 Raven

Controversy had surrounded the F-111 since its inception. The whole concept of a single type of fighter-bomber to meet all the future tactical needs of both the US Air Force and the US Navy seemed to have resulted in an excessively demanding specification, which called for a maximum speed of about Mach 2.5 and enough range to fly between any two airfields in the world in one day, as well as the ability to make short take-offs and landings from rough forward airstrips and to carry a full range of conventional and nuclear weapons. Not altogether surprisingly, perhaps, the F-111A at first proved to be grossly overweight, with excessive drag, and to suffer from severe problems in its propulsion, structure and systems. The F-111A was cleared for service only after a tremendous effort and made its operational début over South-East Asia in March 1968, but the sudden loss of three of the first six aircraft not long afterwards caused further controversy. The losses were eventually ascribed to a faulty weld in the tailplane power unit. Later variants such as the F-111D and F-111F are much

Below: The General Dynamics F-111B was a carrier-based fleet defence fighter variant of the F-111 for which Grumman designed and built the undercarriage, rear fuselage, tailplane and arrester gear. It had a wing span 7ft greater than that of the F-111A and was to carry six Phoenix air-to-air missiles. However, the aircraft failed to meet the US Navy's requirements and was cancelled. (Grumman)

Left: Seen here over RAF Upper Heyford, Oxfordshire, the second prototype EF-111A Raven (66-041) was the first to be fitted with the complete ECM jamming system. The fin tip pod, similar to that of the EA-6B Prowler in shape, houses the Raytheon AN/ALQ-99E receiver and antennae. (Grumman)

Left: Another view of the second prototype Raven. The EF-111A carries a pilot and electronic warfare officer (EWO), and has a more powerful electrical system than that installed in the F-111A, to cater for the extra avionics. (Grumman)

improved, and have enabled General Dynamics to put the early F-111 difficulties behind it.

The F-111A's initial operational deployment in South-East Asia had revealed shortcomings, despite special preparations under the 'Harvest Reaper' programme to provide these aircraft with advanced ECM equipment to penetrate enemy airspace. The lack of adequate and effective ECM jamming was one of several factors contributing to the F-111A's problems in Vietnam and the limited success it enjoyed in this theatre. Its role here had been an essentially supporting one, and included mounting secondary strikes to coincide with the 'Linebacker II' raids over North Vietnam by Guam-based Boeing B-52 Stratofortresses during December 1972.

By this time the growing potential of the Soviet-built air defence systems in eastern Europe, with their updated SAM batteries and their new interceptor fighters with sophisticated ECM equipment, had given the Warsaw Pact countries an acknowledged lead in the field of electronic warfare, and demanded better tactical jamming capabilities for the NATO air forces. In 1972–73 a pro-

gramme was accordingly initiated to convert F-111As into EF-111A electronic warfare aircraft and to evaluate their ability to provide ECM jamming coverage. Design study contracts were awarded to General Dynamics and Grumman by the USAF in 1974, and in January 1975 the award of an $85.9 million contract to Grumman was announced for the conversion of two F-111As into EF-111A prototypes. The EF-111A would feature the Raytheon AN/ALQ-99E tactical jamming system (an updated version of that in the EA-6B Prowler) which, with its associated transmitters, was mounted in the weapons bay, with the transmitter antennae covered by a narrow, 16ft long, canoe-shaped radome. A partially modified F-111A, fitted with the weapons bay radome only, first flew on 15 December 1975; the fully aerodynamic EF-111A prototype, 66-049, with the ventral radome and the fin tip pod similar in shape to that of the EA-6B Prowler, housing the AN/ALQ-99E receiver and antennae, first flew from Grumman's Calverton, New York, facility on 10 March 1977. The complete jamming system was first flown on 17 May that year on the second EF-111A prototype,

66-041. Grumman's flight-testing of the prototypes required 84 sorties covering 215 hours over a period of three and a half months, and further USAF testing involved 78 more flights covering 258 hours over six months.

The AN/ALQ-99E is claimed to be the world's most powerful airborne ECM system, and enables the EF-111A to penetrate the densest known electronic defences; even if multiple enemy radars switch to a variety of frequencies, the system's jamming capabilities can handle them at once. It was earlier feared that the powerful jamming system would also jam radars carried by a friendly strike force being escorted by EF-111As, but flight-tests with the two prototypes dispelled this fear. The EF-111A has a crew comprising a pilot and an electronic warfare officer (EWO); the latter is trained and equipped to handle, through computer management, a tactical workload in the shape of hostile threats that previously required several electronics operators and much more equipment. The total weight of the whole AN/ALQ-99E system is about 6,000lb. The EF-111A also has, amongst its more important items of electronics, an AN/ALR-62 (modified) Terminal Threat Warning System, an AN/ALQ-137 (modified) Self-Protection System, a Texas Instruments AN/APQ-110 terrain-following radar and an AN/APQ-160 attack radar. A more powerful electrical system than the F-111A's is featured, to cater for the greater power consumption of all the extra avionics.

Three basic deployment modes are envisaged for the EF-111A – stand-off, penetration and close air support. In the stand-off role EF-111As would operate within their own airspace at the forward edge of the battle area (FEBA); they would orbit out of range of enemy ground-based weapons, and would use their jamming systems to screen the routes of friendly strike aircraft attacking, in a European scenario, the spearheads of a Soviet armoured thrust into western Europe, and also its resupply areas, reserves and SAM installations. In the penetration role, EF-111As would fly with strike aircraft attacking high-priority targets, while in close air support EF-111A escorts would neutralize anti-aircraft radars while the strike force attacked the target.

The two EF-111A prototypes were subsequently brought up to full production standards, and in April 1979 the first conversion contract, for six EF-111As, was signed. A total of 42 F-111As (of the 86 of this variant still operational at the beginning of 1983) are being converted to EF-111As, equipping two squadrons; 32 of these had been delivered by December 1984, and the 42nd was scheduled for delivery by October 1985. The first EF-111A to be delivered to Tactical Air Command for operational use was the updated first prototype 66-049, which arrived at Mountain Home Air Force Base in Idaho in November 1981. The 390th Electronic Combat Squadron became operational in December 1983 with EF-111As.

On 3 February 1984 the first of twelve EF-111As for the United States Air Forces in Europe, 60037, arrived at RAF Upper Heyford, Oxfordshire, to equip

Below: This view of an EF-111A shows well the long underfuselage radome housing the AN/ALQ-99E jamming system transmitter antennae. (Grumman)

the 42nd Electronic Combat Squadron of the 20th Tactical Fighter Wing, which already had three squadrons of F-111Es. Late in 1985 the 42nd ECS came under the control of the 66th Electronic Combat Wing based at Sembach in West Germany, but for reasons of servicing and maintenance the EF-111As continue to be based at Upper Heyford. They are painted in a two-tone grey colour scheme and are coded 'UH' on the tail. The 42nd ECS also operated some F-111Es, which have now been returned to one of the squadrons of the 20th Tactical Fighter Wing. Updating of the EF-111A's tactical jamming system is being undertaken by Grumman to provide improved capability against early warning radars and in GCIs (Ground Controlled Interceptions), and also in surface-to-air missile acquisition. This updating process will have cost about $200 million when completed.

Grumman Subcontract Work

Apart from the EF-111A conversions, and the design and manufacture of the wings and fin and rudder of the new Israeli Lavi fighter-bomber (mentioned below) Grumman is engaged in several important subcontract jobs for other manufacturers. It is building major components of the Sikorsky CH-53E Super Stallion three-turbine, heavy lift helicopter under a contract announced in the spring of 1978. Later a contract was agreed with Boeing for the building of wing centre-sections of the Model 767 wide-body, twin-jet airliner, seating from

216 to 290 passengers, or up to 330 in the stretched Model 767-300. Under a February 1984 contract Grumman is building 270 ship-sets of Rolls Royce Tay engine nacelles and thrust reversers for the Gulfstream IV and the Fokker 100, the slightly larger successor to the F.28 Fellowship.

In August 1984 Grumman received a contract to design and manufacture complete tail sections of the Bell/Boeing Vertol V-22 Osprey advanced tilt-rotor, vertical lift aircraft. Known at first as the JVX, and now as the Joint Services Advanced Vertical Lift aircraft, the V-22 Osprey is intended as a tactical transport for the US Marine Corps, a fast combat rescue aircraft for the USAF and Navy, and an electronic warfare aircraft for the US Army. There is a total requirement for 1,086 Ospreys for the US services, and the first of eight prototypes is scheduled to fly early in 1988. The Osprey will enter service with the Marine Corps in 1991 powered initially by two General Electric T64 turboshafts. Grumman also manufactured wing skins and fibreglass wing tips at its Milledgeville plant for the Fairchild A-10A Thunderbolt II ground attack aircraft, the last of 713 of which was delivered to the US Air Force in February 1984.

During 1984–85 Grumman completed the refurbishing and updating of 40 McDonnell Douglas A-4M Skyhawks for the Royal Malaysian Air Force; Malaysia had bought 88 'mothballed' ex-US Navy A-4s, and Grumman refurbished 34 of these as single-seater fighters and converted six more to TA-4PTM two-seat trainers very similar to earlier TA-4 variants, these having the forward fuselage lengthened by 27¾in to accommodate a TA-4 type tandem cockpit with seating for a pupil under instruction. This rebuilding of single-seaters was necessary because there were no TA-4 variants available from storage. The Malaysian A-4PTMs have updated avionics, two additional outboard underwing pylons and a tail braking parachute, and are equipped with the Hughes Aircraft Angle Rate Bombing System (ARBS). All the Malaysian Skyhawks can carry AIM-9 Sidewinder air-to-air missiles, and twenty of the A-4PTMs are wired for the Hughes AGM-64 Maverick ASM which may be supplied at a later date. The first refurbished A-4PTM for Malaysia flew in April 1984 and the first three were delivered in December that year. All 40 were scheduled to be in service by December 1985.

During the 1970s Grumman signed two important technical agreements with European companies. The first, announced on 7 May 1973, was between the Grumman Corporation and the Federal German manufacturer VFW-Fokker GmbH, and was for the formation of a new joint subsidiary, Grumman Avio Systems Corporation, based at Grand Prairie, Texas. This was licensed to manufacture, sell and service the Aviobridge range of covered passenger gangways or aerobridges connecting an airliner's cabin door to the airport 'finger' or terminal building. The Aviobridge system had been originally designed by Fokker-VFW's Drechtsteden division in the Netherlands. Simultaneously with the formation of Grumman Avio Systems, an initial US order for the supply and installation of ten Mk. 5M apron-drive Aviobridges was announced from the Massachusetts Port Authority for use at Boston's Logan International Airport.

In April 1974 it was announced that Grumman American Aviation was collaborating with the Federal German company Rhein-Flugzeugbau GmbH (RFB), a subsidiary of VFW-Fokker GmbH, in the design and development of a two-seat, ducted-fan, light aircraft known as the

Above: Grumman refurbished and updated forty ex-US Navy McDonnell Douglas A-4M Skyhawks for the Royal Malaysian Air Force during 1984–85. Six were rebuilt as TA-4PTM trainers and 34 were completed as A-4PTM fighters, like M32-07 seen here. (Grumman)

Fanliner. This evolved from RFB's studies of ducted fans, and was powered by a 114hp Audi NSU Ro 135 Wankel-type, two-chamber, rotating piston engine mounted behind the two pilots and driving a pusher propeller with three plastic blades mounted within an annular duct integral with the centre fuselage. The prototype Fanliner, D-EJFL, first flew on 8 October 1973, its wings and tailplane being identical to those of the Grumman American AA-5A Traveler (later renamed Cheetah). It was later fitted with a Dowty-Rotol ducted fan having propellers with three, five or seven blades, and by September 1976 D-EJFL had made 420 flights.

On the 4th of that month the second prototype Fanliner, D-EBFL, took to the air, powered by a 50hp RFB-modified Audi NSU KM 871 Wankel-type rotary piston engine driving a Dowty-Rotol integral ducted fan. The second prototype had a considerably refined airframe compared to the first. Flight tests of the

Below: In 1974 Grumman American began collaborating with Rhein-Flugzeugbau GmbH (RFB) to develop the two-seat Fanliner light aircraft, which was powered by a ducted fan. The first prototype Fanliner, D-EJFL, is seen here; it had the same wings and tailplane as the AA-5A Traveler. (N. B. Wiltshire)

Fanliner showed that the ducted fan system offered a more efficient use of engine power than a conventional piston engine installation, as well as giving a lower cabin noise level and a much quieter external noise level. The pusher layout combined with the nosewheel undercarriage gave much improved cabin visibility and more convenient access for pilot and passenger. The Fanliner was used to evaluate and prove the ducted fan propulsion system and did not enter production, but it did lead to the RFB Fantrainer armed military trainer with an Allison 250 turboshaft and ducted fan propulsion, of which 47 examples are being supplied to the Royal Thai Air Force.

The X-29 Demonstrator

The development of the jet engine had by 1945 provided aircraft designers with enough thrust to bridge the gap between subsonic and supersonic flight but, whereas what happened at supersonic speeds had been fairly well known for many years from studying the flight of projectiles, aerodynamic phenomena at transonic speeds were still little understood. Wartime German research had shown that drag rise and compressibility effects resulting from the formation of shock waves at near-sonic speeds could be postponed by sweeping the wing forwards or backwards: a normal straight wing of, say, 12 per cent thickness/chord ratio may experience shock waves at about Mach 0.85, but shock wave formation can be delayed to perhaps Mach 0.95 either by making the wing thinner or by sweeping it backwards or forwards, so reducing the chordwise airflow velocity and, in effect, presenting a lower thickness/chord ratio to the line of flight for the same physical wing thickness.

Early in 1943 a Junkers design team under *Dipl. Ing.* Hans Wocke started work on a heavy jet bomber, the Ju 287, intended to be faster than any contemporary Allied fighter, and this was originally proposed with a wing swept back 25 degrees to give a speed exceeding Mach 0.8 in level flight. But the exceedingly poor low-speed characteristics of the swept-back wing led Wocke to propose

reversing the wing configuration to forward sweep, this having the same aerodynamic advantages as backward sweep but avoiding the problem of tip stalling: with forward sweep the wing tips would be the last to stall and the highest lift coefficient would be at the wing root, decreasing towards the tip and enabling aileron control to be maintained beyond the main centre-section flow breakaway. The Ju 287 V1 prototype first flew on 16 August 1944 powered by four 1,984lb s.t. Junkers Jumo 004B-1 turbojets, two under the wings and two in nacelles on each side of the forward fuselage, with a Walter 501 rocket pack under each engine pod for assisted take-off. The Ju 287 V1 proved to be pleasant to fly despite its unorthodox wing, and there were no trim changes when the large slotted flaps extending down to 40 degrees were lowered, the ailerons drooping with them through 23 degrees to provide a completely cambered wing for maximum lift coefficients. Wool tufts mounted on the wing and filmed through a cine camera confirmed the initial centre-section flow breakaway and its progressive outward spread, with nose-down pitch occurring only when it reached the ailerons. Although the war's end cut short its further development, the Ju 287 had proven remarkably successful for such an advanced design, and the only major snag had been the wing's aeroelastic behaviour as speed increased.

When details of wartime German research work on wing sweep became available to the Allies, it was eagerly studied in America and soon adopted for high-speed types such as the North American XP-86 Sabre and Boeing B-47 Stratojet, although Britain was at first much more cautious and hesitant about the claims of wing sweep. But it was backward rather than forward sweep that became almost universal for high-speed aircraft during the 1950s, with the XP-86 Sabre setting the fashion with a wing of 35 degrees sweep, having a thickness/chord ratio of 11 per cent at the root and 10 per cent at the tip, and leading-edge slats for better manoeuvrability and for overcoming tip stall. The original Sabre wing was almost identical to one that Messerschmitt had designed for the Me 262 jet fighter but

never fitted. Leading-edge slats had also been featured by Messerschmitt not only for the Me 262 but also for the piston-engined Bf 109 fighter and Bf 108 Taifun lightplane. On most jet fighters wing sweep was typically about 35 degrees at the quarter-chord line, although the Saab J29 'Flying Barrel', the first swept wing fighter to go into squadron service in Europe when deliveries began in May 1951, had a sweep of 25 degrees. The MiG-19, the first production supersonic fighter to go into service outside the USA, had a sweep of 55 degrees at the quarter-chord line, and the English Electric P.1 and Lightning interceptors had a sweep of 60 degrees.

Although some features of the Ju 287, such as its wing- and fuselage-mounted engines and assisted take-off rocket packs, were adapted for later designs such as the B-47 Stratojet, its forward-swept wing for long remained an isolated example of this wing configuration. Only the HFB 320 Hansa 6–9 passenger executive jet, first flown on 21 April 1964, has followed this trend in recent years. This had a forward sweep of 15 degrees at the quarter-chord line, not for transonic flight but to avoid the necessity of taking the main spar through the passenger cabin. Forward sweep remained an unused option for transonic flight largely because as speed increased to near-sonic values aerodynamic stresses would flex the wing so that it twisted leading edge up, thus increasing the angle of attack (and hence the lift) of the outer wing sections, which in turn would increase the air loads and cause further deformation of the wings. The higher the speed the more these forces would increase, until they eventually exceeded the strength of the wing structure and it would fail. With conventional metal construction a forward-swept wing had to be made strong enough to withstand these twisting loads, and this meant a structural weight penalty sufficient to cancel out any aerodynamic benefits of forward sweep. (By contrast a rearward-swept wing would twist leading edge downwards under aerodynamic loads, so reducing the angle of attack and hence the air loads.)

The growing use of very strong and light composite materials in aircraft struc-

Far left: Designed to explore the aerodynamics and technology of forward-swept wings, the Model 712 or X-29A demonstrator/research aircraft features graphite epoxy composite skins to control the twisting of the wing in flight. Canard foreplanes are fitted to reduce supersonic trim drag, and each wing root trailing edge is extended aft to form a strake down the length of the fuselage. (Grumman)

tures in recent years prompted a fresh look at forward sweep, and in 1975 USAF Colonel Norris Krone, on sabbatical leave, completed a Master's thesis entitled 'Divergence Elimination with Advanced Composites'. This showed that the directional properties of carbonfibre laminates could be used to control the twisting of a wing, and thus to overcome the basic structural problem of forward sweep. This became known as aeroelastic tailoring, and meant that the carbonfibre laminates making up the wing skins were swept forward relative to the structural axis along which the wing bent, so that as it twisted upwards the wing upper surface was compressed and the lower surface stretched. The laminated skins, lying at an angle to the wing bending axis, would shear forwards under compression and backwards under tension, the effect of this shearing under load being to generate a nose-down torque which would oppose the forward-swept wing's upward-twisting tendency.

Colonel Krone's Master's thesis served as the germ for the Grumman Model 712 or X-29A FSW (forward-swept wing) demonstrator aircraft intended to explore forward-sweep aerodynamics and technology. The aerodynamic advantages of this include better manoeuvrability, with virtually spin-proof characteristics, better low-speed handling and reduced stalling speeds, and lower drag across the entire operational envelope, particularly at speeds approaching Mach 1 as well as supersonic speeds, thus allowing the use of a less powerful engine. Of especial interest to Grumman was the improvement in transonic performance and manoeuvrability offered by forward sweep, and the X-29A could foreshadow a new generation of FSW tactical aircraft and fighters that will be smaller, lighter, less costly and more efficient than contemporary designs.

Grumman had been studying the benefits of forward sweep for some time, and conducted a series of wind tunnel test programmes on FSW designs funded by the US Defense Advanced Research Projects Agency (DARPA) from 1977, General Dynamics and Rockwell International as well as Grumman receiving FSW feasibility study contracts. Basic design work on the Model 712 FSW demonstrator began in January 1981, this being funded by DARPA and administered by the USAF's Flight Dynamics Laboratory at Wright-Patterson Air Force Base; in September that year the Model 712 was given the USAF designation X-29A. On 22 December 1981 the award of an $80 million contract to Grumman was announced, to build, ground-test and flight-test two single-seat X-29A demonstrators, and construction of the first began the following month. No. 2 X-29A was used for the formal roll-out ceremony on 27 August 1984, and the next day the first prototype started taxiing trials. The latter made its first flight on 14 December 1984 at NASA's Dryden Flight Research Center at Edwards Air Force Base in the hands of Grumman chief test pilot Chuck Sewell, who described its handling as 'absolutely flawless – outstanding'.

On 12 March 1985 the X-29A prototype was delivered to the USAF Aeronautical Systems Division, which handed it over to NASA, the first flight by a NASA pilot being made on 2 April. By September 1985 the X-29A had made nineteen flights, in which it had reached speeds up to Mach 0.75 and maximum loadings of 5.2g. An improved back-up flight control system was then installed, and the NASA test programme began to explore stability and controls loads, flutter and wing divergence at speeds up to Mach 1.5 and heights up to 40,000ft.

The X-29A's low/mid-set wings have a forward sweep of 33° 44' at the quarter-chord line and no dihedral. They are of supercritical section (i.e. designed to cruise at above the critical Mach number) and are exceptionally thin, with a thickness/chord ratio of 6.2 per cent at the root, tapering to 4.9 per cent at the tip. A variable-camber trailing edge consisting of full-span, three-section hinged flaps/ailerons ('flaperons') changes the wing shape to match flight conditions, these being operated symmetrically for pitch control and asymmetrically for control in the rolling plane. The flaperons are hinged at two chordwise locations to provide discrete variable camber. To reduce cost, no leading edge flaps or slats are fitted, and there is no wing de-icing system. The wing roots are swept aft to alleviate some of the root stall problems associated with forward sweep, and each wing root trailing edge is extended aft to form a strake down the length of the fuselage, each strake terminating in a controllable flap. These strakes add area behind the centre of gravity, thus improving directional stability. Close-coupled, variable-incidence, aluminium alloy canard foreplanes are fitted to reduce supersonic trim drag. No tailplane is fitted, the fin and rudder being swept back and like the foreplanes, having no de-icing.

The wings are of safe-life metal/composite construction, with a titanium front spar located at 15 per cent chord, this material being chosen to cater for the high loadings that forward sweep imposes on the front part of the wings. The root attachment ribs are also of titanium, but the rest of the wing substructure is of aluminium, including the rear spar at 70 per cent chord. To achieve the aeroelastic tailoring necessary for forward sweep, graphite epoxy composite skins are used, a total of 752 plies or thicknesses being employed, each wing comprising 156 layers at its thickest part. These skins are set at an angle to the wing's structural or bending axis to generate nose-down torque, and are mechanically fastened to the one-piece wing substructure, which is then attached to the fuselage.

A standard Northrop F-5A provided the forward fuselage and cockpit, this actually being taken from US Air Force surplus F-5A stocks held in storage at

Davis-Monthan Air Force Base in Arizona. An F-5A nose landing gear is fitted, and small strakes have been added to the tip of the nose, which has a probe with pitch and yaw vanes. The pilot has a Martin-Baker GRQ7A ejection seat. The fuselage is new aft of the cockpit bulkhead, and is a semi-monocoque, fail-safe, aluminium alloy structure. To reduce costs many off-the-shelf components such as General Dynamics F-16 main landing gear units are used, as well as F-16 integrated servo actuators for the canard foreplanes, flaperons and rudder. All the undercarriage units retract forwards, and there is a small notch in the trailing edge of each canard surface to clear the mainwheel doors. Goodrich air-cooled carbon disc brakes are fitted, with Goodyear anti-skid units. The powerplant is a General Electric F404-GE-400 afterburning turbofan of about 16,000lb s.t., this same engine powering the McDonnell Douglas

Below: The first prototype X-29A takes off on its first flight at NASA's Dryden Flight Research Center, Edwards Air Force Base, 14 December 1984. (Grumman)

Left: The second prototype X-29A. A standard Northrop F-5A forward fuselage and cockpit is incorporated into the airframe, and to reduce costs many off-the-shelf components such as F-16 main landing gear units have been used. (Grumman)

F-18 Hornet. There are two fuel cells in the fuselage and an integral tank in each wing strake, giving a total capacity of 3,978lb. There is no provision for in-flight refuelling.

The X-29A has an advanced Honeywell triple-redundant, digital, fly-by-wire control system, and the aircraft is designed to be highly unstable longitudinally. The centre of gravity (CG) is located at no less than 35 per cent of the MAC (mean aerodynamic chord) aft of the combined wing and foreplane aerodynamic centre. It was originally planned to make the aircraft only 20 per cent unstable, and the canard foreplane was sized accordingly at 15 per cent of the wing area, but tunnel tests showed this to be too small, the foreplane running out of control power in transonic manoeuvres, and so its size was increased to 20 per cent of the wing area (or 35.96ft^2), thereby increasing longitudinal static instability to 35 per cent. At supersonic speeds the X-29A becomes neutrally stable, ensuring minimum trim drag throughout the flight envelope.

The canard foreplane's purpose is not only to act as the primary pitch control and to reduce supersonic trim drag, but also to overcome the disadvantageous root stall characteristics of a forward-swept wing, which leads it to generate less lift than an aft-swept wing. The canard foreplane does this because its downwash reduces the effective angle of attack (AOA) on the wing behind it, thus delaying the root stall and enabling the main wing to achieve its full lift potential. With the wing tips remaining effective at angles of attack beyond 80 degrees, the X-29A is virtually spin-proof, and the high approach angles made possible by forward sweep would be an obvious asset for carrier-based aircraft. The wing strake flaps can be raised or lowered 30 degrees each way, and act in a similar fashion to elevators, augmenting the foreplanes at low speeds, to rotate the X-29A on take-off or to apply nose-down pitch from a deep stall. Later in the flight test programme these flaps will be separated from the automatic camber control of the flaperons for high AOA trials.

Grumman has invested $40 million of its own funds in the X-29A programme, and in due course the aircraft will be used to explore other advanced concepts relating to cockpits, weapons carriage, two-dimensional exhaust nozzles and techniques to reduce the landing speed of FSW aircraft still further. Grumman has estimated that an FSW design could generate between 10 and 20 per cent less drag for a given mission, and could be made between 5 and 25 per cent smaller than an equivalent aircraft with backswept wings, because, as noted earlier, less drag means that a smaller engine (requiring less fuel) can be installed.

An important 'spin-off' from the X-29A programme is that in mid-1983 Grumman was chosen to design, develop and build the graphite-epoxy composite wings, fin and rudder for the new Israel Aircraft Industries Lavi single-engined, multi-role, canard delta fighter-bomber. The first prototype Lavi is scheduled to make its maiden flight in early 1987, and the type will replace A-4 Skyhawks and Kfir fighter-bombers in the *Heyl Ha'Avir*. Grumman is responsible for the initial production of twenty wing and fin ship-sets for the Lavi, which will feature, among other advanced technologies, a quadruplex-redundant, digital fly-by-wire control system allowing relaxed stability.

Grumman in Space

Grumman was early into the space race, and was given the task of designing and building the Lunar Module *Eagle* from which Neil Armstrong became the first man to set foot on the Moon's surface on 21 July 1969. But the company's first major space project was the Orbiting Astronomical Observatory, known as OAO, which was initiated in February 1959 when NASA called a meeting of astronomers interested in the concept of an observatory in space able to track distant stars and measure such phenomena as ultra-violet radiation in space free from the Earth's atmosphere with its cloud cover, haze and industrial pollution.

The Orbiting Astronomical Observatory

In August 1959 preliminary specifications for the OAO, which had been drawn up by NASA's Ames Research Center, were circulated to US industry, and engineers at Ames also built a prototype full-scale stabilized platform to study the problems involved in orientating the satellite. The final specification for the OAO was drawn up in December 1959, and eleven companies submitted formal proposals, Grumman being selected as prime contractor and systems manager for the OAO during the following October. Contracts were later placed for four flight models of the OAO.

Designed to be launched from an Agena or Centaur upper-stage rocket mounted on an Atlas intercontinental ballistic missile converted to a launch vehicle, the OAO consisted of a standard eight-sided aluminium shell measuring 9ft 10in long and 6ft 8in wide. Into this shell one or more separate experiments, with appropriate measuring devices, could be fitted for each flight; also installed were General Electric stabilization and control equipment, an IBM and Radiation data

processing system, telemetry instruments and a command system enabling it to be 'locked' on to any selected star by remote control from the ground. Paddles at the sides, with a total area of 264ft^2, were covered with more than 108,000 solar cells to generate the power required by the OAO and its payload. The total weight of the OAO, with about 1,000lb of payload, was approximately 4,400lb, and the maximum span over the paddles was 21ft 2in. A 48in diameter cylindrical chamber running the full length of the OAO could be used to house astronomical equipment such as telescopes, with reflecting mirrors up to 38in in diameter. The cover plate over the end of this chamber was designed to function as a sunshade when open in orbit.

A major advantage of the OAO was that it was potentially stable enough to track a star with an accuracy as high as one-tenth of a second of arc. Results of experiments on board were transmitted to

Below: The Orbiting Astronomical Observatory was designed to make observations and measurements in space, free from the Earth's cloud cover and haze. The solar cell-covered paddles at the sides generated the power for the OAO's payload of scientific experiments carried in the octagonal aluminium shell. (Grumman)

the ground by the telemetry system in digital data on wide band, and information on experiments and satellite orientation in real time on narrow band. A memory system could store up to 102,400 items of information for later read-out when the OAO was over ground stations, and an on-board tape recorder enabled the continuous recording of spacecraft and experiment status data to be made for subsequent playback to ground stations. The first OAO, designated OAO-1, was launched from Cape Kennedy on 8 April 1966 by an Atlas-Agena, but unfortunately it suffered a power failure and no experimental data were transmitted, although, except for the component failure that caused the loss of power, the subsystems were shown to operate as designed. OAO-1 carried four experiments to study stars and other celestial objects in the ultra-violet, X-ray and gamma ray spectral regions.

Its successor, OAO-2, launched on 7 December 1968 by an Atlas-Centaur, was much more successful. It carried eleven telescopes, and when it was finally shut down on 13 February 1973 during its 22,000th orbit of the Earth it had completed one of the most productive careers of any unmanned spacecraft up to that time. OAO-2 carried two major experiments on board, that devised by the University of Wisconsin to measure the brightness of ultra-violet emissions from the stars, and that of the Smithsonian Astrophysical Observatory to map ultra-violet radiation over the entire sky. For the latter task OAO-2 carried four independent, electronically recording, telescopic Schwarzschild sensing units, each employing an imaging uvicon system to map the radiations. The Smithsonian experiment completed its mission on 7 January 1972 after making more than 8,500 observations, while the Wisconsin experiment viewed 1,920 celestial objects during 14,060 observations up to OAO-2's final shut-down. A great advantage of the 'observatory in space' concept was that during its long lifetime the space environment did not in any way degrade the OAO-2's telescopes, whereas telescopes on Earth are adversely affected by pollution and the effects of gravity.

The third in the OAO series, desig-

nated OAO-B, was launched on 30 November 1970, but because of problems with the Atlas-Centaur launch vehicle it failed to achieve the correct altitude and velocity. Apparently one half of the protective shroud did not release, and the added weight of this precluded the success of the mission. The fourth and last OAO, designated OAO-C, was named *Copernicus* after the famous Polish astronomer who lived from AD 1473 to 1543. It was launched by an Atlas-Centaur D on 21 August 1972 into a near-circular orbit at a height of 460 miles, and weighed 4,900lb compared to the 4,400lb of OAO-2, which represented the heaviest scientific payload launched by the United States up to that time. It carried a 32in reflecting ultra-violet telescope developed by Princeton University space scientists to study cosmic gas and dust by observing them against the stars and claimed to be capable of viewing an object the size of a football at a distance of 400 miles.

Copernicus also carried a battery of three smaller X-ray telescopes developed by University College, London, and after an eight-day check-out period this OAO became fully operational on 29 August 1972. By February 1974 it had exceeded its mission objectives by one year, and the two Princeton and University College experiments had made a total of 7,906 observations of 415 unique objects in space. *Copernicus* still had many months of

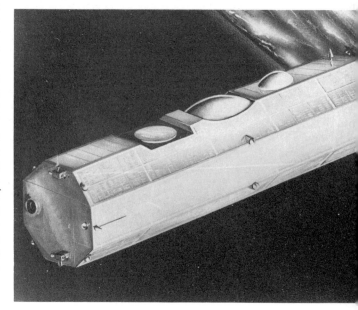

Below: An artist's impression of the projected High Energy Astronomy Observatory (HEAO). About three times as big as the OAO, it would have carried a payload of about 12,500lb of scientific experiments when launched by a Martin Titan IIIC in 1974, but it remained a project only. (Grumman)

useful life ahead. Experience both with OAO-C and with OAO-2 showed that the pointing accuracy by which the telescopes were aimed, designed to be maintained at one-tenth of a second of arc, has proven to be three times more precise than this objective, thus permitting the optics on board to be pointed with an unusual degree of precision and contributing much to the success of experimental observations. The pointing of the optics was programmed remotely from the Goddard Space Flight Center, through delicate adjustments to the attitude of the OAO itself.

Following the success of the OAO series, Grumman acted as prime contractor for a much bigger observatory in space known as the High Energy Astronomy Observatory, or HEAO, for which NASA requested initial funding of $11 million in FY72. HEAO would have been the largest unmanned spacecraft ever to be launched by NASA, with a total weight of approximately 20,000lb, of which 12,500lb would have been made up by the payload of scientific experiments. HEAO would have been 30ft long and 9ft in diameter over its octagonal cross-section – about three times the size of the OAO – and would have been launched by a Martin Titan IIIC in 1974. HEAO, however, remained a project only, partly because manned spacecraft such as the S-IVB Orbital Workshop, or Skylab, were to assume a position to take over from unmanned spacecraft in making scientific observations from space.

The Lunar Excursion Module

The Apollo project had as its goal to land two men on the surface of the Moon by 1970 and to return them safely to Earth, using a lunar rendezvous technique. It was announced by NASA on 28 November 1961 that the organization chosen to develop the Apollo three-man spacecraft, after an evaluation of five industry proposals, was North American's Space and Information Systems Division, which became North American Rockwell's Space Division in September 1967. Contracts were later placed for the production of twenty Apollo spacecraft, sixteen so-called 'boilerplate' versions of the Apollo, ten full-scale mock-ups, five engineering

simulators and evaluators, and two mission simulators. The design of the Apollo spacecraft was based on the 'building block' or modular concept, in which there were three major components or modules. These were the Command Module housing the three-man crew, the Service Module housing fuel, electrical power supplies and propulsion units, and the Lunar Module (LM), designed to be detached from the Command/Service Modules in orbit and carry two astronauts down to explore the Moon's surface.

The choice of Grumman from nine competing companies to design and produce the Lunar Module, the contract covering the manufacture of fifteen flight models and ten test vehicles, was announced on 7 November 1962. The Command Module was 10ft 7in high, with a launch weight of about 13,000lb, and consisted of an inner pressurized compartment of aluminium honeycomb construction and an outer structure of stainless steel honeycomb, with a plastic ablative heat shield coating over the entire

Above: This model of a Lunar Module shows the egress platform unfolded and an astronaut with survival pack on the descent ladder. Note the clusters of four very small Marquardt R-4D single chamber rocket engines at each corner of the ascent stage for precise manoeuvring and control of the Lunar Module. (Grumman)

outer surface. The Service Module was 24ft 9in high and of aluminium honeycomb construction, and weighed about 53,000lb. The total weight of the Apollo spacecraft on the first Moon journeys was about 95,000lb. North American Rockwell was responsible for the design and production of the Command and Service Modules.

Apollos 5 and 7 were launched by the very large Saturn 1B launch vehicle, made up of an S-1B first stage by Chrysler and an S-IVB stage by McDonnell Douglas; this could put a payload of 45,000lb into a 120-mile orbit. The Apollo 4, 6 and later missions from No. 8 onwards were launched by the even larger three-stage Saturn 5, which had an S-1C first stage by Boeing, an S-II second stage by North American Rockwell, and an S-IVB third stage by McDonnell Douglas. The Saturn 5 could send a payload of 50 tons to the vicinity of the Moon, and its height with payload was no less than 353ft 5in.

The Lunar Module was, in effect, a two-stage vehicle, each stage having its own liquid-propellant rocket engine, the 10,500lb s.t. TRW Systems descent engine in its lower (descent) stage effecting a gentle touch-down on the Moon's surface. When their lunar mission was completed, the two astronauts took off in the ascent stage (the Module's upper half), the descent stage being left on the Moon's surface and serving as a launch platform. The two stages were separated by firing four explosive bolts at the stage interconnections, and the interstage wiring was also severed explosively. The ascent stage was powered by its 3,500lb s.t. (maximum thrust in vacuum conditions) Rocketdyne RS18 engine to rendezvous again with the Command/Service Modules, after which the Lunar Module was jettisoned and the Apollo returned to Earth, and to a splashdown in the Pacific. In addition to the main ascent and descent engines, the Module was controlled on its way down to and away from the lunar surface by four clusters of Marquardt R-4D liquid-propellant, reaction-control, single-chamber rocket engines, each of which produced a maximum thrust of 100lb in a vacuum and was only 13.5in long overall; a cluster of these was mounted at each corner of the ascent

stage, thus enabling the Module to be manoeuvred with great precision.

The LM was stowed behind the Command and Service Modules and in front of the S-IVB third stage, being housed in a cylindrical adapter fairing (the Adapter Module) on the S-IVB; this fairing was 28ft long, with a diameter of 22ft at the base tapering to 12.8ft at the top, and was made up of eight panels that hinged backwards like petals to allow the LM to be extracted by the Command Module after a transposition and docking manoeuvre. This involved separating the Command/Service Modules from the expended S-IVB stage, blowing away the adapter panels around the LM. The Command/Service Modules were then flown out a short distance ahead, turned through 180 degrees by the use of gas-jet controls, and gently brought back so that a probe on top of the Command Module entered a drogue with a twelve-position latch in the top of the LM ascent stage; the LM was then pulled away and extracted from the S-IVB stage, which separated from the rest of the spacecraft. After docking a mid-course correction was applied to achieve the correct trajectory for the Moon.

The action of docking now made a pressure-tight seal between Command and Lunar Modules, and to pass freely from one to the other along the connecting tunnel between them the astronauts had first to open the latch covers at each end of it and remove the docking fixture. The tunnel was now free of obstruction and transfer was simply a matter of crawling through to emerge into the LM via the hatch in the roof of the compartment aft of the control cabin. The LM cabin was pressurized at the same value, 5lb/in^2, as the Command Module, and both hatches opened inward, the normal cabin pressure forcing each hatch into its seal. To open either hatch it was necessary to depressurize the cabin by means of a dump valve. The ECS (Environmental Control System) supplied the cabin atmosphere, and maintained its pressure, temperature and humidity for a maximum of 48 hours (a figure later extended), and was supplied by two gaseous tanks. To rendezvous with the Command/Service Module after separation, the astronauts had an overhead docking window in the left side of the Lunar Module.

The Lunar Module was completely self-sufficient, being equipped with all the subsystems necessary for life-support, guidance and navigation, attitude control, and communications. The two astronauts stood side by side, facing two triangular windows that gave them forward and downward vision, and they were supported in a harness that provided stability under varying conditions of gravity and helped them to withstand the impact of a lunar landing. Instrumentation was mounted on a large central panel, and the astronauts' cabin, which had a volume of $235ft^3$, was of course pressurized. A forward hatch opened on to a small egress platform and ladder mounted on one of the descent stage's four landing legs, this enabling the astronauts to climb down on to the lunar surface. The landing legs remained folded until the Module arrived in lunar orbit; the landing gear uplocks were then explosively released and springs in each drive-out mechanism extended the landing gear, each leg being locked into place by its two down-lock mechanisms.

The LM ascent stage was 12ft 4in high and the descent stage 10ft 7in, the Module's overall width being 14ft 1in. Its weight on launching from Earth was 32,000lb (and 33,205lb for the Apollo II Moon landing). Apart from its engine, which was gimballed and could be throttled, the descent stage also housed the ALSEP (Apollo Lunar Surface Experiment Package).

After some preliminary testing of Apollo components and systems, with particular reference to the escape system, had been carried out with the use of Little Joe II boosters produced by the Convair division of General Dynamics, the first launch into orbit of a 'boilerplate' Apollo Command Module was made on 28 May 1964 by a Saturn SA-6. The first three flights by Saturn 1B, the developed and uprated Saturn 1, took place on 26 February, 5 July and 25 August 1966 and were designated AS-201, AS-203 and AS-202 respectively. These flights were all successful and unmanned, and served to test the space vehicle's compatibility and structural integrity, the Command Module heat shield's suitability for re-

entry speeds and tempeatures, S-IVB second-stage restart and cryogenic pro-pellant storage in zero-gravity conditions, and pressure-testing of the S-IVB liquid hydrogen propellant. The orbital restart capability was essential to the S-IVB's task of injecting the Apollo spacecraft into its lunar trajectory.

These were the first three Apollo launches. On 9 November 1967 Apollo 4 became the first to be launched by the very big, three-stage Saturn 5, which could put a payload of 120–140 short tons into Earth orbit and had a launching weight of no less than 6,100,000lb (3,050 short tons). This placed Apollo 4 into an Earth orbit of 11,234 miles apogee, and demonstrated the Saturn 5's performance on this, its first flight, as well as the Command Module heat shield's suitability for lunar mission re-entry speeds. The mission was the first to be conducted following the major setback to the programme on 27 January when astronauts Virgil Grissom, Edward White and Roger Chaffee perished in a fire during a practice count-down on the launching pad in preparation for the Apollo 1 flight scheduled for 21 February. A flash fire originated in the spacecraft which spread with uncontrollable speed because of the 100 per cent oxygen atmosphere inside it.

To the Moon
The first Lunar Module flight vehicle, designated LM-1, was launched into un-

Below: The crew of Apollo 9, the first manned flight to test the Lunar Module: (left to right) Col. James A. McDivitt, Col. David R. Scott, and Russell Schweickart. The crew successfully tried out the LM's critical rendezvous and docking manoeuvre. (NASA)

manned orbit 100 miles above Earth by Saturn 1B on 22–23 January 1968; this was the Apollo 5 mission, the Lunar Module being the last of the three Apollo components to be flight-tested, and subsequent Lunar Modules that flew on missions up to Apollo 17 were designated LM-3 to LM-11. During LM-1's orbit both ascent and descent engine firings were made, the latter engine also being restarted, and LM-1's systems performance, structure and staging were also evaluated. The LM-1's first flight was described by the Kennedy Space Center as a 'qualified success'. The engine tests were of briefer duration than planned because after LM-1's robot pilot prematurely cut short the ascent engine's first burn, ground controllers had to take over the engine firings. However, both engines were subsequently fired twice more for precisely planned times and run at various power levels, the final burn of the ascent engine lasting more than six minutes. The LM-1 was not recovered but left in Earth orbit, where it was scheduled to remain for about two years before disintegrating in the Earth's atmosphere.

Apollos 6, 7 and 8 did not carry a Lunar Module, but Apollo 8, crewed by astronauts Frank Borman (commander), James Lovell and William Anders and launched on 21 December 1968 by a Saturn 5, was historic in being the first manned spaceflight from Earth to another body in the solar system, making ten two-hour orbits of the Moon and proving outstandingly successful. Apollo 9, launched from Cape Kennedy on 3 March 1969, also by Saturn 5, was the first manned flight with the Lunar Module, designated LM-3; this Apollo mission was crewed by Co. James A. McDivitt, Col. David R. Scott and Mr. Russell Schweickart. The primary task of this Earth-orbital flight was to test the LM and perform rendezvous and docking manoeuvres. The first exercise, the transposition and docking of the Command Module with the LM (still attached to the S-IVB third stage) was successfully begun during the second orbit, and the LM was then extracted. McDivitt and Schweickart climbed into the Lunar Module, the latter acting as LM pilot and, on his first space flight, experiencing some nausea and vomiting during

this part of the operation. With the LM still attached to the Command Module, its descent engine was fired for a burn of nearly six minutes, the first time this had been achieved in space. For the purposes of radio and TV transmissions, the LM was given the call-sign *Spider* and the Command Module was known as *Gumdrop*, and following the descent engine burn, the crew busied themselves intensively taking photos of each other, of the LM's interior and of the Earth, while live TV transmissions to Earth were also made.

Because of Schweickart's earlier nausea, a planned two-hour EVA (Extra Vehicular Activity) mission was cancelled and instead, with both modules depressurized, the LM and Command Module hatches were opened simultaneously. Schweickart climbed out of the LM and on to the ladder on the landing leg, so as to test his EVA suit under space conditions, while Scott reached out of the Command Module to retrieve some thermal samples which Schweickart was to have collected during his programmed EVA. On the third day of flight, the LM was separated from the Command Module, and the critical rendezvous and docking manoeuvre was accomplished successfully in orbits simulating those to be used on the coming lunar mission. The horizontal separation between the two modules reached 113 miles during this manoeuvre when the LM descent stage was jettisoned and the non-throttling ascent engine fired, to begin the rendezvous. Some other mission tasks were accomplished, and Apollo 9 splashed down successfully on 13 March only three miles from the recovery ship *Guadalcanal* and only eleven seconds late.

Apollo 10, launched on 18 May 1969 and crewed by Thomas Stafford as commander, Eugene Cernan as Lunar Module pilot and John Young, was a 'dress rehearsal' for the actual lunar landing, the mission closely following the flight plan for Apollo 11. For the flight the Lunar Module was designated LM-4 and named *Snoopy*, while the Command Module was called *Charlie Brown*, after the characters in the strip cartoon by Charles Schulz. An eight-hour sequence of undocked activities was accomplished in *Snoopy*, in which

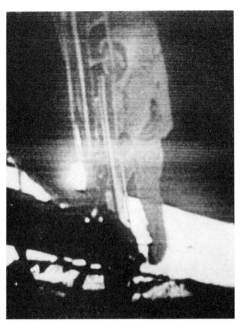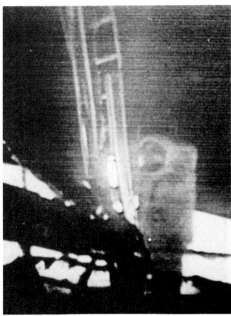

Stafford and Cernan descended to within 50,000ft of the lunar surface, later rejoining the Command/Service Module in a 69-mile circular lunar orbit. All aspects of the flight duplicated as closely as possible the projected lunar landing, including the out-and-back flight path to the Moon, the time of mission events and the sun angles at Apollo Site 2, the intended landing site. Apollo 10 also provided additional operational experience in navigating around the Moon and in mission support facilities during a simulated lunar landing.

While preparing for the undocking manoeuvre, the astronauts found that they could not depressurize the tunnel linking the Lunar and Command/Service modules; the unvented pressure might have imparted too much velocity to *Snoopy* as it undocked. To solve this problem, Stafford and Cernan re-opened the LM's hatch and released the excess pressure through a vent in the LM to space. A potentially much more serious snag occurred after the close approach to the Moon had been completed and the LM descent stage was jettisoned prior to firing the ascent engine to rejoin the Command/Service Module. Immediately after the descent stage had been detached by the blowing of explosive bolts, the ascent stage began to gyrate violently, pitching up and down, and the heartbeat rate of Eugene Cernan, piloting it, went

up from a normal 60 to 129. Stafford was able to stabilize the LM after about one minute, and it was later concluded that a control switch, omitted from the detailed check list and left in the wrong position, had caused the gyrations. Many TV broadcasts were made during the eight-day Apollo 10 flight, including the first colour transmissions and some memorable shots of the undocked LM firing its Marquardt R-4D reaction control rockets to move it away from the Command Module prior to its descent to the lunar surface. Splash-down was made on 26 May, about four miles from the recovery ship, *Princeton*.

'The Eagle has Landed'

The great day of Wednesday 16 July 1969, which saw the launch of the historic Apollo 11 mission to land two astronauts on the Moon's surface, dawned fine and clear at Cape Kennedy. At 1432hrs BST, after the long and elaborate countdown was completed, Apollo 11, crewed by Neil Armstrong (commander), Edwin Aldrin (LM pilot) and Michael Collins, rose on its Saturn 5 launcher as a million people on the ground watched the blast-off. The television networks were to show 230 hours of pictures of the Apollo 11 mission to an audience of some 500 million people all over the world. As the Saturn 5 rose away from the launching pad its mighty rocket exhausts crackled loudly, and shock diamonds could be plainly seen; within 12 minutes of lift-off (T+11min 50sec) it had carried Apollo 11 safely into a 105.4 by 103.6 mile Earth orbit. One and a half orbits were completed while the crew and Mission Control made checks, and then, 2 hours 44 minutes after lift-off, the S-IVB third stage of the Saturn 5 was ignited a second time to inject Apollo 11 into a trans-lunar trajectory. Thirty-six minutes after this burn, the Command/Service Module separated for the transposition and docking manoeuvre and the extraction of the Lunar Module, designated LM-5, from the S-IVB stage. This was successfully completed, although Aldrin used slightly more fuel than had been predicted. The Command/Service Module was now known as *Columbia*, and the LM as *Eagle*, and together they made the 250,000-mile journey to the Moon uneventfully except for a three-second mid-course correction, arriving in the Moon's vicinity on Friday 18 July. That day Armstrong and Aldrin donned their spacesuits and climbed into the LM for initial checks, and while there they also made one of the best TV transmissions of the entire Apollo series.

The next day, Saturday, the critical burn for insertion into lunar orbit was made after Apollo 11 had disappeared behind the Moon at 1813hrs BST, and this later became the 69-mile circular orbit required for the LM to rendezvous with the Command/Service Module on its return from the lunar surface. The landing area in the Sea of Tranquillity was known as Site 2. Armstrong and Aldrin entered the LM at 1520hrs BST on Sunday 20 July for a final series of checks, and at 1847hrs *Columbia* and *Eagle* undocked, the two craft staying close together while Collins in *Columbia* inspected *Eagle* visually for any damage that might have occurred in undocking. While *Eagle* was behind the Moon on the thirteenth orbit, at 2011hrs, the descent engine was fired to begin the journey to the lunar surface. At 2106hrs *Eagle* arrived at the so-called 'high gate', 50,000ft above the lunar surface and 300 miles from the predicted touch-down point at Site 2. The LM's landing radar was activated at about 40,000ft to update the height data in its guidance computer, and near the surface Armstrong took over manual control to negotiate an area the size of a football pitch strewn with rocks and boulders.

The excitement of those last few historic moments before touch-down is captured in these exchanges between Armstrong and the Capsule Communicator, or Capcom, at Houston Mission Control, who was the only ground controller to speak directly with the crew:

EAGLE (ARMSTRONG): Lights on. down 2–½. Forward. Forward. Good 40 feet, down 2–½. Picking up dust. 30 feet, 2–½ down. Faint shadow. 4 forward. 4 forward, drifting to the right a little. 6 [garbled] down a half.

CAPCOM: 30 seconds.

EAGLE: [Garbled] Forward. Drifting right [garbled]. Contact lights. Okay, engine stop. ACA out of detent. Modes control both auto, descent engine command override off. Engine arm, off. 413 is in.

CAPCOM: We copy you down, Eagle.

EAGLE: Houston, Tranquillity Base here. The *Eagle* has landed.

CAPCOM: Tranquillity, we copy you on the ground. You've got a bunch of guys about to turn blue. We're breathing again. Thanks a lot!

So it was that Man landed on the Moon, at 21hrs 17mins 42secs BST on Sunday 21 July 1969, and President Kennedy's goal was achieved. The *Eagle* had landed with less than 2 per cent of its descent engine propellant remaining, and the first few moments after landing were spent in checking the LM in case an immediate ascent was advisable. But there

was no damage evident, and no cause for ascent, and the two astronauts embarked on an arduous two-hour programme of exploration and of setting up scientific experiments on the lunar surface.

At 0356hrs BST Neil Armstrong became the first man to set foot on the Moon, saying as he did so, 'That's one small step for [a] man, one giant leap for mankind'. He and Aldrin took their first tentative steps, practised running and did some exuberant kangaroo hops in the reduced gravity. They ceremonially implanted an American flag, received a telephone call from President Nixon, and packed two boxes with samples of lunar soil and rock, which they found to be powdery but cohesive. A plaque was unveiled bearing the words 'Here men from the planet Earth first set foot upon the Moon. July 1969 AD. We came in peace for all mankind', which message was followed by the signatures of the three astronauts and President Nixon. The plaque was fixed to *Eagle*'s descent stage, which was left behind on the Moon.

Several scientific experiments were set up, including a Solar Wind Composition experiment, which was basically a sheet of aluminium foil deployed to measure the elemental and isotopic constituents of the inert gases in the solar wind; this was brought back to Earth for analysis. Other experiments left on the lunar surface included a Laser Ranging Retro Reflector for precise measurement of Earth-to-Moon distances, and a Passive Seismic Experiment Package (PSEP) to measure moonquakes and meteoroid impacts. The PSEP featured an isotopic heater system to protect the recorder during the very cold lunar nights.

After a total EVA time of 2hrs 31mins 40secs on the lunar surface, Armstrong and Aldrin re-entered *Eagle* and removed their bulky spacesuits and the personal life support system (PLSS) back packs. They rested for some seven hours, and then began their preparations for the lift-off of the ascent stage and its rendezvous with the Command Module *Columbia*, in which Collins had been orbiting the Moon while his colleagues were on its surface. *Eagle* lifted off on schedule at 1854hrs BST on 21 July, some 21½ hours after *Eagle* had touched down, and

just after *Columbia* had emerged from behind the dark side of the Moon on its twenty-fifth orbit. The ascent engine burned for just over seven minutes to place *Eagle* in the desired orbit of 10.5 by 54.4 miles. The descent stage was left behind on the lunar surface, along with several other items of discarded equipment. Also left on the Moon were medallions of two Soviet cosmonauts and three US astronauts who had been killed in the course of their duties, and numerous microfilmed messages, including one of President Kennedy's speech that had made the lunar landing a national goal.

Eagle and *Columbia* went behind the Moon for the complicated set of manoeuvres that preceded rendezvous and docking about 3½ hours later, out of contact with Mission Control at Houston. During the actual docking Collins was heard to say, 'That was a funny one. You know, I didn't feel us touch. I went to retrack there and that's when all hell broke loose'. When docked, the Command and Lunar Modules reverted to using Apollo as their call-sign. Before re-entering the Command Module Armstrong and Aldrin spent some time vaccum-cleaning their clothing and equipment, as a precaution against bringing back contamination when they returned to Earth. After they were back in the Command Module the Lunar Module was jettisoned, and at 0557hrs on 22 July the Service Module propulsion engine was fired to bring Apollo 11 out of its lunar orbit and into a trans-Earth trajectory.

The return flight was uneventful, although just before re-entry the target impact point was shifted some 250 miles to avoid potential storms. Splashdown occurred at 1750hrs BST on Thursday 24 July, only about 30 seconds later than had been predicted at the start of the 195-hour mission, and about 13 miles from the prime recovery ship, the carrier *Hornet*. Before leaving the Command Module the astronauts donned Biological Isolation Garments, to prevent any possible contamination, and went straight from the helicopter which lifted them from the sea into a Mobile Quarantine Facility, which was finally delivered to Houston; here the three men remained in

Far left: Neil Armstrong and 'Buzz' Aldrin in front of the American flag they ceremonially implanted at the Sea of Tranquillity landing site, with *Eagle* in the background. The two astronauts appear ghostlike in this TV image. (Grumman)

the isolation of quarantine for 18 days. This was rather an anti-climax compared to the traditional ticker-tape welcome given to past heroes such as Charles Lindbergh, but for the first time a great voyage of discovery, as Apollo 11 was, had been presented to millions of people all over the world through the medium of television, as it was actually happening.

The Second Moon Landing

Apollo 12 was launched for the second Moon landing just four months after Apollo 11, on 14 November 1969, and it was crewed by Capt. Charles Conrad Jr. USN, Capt. Alan L. Bean, and Richard F. Gordon Jr. (the command pilot). The launch by Saturn 5 took place in conditions of rain and cloud, and barely 50 seconds after lift-off two lightning flashes were seen from the ground. At almost the same time Conrad said, 'Just lost the platform . . . Everything in the world just dropped out' – the Saturn 5 had been struck by lightning twice, and scorch marks could be seen on the side of the Service Module. As a result of this NASA later revised the launch weather regulations for Apollo missions to avoid a similar incident happening again, with possibly serious consequences. The first lunar orbit insertion burn was started at 0452hrs BST on 17 November behind the Moon, and was followed by a second burn two orbits later. The next day Conrad and Bean entered the Lunar Module, designated LM-6 and named

Intrepid, the Command/Service Module being called *Yankee Clipper*. These separate identities were assumed after the LM had undocked at 0520hrs on 19 November, and 34 minutes later the descent-orbit insertion burn was made, again behind the Moon, and *Intrepid* was on its way to the designated landing place, Site 7 in the Ocean of Storms. As it re-appeared from behind the Moon the trajectory seemed to be adrift, but this was put right by corrections fed by Mission Control into *Intrepid*'s navigation/guidance system.

The descent engine was fired at 0740hrs, and twelve minutes later *Intrepid* entered the 'high gate'. The last moments before touch-down were recorded in this light-hearted exchange between Charles (Pete) Conrad and Alan Bean in *Intrepid*:

'. . . You're looking good . . . 124 feet . . . 120 feet coming down at 6 . . . you got 9 per cent, 8 per cent, you look okay . . . slow down your descent rate . . . 80 coming down at 4 . . . You're looking good . . . 70 feet . . . 63 . . . 60 coming down at 3 . . . Watch for the dust . . . 46 . . . 42 coming down at 2 . . . 40 coming down at 2 . . . 31 . . . 32 . . . 32 . . . plenty of gas, plenty of gas . . . he's got it made . . . come on in there . . . 24 feet . . . Contact lights on . . . Roger, copy contact light . . . You got your command override on? . . . Yes . . . Man oh man, Houston, that was an IFR landing'.

The landing, made at 0754hrs BST, was very smooth, although it raised a dense cloud of dust, and of pin-point accuracy – a triumphant vindication of the navigation/guidance refinements that had been made since Apollo 11. There was a full 90 seconds of fuel remaining, and *Intrepid* had landed at the edge of a 300ft crater, within walking distance (actually 656ft) from the Surveyor 3 Moon probe that had landed there over two years before, on 19 April 1967.

First out of *Intrepid* was Conrad, who alighted on the Moon at 1244hrs BST and, shortly afterwards, was heard to be humming away to himself. The television camera that was to record the setting up of experiments developed a snag that prevented it screening pictures, so Bean gave it a hit with his hammer. But this failed to do the trick, and viewers all over the world, including Mission Control, were deprived of their TV coverage. The astronauts deployed the first nuclear-powered ALSEP (Apollo Lunar Surface Experiments Package), and soon its seismometer was recording their footsteps. Their first period of EVA, or excursions on foot outside *Intrepid*, lasted about 4hrs and the second 3hrs 49mins; during this time they obtained 75lb of lunar rock and soil samples. Back in *Intrepid* between the two EVA periods, the two astronauts ate a meal and then slept in two hammocks slung across the walls of the LM. During the second EVA period, they visited the Surveyor 3 probe lying in a crater, photographed it and removed its TV camera (which had earlier returned over 6,000 pictures of the Moon's surface) and one or two other parts for return to Earth. The camera yielded valuable information on how a man-made object had stood up to the very high vacuums and large temperature range of the lunar surface over a long period.

At 1526hrs BST the astronauts left the Moon in *Intrepid*'s ascent stage after a total of 31hrs 31mins on the lunar surface, and docked with the Command Module *Yankee Clipper* at 1858hrs. Conrad and Bean having transferred to the Command Module, the now empty LM ascent stage was undocked and separated from the latter at 2043hrs, and, just under two hours later, the ascent engine was fired by remote control, placing the LM on a descent orbit to the Moon, where it crashed 28 minutes later about 45 miles from Site 7. The impact was recorded by the ALSEP seismometer, and provided important information about the Moon's structure. After an uneventful return journey, the Command Module splashed down in the Pacific near Samoa on 24 November, the recovery ship being the carrier *Hornet*. The Apollo 12 mission had lasted 10 days 4hrs 36mins 25secs, and had been extremely successful.

Unlucky Thirteen

To the earthbound TV watcher Apollo 12 must have seemed something of a fun-packed mission, with continuous light-hearted banter between Conrad and Bean, but Apollo 13 would be a warning that space travel was not yet to be taken for granted. Launched on 11 April 1970 by Saturn 5, Apollo 13 was crewed by James A. Lovell Jr., Fred W. Haise and, as Command Module pilot, John L. Swigert. Lovell and Haise were to land on the Moon in the hazardous hilly region of the crater Fra Mauro, named after the seventeenth-century Venetian geographer. It was also planned to fly the S-IVB third stage of the Saturn 5 all the way to the Moon, instead of jettisoning it at the beginning of the flight, and to fire it at the lunar surface, which would result in a much greater impact than that of *Intrepid*'s ascent stage. The S-IVB impact, recorded on the ALSEP seismometer, would provide further important data on the Moon's structure.

During the Apollo 13 launching the centre engine in the S-II second stage's cluster of five Rocketdyne J-2 rocket engines was shut down prematurely, 2mins 12secs early. This necessitated burning the four outer engines for a correspondingly longer period, and the single 200,000lb s.t. Rocketdyne J-2 engine of the S-IVB third stage also had to run longer than planned. The S-II shutdown problem was overcome, and Apollo 13 was successfully injected into its lunar trajectory.

On 14 April, at 0417hrs BST, with Apollo 13 some 205,000 miles from the Earth, Lovell was heard to report 'Hey! We've got a problem!', and a major malfunction was registered at Mission Control at Houston. At first it seemed as if a meteoroid had struck the spacecraft, but what had happened was that an oxygen tank of the Service Module's fuel cells had exploded, causing a failure of the tank and some damage inside the equipment bay, as well as an immediate loss of electrical power. The planned Moon landing was now out of the question, but Apollo 13 could not be recalled to Earth immediately. Technical staffs of NASA and the various spacecraft contractors were hurriedly summoned from their homes to report back to Mission Control and work out rescue procedures. An entirely new set of flight instructions was computed at Houston and passed on to the Apollo 13 crew, who had to continue on round the Moon and then return. While this was happening the world watched and wondered: would Apollo 13 be the first spaceflight tragedy? Would its crew be carried on beyond the Moon, into the unknown vastness of outer space, never to return?

Happily this did not occur, because the crew agreed with Mission Control that the Lunar Module, named *Aquarius*, would be retained for as long as possible so as to utilize its oxygen and electrical supplies for the Command/Service Module, named *Odyssey*. The latter's three fuel cells worked by feeding liquid hydrogen and oxygen from separate tanks into the fuel cell battery to generate electrical power and, with one tank gone, the oxygen supply to the fuel cells was cut off to conserve this precious gas. To conserve the remaining electrical power (supplied by three silver-zinc storage batteries) for re-entry, and to make use of the Lunar Module's oxygen and life-support systems, Lovell and Haise left the Command Module for the LM, making their way to it through the connecting tunnel from the Command/Service Module, leaving Swigert in the latter to carry out a power-down procedure, the tunnel remaining open so that oxygen from the LM could enter the Command Module. Shortly afterwards the LM's electrical system was switched on, and its radio enabled control to be made with Houston. The water supply, necessary for cooling and other purposes as well as for drinking, also gave cause for concern, but it turned out that there was more than enough water: steps had to be taken to avoid an excessive build-up of carbon dioxide in the craft, as well as contamination of the atmosphere.

The Service Module engine, of 20,500lb s.t., obviously could not be used for the journey back to Earth, and the LM descent engine, of half its thrust, would now have to be used for all the main trajectory changes. At 0943hrs BST on 14 April the descent engine burn was initiated that put Apollo 13 into orbit round the Moon, and at 0121hrs BST on 15 April the craft passed behind the Moon and out of radio contact. This was a tense and dramatic period, and at 0341hrs the second descent engine burn, lasting 4mins 20secs, started, to put Apollo 13 on course for its Pacific splashdown. Twenty-five minutes later Mission Control was able to report to the astronauts and the

world at large that 'it looked good'. Meanwhile the S-IVB third stage of the Saturn 5 was, as previously planned, aimed towards the lunar surface for its impact to be recorded by the ALSEP seismometer and, to combat mounting carbon dioxide contamination, the astronauts, advised by Mission Control, rigged up a device using flexible hose from their space suits, a plastic bag and adhesive tape, and this proved to be successful. At 1352hrs BST on 17 April the final course correction prior to re-entry was made by a short burn of the LM engine. With all three astronauts in the LM, Houston authorized the Service Module to be jettisoned at 1417hrs.

It was only now that the full extent of the damage could be seen. The 13ft by 6ft access panel was missing, having been blown out by the explosion. Quite severe damage was also evident to a section of the equipment bay, which had some debris hanging out of the side, and there were also signs of damage to the Service Module engine. Had all this occurred when the LM was down on the Lunar surface or during the return journey to Earth, the Apollo 13 mission would have ended in disaster as there were only a few hours of emergency oxygen and battery power available in the Command Module. The latter flew on for just over three hours with the LM attached after the Service Module had been jettisoned, and the Comand and Lunar Modules flying together were a combination that had never been tested before nor anticipated. At 1744hrs BST the crew, now back in the Command Module and having sealed the hatch, jettisoned the LM which had served them so well as a 'lifeboat', the module blasting itself away to avoid collision and burning up during its re-entry over the Pacific. The Command Module went into the re-entry corridor at a speed of 24,000mph, one of the fastest of any Apollo re-entries, and at temperatures building up to some 4,000°F. Then at 1900hrs, over the Pacific, television cameras picked out the three orange and white parachutes bearing Apollo 13 to its splashdown, which took place seven minutes later, only four miles away from the waiting assault ship *Iwo Jima*, to universal sighs of relief. The flight had lasted 142hrs 54mins 41secs. Although it failed in its task of landing on the Moon, Apollo 13 was a resounding success as a demonstration of technical improvisation, conducted in the fullest possible glare of publicity, in overcoming a major malfunction.

Only two months later the Apollo 13 review board's findings were announced. A short circuit had ignited insulation in the No. 2 oxygen tank, causing its failure and the explosion, and it was recommended that Command and Service Module systems be modified and re-designed to eliminate potential combustion hazards in high-pressure oxygen as revealed by the accident. All later Apollos incorporated a number of modifications to this end, which included reducing to a minimum the use of Teflon, aluminium and other materials that were potentially combustible in the presence of high-pressure oxygen. Furthermore, all electrical wires were now sheathed in stainless steel, and a number of other changes were made.

The Last Four Missions

The delays caused by incorporating the modifications resulting from Apollo 13 meant that it was not until 31 January 1971 that Apollo 14 was successfully launched by Saturn 5, after a 40-minute delay caused by bad weather. Crewed by Capt. Alan B. Shepard Jr. USN, and Maj. Edgar J. Mitchell USAF (the LM pilot), with Cdr. Stuart A. Roosa USN as Command Module pilot, Apollo 14's objective was a landing north of the Fra Mauro crater in the Sea of Rains which Apollo 13 had been meant to visit. The transposition and docking manoeuvre proved to be troublesome, when probe catches on the nose of the Command Module, named *Kitty Hawk*, failed to capture the Lunar Module, named LM-8 *Antares*, satisfactorily. Six attempts had to be made before docking was achieved and *Antares* could be withdrawn from the S-IVB third stage. By combining the second lunar orbit insertion burn with the descent orbit insertion, sufficient of the LM's fuel was saved to provide an additional 15 seconds' hovering time, so providing more accurate position and velocity data for the landing. But the LM's computer gave trouble

just before the descent manoeuvre, indicating that the abort system had inadvertently been activated, so that when the descent engine was fired the computer would automatically abort the landing. This was overcome by a rapid programme change by Mission Control, which enabled the crew to feed fresh information into the computer to get round the fault. Another snag was that the landing radar did not operate at the programmed height of 50,000ft, and did not switch on until the LM had descended below 25,000ft.

But in spite of these snags a successful landing was made at Fra Mauro only 87ft from the nominal target centre, at 1018hrs BST on 5 February, less than two minutes later than planned but with 60 seconds of fuel remaining. The LM settled at an angle of 8 degrees to the horizontal. Shepard and Mitchell spent two EVA periods totalling 9hrs 29mins on the lunar surface, during which they set out another ALSEP package similar to that left by Apollo 12 and made an extensive geological survey of the area around the landing site. To assist in this, they used a small trolley like a golf cart called the Modular Equipment Transporter (MET) to carry cameras, geological tools and samples of lunar rock, of which 96lb was collected, including two rocks weighing about 10lb each. During this survey the astronauts walked a mile to the nearby Cone Crater, but the upper slopes of this were too steep for them to reach the top of the rim as they had hoped. While on the Moon Shepard also played a golf shot which landed in a crater 60ft away and which, like the other EVA activities, was shown worldwide on television.

The LM ascent stage lifted off at 1948hrs BST on 6 February, and docking was achieved at 2134hrs. This time many of the intermediate manoeuvres leading up to the rendezvous and docking with the Command/Service Module were omitted. After the LM had been jettisoned its ascent engine was re-ignited to direct it on to a collision course with the Moon, which it hit at 0145hrs on 7 February to activate the seismometers of the Apollo 12 and 14 ALSEP packages. The S-IVB third stage had earlier impacted on the Moon for the same reason. A safe splashdown was made in the Pacific at 2005hrs on 9 February near the recovery ship *New Orleans*, the mission having lasted 216hrs 1min 57secs. The LM had spent 33hrs 31mins on the Moon.

Apollo 15 was launched on 26 July 1971 and crewed by David R. Scott and James B. Irwin, with Alfred M. Worden piloting the Command/Service Module *Endeavour* (itself equipped for extensive lunar surface survey). Scott and Irwin landed the Lunar Module *Falcon* in the Apennine Mountains/Hadley Rille area, and they carried out three EVAs totalling 18hrs 36mins. During these a third ALSEP package was set up, a sub-satellite was released into lunar orbit, and the Boeing Lunar Rover Vehicle was used for the first time on the Moon in the course of collecting 169lb of lunar rock and soil samples. The Lunar Rover was an electrically driven, four-wheel chassis with seats for the two astronauts, and could carry, besides them, 170lb of lunar rock and scientific experiments. It was stowed in the storage bay of the LM's descent stage. The LM's lift-off, made after 66hrs 55mins on the Moon, was the first to be covered live on TV. During the return to Earth, Worden made the first EVA 'space walk' in deep space when he recovered film cassettes from the Service Module's lunar cameras while 196,000 miles from Earth. Apollo 15 splashed down on 7 August after a highly successful mission lasting 295hrs 11mins 53secs.

Apollo 15 was the first J-class mission of the series, in which some modifications were made to enable a greater useful load to be carried. The three Modules were nearly 6,400lb heavier than Apollo 11, and Apollo 15 now weighed 103,311lb, or 5,200lb more than Apollo 14 (for comparison, the maximum take-off weight of the Douglas DC-6B four-engined airliner was 107,000lb). The Service Module now featured a Scientific Instrument Module (SIM) bay, and carried cameras for recording the lunar surface, whilst various modifications were also made to the Saturn 5 launcher.

The Lunar Module was also modified in several ways. By a major re-arrangement of the four outer 'quads' or compartments of the descent stage, oxygen and water supplies were increased and the electrical life raised. The Lunar Rover Vehicle was stowed in Quad 1, while Quad 4 held a new 50kg water storage tank, a waste container and a gaseous oxygen module. A new MESA (Modularized Equipment Stowage Assembly) held sample containers, a tool pallet, and batteries for personal life support systems, and a cosmic ray detector was carried externally on the 'quad'. Some changes were made to the descent engine to allow for a longer burn period, and propellant tank capacity was increased to carry an extra 1,150lb fuel and oxidant. Several changes were also made to the LM's ascent stage, which now featured a new method of stowing the astronauts' re-designed pressure suits, the latter having greater arm and leg flexibility and increased oxygen and water capacity for longer EVA periods.

Apollo 16, the second J-class mission, was launched on 16 April 1972 by Saturn 5, with John W. Young and Charles M. Duke Jr. as crew and Thomas K. Mattingly II as Command Module (*Casper*) pilot. On 20 April at 2135hrs EST Young and Duke landed in the Descartes highlands in the Lunar Module *Orion* and set up the fourth ALSEP package of experiments. Three EVAs were undertaken, totalling 20hrs 14mins (the longest EVA period so far) and the Lunar Rover Vehicle was used in the process of gathering 210lb of rock and soil samples. A sub-satellite was also released into lunar orbit. *Orion* lifted off after the astronauts had spent 71hrs 6mins on the Moon. On the return to Earth Thomas Mattingly conducted another 'space walk' when he retrieved film canisters from the Service Module's cameras. Splashdown occurred on 27 April after a successful mission lasting 265hrs 51mins 0.5secs.

Apollo 17 was the third J-class mission and the last in the historic Apollo series. It was also the first night launching, and as it lifted off at 0033hrs EST on 7 December 1972 thousands of people watched from roadside car parks near the Kennedy Space Center and along Cocoa Beach as, like an immense torch, the Saturn 5's rocket exhausts lit up the area as brightly as day, a spectacle visible in places as far away as Cuba. Crewed by Eugene A.

Cernan, Harrison H. ('Jack') Schmitt (Lunar Module pilot), who was a qualified geologist, and Ronald E. Evans (Command Module pilot), Apollo 17 was launched at night to ensure a low sun angle at the time of landing on the Moon.

The Lunar Module *Challenger* separated from the Command Module *America* during the twelfth lunar orbit, and at 1855hrs GMT on 11 December it landed, rather heavily, at the Taurus-Littrow site in a lunar valley about eight miles wide between rather high mountains on the south-eastern rim of the Sea of Serenity. Three EVAs were undertaken, totalling 22hrs 5mins 6secs, the longest of any Apollo mission; one of these, at 7hrs 37mins 21 secs, was the longest single EVA. A fifth ALSEP scientific package was set up, the Lunar Rover Vehicle was used in the course of collecting 257lb of rock and soil samples, and the Rover made its longest trip on one EVA when it covered a distance of 12nm. Two 8ft deep holes were drilled into the lunar surface for an important heat-flow experiment, and a sub-satellite was released into lunar orbit. The LM lifted off, amid a shower of sparks, at 2255hrs GMT on 14 December after 74hrs 58½mins on the Moon, and, after a hard docking with *America* was achieved at the third attempt, the LM was programmed to crash back on to the Moon, which it did some 10 miles from the landing site. A near-perfect splashdown was made by Apollo 17 near the recovery ship *Ticonderoga* at 1924hrs GMT on 19 December, after a highly successful mission lasting 12 days 13hrs 51mins 59secs. The astronauts left behind a plaque fixed to the LM's descent stage that commemorated the end of the Apollo missions and included a message from President Nixon.

So ended the historic first chapter of space exploration, in which Man had demonstrated his ability to travel to another body in the solar system and land upon it. Grumman-designed and -built Lunar Modules had set down a total of twelve astronauts on the lunar surface, and returned all of them safely, while the LM *Aquarius* had been instrumental in saving Apollo 13 from disaster. By the time of the last Apollo mission, space-flights to the Moon were coming to seem almost as routine as jet travel, in spite of the drama of Apollo 13.

Below: Seen from the Command Module *Columbia* piloted by Michael Collins, the LM *Eagle*'s ascent stage makes its docking approach to the Command/Service Module for the return flight while carrying Armstrong and Aldrin. This photograph shows the Earth rising above the lunar horizon; the large dark area of lunar surface behind the LM is known as Smith's Sea. (NASA)

Appendix

GRUMMAN AIRCRAFT SPECIFICATIONS

Aircraft	Span (ft–in)	Length (ft–in)	Height (ft–in)	Wing area (ft²)	Empty weight (lb)	Gross weight (lb)
FF-1	34–6	24–6	11–1	310		4,828
F2F-1	28–6	21–5	9–1	230		3,847
F3F-3	32–0	23–2	9–4	260		4,795
J2F-5 Duck	39–0	34–0	15–1	409		6,711
JRF-5 Goose	49–0	38–4	16–2	375		8,000
McKinnon G-21D Goose*	50–10	39–7	14–6	377.64	9,000	
McKinnon G-21D Turbo Goose	50–10	39–7		377.64	8,200	
Grumman G-44A Widgeon	40–0	31–1	11–5	245		4,525
McKinnon Super Widgeon	40–0	31–1	11–5	245		
G-73 Mallard	66–8	48–4	18–9	444		
Turbo Mallard	66–8	48–4	18–9	444		
SA-16A Albatross	80–0	60–8	24–3	833	20,100	27,025
HU-16B Albatross	96–8	61–3	25–10	1,035		
F4F-4 Wildcat	38–0	29–0	8–11	260	4,649	6,100
FM-2 Wildcat	38–0	28–11	11–5	260	4,900	8,271
XF5F-1 Skyrocket	42–0	28–11				10,892
F6F-3 Hellcat	42–10	33–7	13–1	334	9,042	12,186
F6F-5 Hellcat	42–10	33–7	13–1	334	9,238	15,413*
TBF-1 Avenger	54–2	40–0	16–5	490	10,100	15,905
TBM-3E Avenger	54–2	40–11½	16–5	490		14,160
AF-2S Guardian	60–8	43–4	15–2	560		25,500
F7F-3 Tigercat	51–6	45–4	16–7	455		25,720
F8F-1 Bearcat	35–10	28–3	13–10	244	7,070	12,947
F8F-2 Bearcat	35–6	27–8	13–10			13,494
F9F-2 Panther	38–0*	37–3	11–4	250		19,494
F9F-5 Panther	38–0*	38–10	12–3	250	10,417	18,721
F9F-6 Cougar	36–5	41–7	15–10			
F9F-8T (TF-9J) Cougar	34–6	44–5	12–3			20,600
XF10F-1 Jaguar	36–8*	55–8	16–4	450†	20,426	27,451‡
F11F-1 (F-11A) Tiger	31–7½	46–11½	13–2¾	250	13,428	22,160
F-14A Tomcat	38–2½*	62–8	16–0	565	40,104†	59,714†‡
S-2A Tracker	69–8	42–3	16–3½	485	17,357	26,300
S-2E Tracker	72–7	43–6	16–7	499	18,750	29,150
TF-1 (C-1A) Trader	69–8	43–6	16–7			27,000
WF-2 (E-1B) Tracer	69–8	45–4	16–10		21,024	27,000
E-2C Hawkeye	80–7	57–7	18–4	700	37,616	51,669
C-2A Greyhound*	80–7	56–8	15–11	700	31,154	
OV-1A Mohawk	42–0	41–0	12–8	330	9,937	
OV-1D Mohawk	48–0	44–11*	12–8	360	12,054	18,448
A-6A Intruder	53–0	54–7	15–7	529	25,684	
A-6E Intruder	53–0	54–7	16–3	529	26,746	
EA-6B Prowler	53–0	59–10	16–3	529	32,162	
G-164 Ag-Cat*	35–8	24–4	10–9	326	2,201	
G-164 Ag-Cat*	35–11	24–4¼	10–9	328	2,239	
G-164A Super Ag-Cat A/450	35–11	24–4	10–9	328	2,796	
G-164B Ag-Cat Super-B/600	42–5	24–6	11–6	392	3,650	
G-164D Turbo Ag-Cat D/ST	42–3	34–4	11–8	392	3,450	8,500
G-159 Gulfstream I	78–6	63–9	22–9	610.3	21,900	
GAC 159-C Gulfstream I-C	78–6	74–3	22–9	610.3		
G-1159 Gulfstream II	71–9*	79–11	24–6	809.6	30,938*	
Gulfstream II-B	77–10	79–11	24–6	934.6	39,100	
Gulfstream III	77–10	83–1	24–4½	934.6	38,000	
Gulfstream IV	77–10	87–7	24–4	950.39	39,300*	
Grumman American AA-1C Trainer	24–5½	19–3	7–6	100.92	1,002	
Grumman American AA-5B	31–6	22–0	7–6	139.7	1,360	
Grumman American GA-7	36–10¼	29–10	10–4¼	184	2,588	
Grumman X-29A	27–2½	53–11¼	14–3½	188.4	13,800	
General Dynamics/Grumman EF-111A	31–11.4*	76–0	20–0	525†	55,275	

Max. take-off weight (lb)	Max. speed (mph)/at (ft)	Cruising speed (mph)/at (ft)	Initial climb rate (ft/min)	Service ceiling (ft)	Range (miles)	Remarks
	207/4,000			21,000	921	
	231/7,500		2,050	27,100	985*	*Max. figure
	264/15,200		2,750	33,200	980	
	188	150			780	
	201/5,000	191/5,000			640	
499	264/sea level	240/10,000	2,500		600	*With 4 Lycomings
200	220				c.1,200	
	160	130				
00	190/sea level	180/10,000	1,750	18,000	1,000	
750	215/6,000	180/8,000				
000	240	215				
	264.5/18,800	225	1,400		2,700*	*With 600 US gals in drop tanks
700	236/18,800	224			2,850*	*With drop tanks
	320/18,800		2,190	34,000	1,050*	*At 157mph with 2 drop tanks
	332/28,800		3,650		900	
					1,170	
	376/22,800		3,240	37,500	1,085*	*At 179mph
	380/23,400		2,980	37,300	945	*Max. figure
	278		1,075		1,010	
895	276/16,500	147		30,100	1,010*	*With torpedo; 1,920 as scout
	317/16,000		1,850		1,500	
	435/22,200		4,530	40,700	1,200	
	421/19,700		4,570		1,105	
	447				865	
	526		5,000	44,600	1,353†	*Exc. tip tanks †With ext. tanks
	579/5,000		5,090	42,800	1,300†	*Exc. tip tanks †With ext. tanks
	690/sea level			50,000	1,000	
	705/sea level				1,000*	*With drop tanks
450	720					*Swept; 50–7 unswept †Swept; 467 unswept ‡Combat weight
	890/40,000*		5,130	50,500	700	*Mach 1.35
349†	1,544§		30,000†		c.2,000	*Swept; 64–1½ unswept †With TF30-P-414As ‡With 4 Sparrows §Mach 2.34; 910mph/sea level
	287	172/5,000	1,920	23,000	900	
	267	149/1,500	1,390	21,000	1,300	
	290/4,500	250	2,000		800	
	265			20,000		
	374	310			1,600	
350	352	296/30,000	2,330			*First production batch
031	Up to 310	207	2,950	31,000	1,410*	*With drop tanks
	Up to 310	207	3,618	25,000	1,011†	*With SLAR †With drop tanks
626	685/sea level	480		41,660	3,225*	*Ferry range
400	648/sea level	557	8,600	44,600	1,077*	*With full combat load
000	651/sea level*	481		41,200	2,399†	*Clean †Combat range with max. ext. fuel
00	131		435			*With Continental W670
50	131		700			*With Jacobs R-755
75	147	132	580			
20	124					
00		130				
100	348/25,000					
000		356*			715†	*Estimated figure †Max. payload
500*		581/25,000		43,000	3,662*	*With tip tanks
700		Mach 0.85/30,000	3,800			
700		576	3,800		4,721*	*With 8 passengers and VFR reserves
700*		564/35,000*	4,350*		4,201†	*Estimated figure †With max. payload and IFR reserves
00		129/3,000			434	
00	170/sea level	160/8,500			638	
00	193/sea level	184/8,500			1,347*	*Max. fuel
800	c.Mach 1.6					
000‡	1,412	1,377§				*Swept; 63–0 unswept †At 16° sweep ‡Combat weight §Max. combat speed

Bibliography

Andrade, John M. *US Military Aircraft Designations and Serials since 1909*. Earl Shilton, Leicester: Midland Counties Publications, 1979.

Francillon, René J. *Grumman (Eastern) TBF (TBM) Avenger* (Profile No. 214). London: Profile Publications Ltd., 1970.

Green, W. *Famous Fighters of the Second World War*. Abingdon, Oxon.: Purnell Book Services Ltd., 1977.

Green, W. *The World's Fighting Planes*. London: Macdonald & Co. (Publishers) Ltd., 1964.

Green, W. *War Planes of the Second World War: Vol. 5, Flying Boats*. London: Macdonald & Co. (Publishers) Ltd., 1962.

Gunston, Bill. *Fighters of the Fifties*. Bar Hill, Cambridge: Patrick Stephens Ltd.

Gunston, Bill. *The Encyclopedia of the World's Combat Aircraft*. London: Salamander Books Ltd., 1976.

Kinert, Reed. *Racing Planes and Air Races*. Vols. IV, VI, VII, IX, X and XII. Fallbrook, California: Aero Publishers Inc., 1969–76.

Swanborough, G. and Bowers, Peter M. *United States Military Aircraft since 1908*. London: Putnam & Co. Ltd.

Swanborough, G. and Bowers, Peter M. *United States Navy Aircraft since 1911*. London: Putnam & Co. Ltd., 1976.

Taylor, John W. R. (Ed.). *Jane's All The World's Aircraft*. London: Jane's Yearbooks, annual editions.

Thetford, Owen G. *British Naval Aircraft since 1912*. London: Putnam & Co. Ltd., 1982.

Index